KINDRED SPIRITS

A Year of Readings

KINDRED SPIRITS

A Year of Readings

Lionel Blue
and Jonathan Magonet

HarperCollins*Publishers*

HarperCollins*Religious*
Part of HarperCollins*Publishers*
77–85 Fulham Palace Road, London W6 8JB

First published in Great Britain
in 1995 by HarperCollins*Religious*

1 3 5 7 9 10 8 6 4 2

A catalogue record for this book is
available from the British Library

000627819 1

Printed and bound in Great Britain by
Redwood Books, Trowbridge, Wiltshire

To Jim, Peter and Rose, Jack and Ella who cared for my mother and my aunt. To Henk and Theo who helped me with this book. To my 'family' of friends, Ulrica and Marcus, Barry and Sandy, André and Robin. *Lionel Blue*

For Doro, Gav and Avi, who, as usual, suffered most from my 'absences' during the compiling of this book.

Jonathan Magonet

PROLOGUE

I wake up each morning hopeful but apprehensive. Sometimes I can launch into prayer but not often. I'm too preoccupied wondering what will hit me in the morning post. Like most middle-class people I live in a comfortable world but an insecure one.

As I surface from sleep I manage to repeat a blessing about God removing the bands of sleep from my eyelids, and, as I munch a piece of chocolate, consider a piece of wisdom from someone else's life experience which may help me make sense of mine.

I don't care where that wisdom comes from, provided it's to the point and it works. Labels are luxuries a sensitive soul like me can't afford. The Roman Emperor Marcus Aurelius has always been a great help once I discovered him in a second-hand bookstall in early adolescence – though he didn't like Jews much and Christians even less. Still, like him, I review the sordid characters I'm bound to meet in the course of the day, and before I get worked up, consider why they are the way they are, and I am the way I am (and indeed if we are the same seen from different points of vantage). I remember Jewish lullabies, Carmelite cooks, Anglican clergymen, disappearing Chinese sages, Quaker samplers and my own long-suffering friends. All have provided the slices of daily bread that form the uneven loaf that is this book. What they have in common is that they work, and I live my day on a deeper level than the pluses and minuses to my ego.

This book includes the religious testimony not just of Jews like us but of Christians, Muslims, Vedantists and people of many faiths and none. They speak the truth they have discovered in their own voice. We have not tried to tidy up their richness and variety.

Now they are not a fashionable lot. Some are so overquoted they may seem trite and some banal because the incidents seem small and the authors unknown. Some seem past their expiry date like minor

Victorian poetesses, and a few are just jokes – but jokes are not just joking matters.

The hope of Jonathan and me is that this book, like the Commonplace Books of years gone by, will be your commonplace companion too, and that you will go on to enrich it with your life-experience and share it. Experience of this life and of the life beyond is distilled out of so much pain and joy; it is a pity to waste it. In our time revelation does not come as a thunderbolt from above with dramatic effects, like trumpet blasts, lightnings, heavenly voices. Instead it gently seeps up from the little things of life. Revelation has had to become humble too.

In the books we have composed together Jonathan and I have taken it in turns to write the prologue. (The other writes the epilogue.) We have worked together constructively for over thirty years, though we're not a bit alike. And yet the only time we nearly came to blows was over my driving not divinity. For the rest it's a case of 'creative tension' as the in-words would have it.

I think he's too consciously Jewish. He thinks I'm too unconsciously Christian. We are from different generations, which is important in the way we see World War II and the Holocaust. He is from public school and London's West End. I am from London's disintegrating East End, though I did make it to Oxford, Balliol no less! I feel consciously English, he is unconsciously English. For both of us, though for different reasons, Germany is important. We both believe in God – critically! He has put up with me for over thirty years, as I've said, and deserves a medal!

So if you have difficulty in bouncing out of bed, and not bouncing back in again, here are two rabbis to ease you into life with the common and uncommon experiences of themselves and many others in their modern Commonplace Book. God bless you. Life is addictive if you don't weaken.

Lionel Blue

CONTENTS

JANUARY

1 JANUARY

Blessing the new

This blessing is recited on the first day of festivals but also when acquiring something new, like clothes, or celebrating any kind of 'first'.

Blessed are You, our Living God, Sovereign of the universe, who has kept us alive and supported us and brought us to this season. JM

2 JANUARY

Ghosts

In Bedford I stood on the banks of the River Ouse, as Bunyan must have done, thinking of his pilgrims summoned to cross the river of death to reach the Celestial City on the other side. I identified not with Mr Valiant-for-Truth and his courage but with Mr Despondency and his daughter Much-afraid, for I too had suffered from self-doubt and depression.

> When days had many of them passed away Mr Despondency was sent for. For a post was come, and brought this message to him, 'Trembling man, these are to summon thee to be ready with thy King, by the next Lord's day, to shout for joy for thy deliverance from all thy doubtings . . .'
>
> Now Mr Despondency's daughter, whose name was Much-afraid, said, when she heard what was done, that she would go with her father. Then Mr Despondency said to his friends, 'Myself and my daughter, you know what we have been and how troublesomely we have behaved ourselves in every company. My will and my daughter's is that our desponds and slavish fears be by no man ever received, from the day of our departure, forever; for I know that after my death they will offer themselves to others. For, to be plain with you, they are ghosts, the which we entertained when we first began to be pilgrims and could never shake them off after. And they will walk about and seek entertainment of the pilgrims, but for our sakes shut ye the doors upon them.'
>
> When the time was come for them to depart they went to the brink of the river. The last words of Mr Despondency were, 'Farewell, night; welcome, day.' His daughter went through the river singing but none could understand what she said.
>
> (*John Bunyan* 1628–1688)

Fears can turn inside out, when you accept death as a friend not an enemy. I know this as a hospital chaplain. LB

3 JANUARY

Heine

Heinrich Heine would probably be amused at finding himself in a book like this. He was such a complex figure. Born into a Jewish family (probably in 1797) he converted to Christianity, the gateway into the university. A disastrous business man (he bankrupted his uncle!), he became celebrated as an essayist and poet. His satirical writings on religion and politics got him into trouble with the authorities and forced him to flee from his native Germany to Paris in 1831.

Even after his death in 1856 he remained a figure of controversy – a statue of him in Hamburg was the scene of a riot in 1919 and was used for target practice by the Nazis. (See what they thought of his poem 'The Lorelei' elsewhere in this book.) It was Heine who prophesied that 'where they burn books, they will one day burn people.'

The following little poem, translated from the German by the American poet Emma Lazarus (one of whose poems adorns the Statue of Liberty) is a more lyrical Heine, offering a sad reminder of the passing of love and of life.

Shadow-love and shadow-kisses,
Life of shadows, wondrous strange!
Shall all hours be sweet as this is,
Silly darling, safe from change?

All things that we clasp and cherish,
Pass like dreams we may not keep,
Human hearts forget and perish,
Human eyes must fall asleep. JM

4 JANUARY

Hymn

When I was evacuated during the war, I decided to attend school prayers, though I was the only Jewish child present. I was curious and overrode my parents' hesitations. I preferred bellowing out English hymns to cantors sobbing in synagogues. I used to stand with legs apart, cheerfully bawling out verse after verse with a couple of hundred other little boys.

Some of the faith in them must have seeped into me because I still sing them in the bathroom to help me face a new day.

This one was written by John Newton (1723–1807), a slave trader, who saw the light and helped Wilberforce in his fight for abolition. He is his own proof of amazing grace.

Amazing grace! (how sweet the sound!)
  That sav'd a wretch like me!
I once was lost, but now am found,
  Was blind, but now I see.

'Twas grace that taught my heart to fear,
  And grace my fears reliev'd;
How precious did that grace appear,
  The hour I first believ'd.

Through many dangers, toils and snares,
  I have already come;
'Tis grace has brought me safe thus far,
  And grace will lead me home.

The Lord has promis'd good to me,
  His word my hope secures
He will my shield and portion be,
  As long as life endures.

Yea, when this heart and flesh shall fail,
  And mortal life shall cease;
I shall possess, within the vail,
  A life of joy and peace.

The earth shall soon dissolve like snow,
  The sun forbear to shine;
But God, who call'd me here below,
  Will be forever mine. LB

The Nudnik

Some words just don't translate into English. ***Nudnik*** is a good Yiddish word that describes the sort of person who is always out of step and in the way. The type who gatecrashes your party and will never take the hint that he ought to go. A subcategory of ***nudnik*** would be a ***besser-wisser***, the one who always knows better and insists on telling you. A ***nudnik*** cannot help being a ***nudnik***, but a ***besserwisser*** ought to know better – except that being a ***nudnik*** he probably cannot help himself either.

How do you classify the Rabbi Jeremiah mentioned in the following story?

The Rabbis discussed what happens when people live next door to each other. For example what kind of businesses may be built next to someone's property, in case, say, the smell (from a tannery) or the noise, from the shoppers, might disturb? The Rabbis were into environmental concerns already some two thousand years ago.

But what about the case of a dovecot? How much space do you need around it, so that the owner has access to put up a ladder to clean it, but also so that it is far enough away from town not to be a nuisance? The ideal distance from the nearest property, they decided, is fifty cubits. Then comes the following discussion.

> If a young pigeon is found within the fifty cubits, it belongs to the owner of the dovecot. But if it is found beyond the fifty cubits, then it belongs to whoever finds it.

At this point enter Rabbi Jeremiah with a question. 'If a pigeon is found exactly fifty cubits away from the dovecot, but one foot is within the boundary and the other is outside it, who owns the pigeon?' The Talmud concludes: for this reason they threw Rabbi Jeremiah out of the academy. (*Baba Batra 23b*)

(In defence of the Rabbis who thew him out it must be pointed out that this was not the first time Rabbi Jeremiah had asked a kind of absurd question. Some even think that he meant them seriously. Would that make him a ***nudnik*** or a ***besserwisser***? What if half of him was a ***nudnik*** and half of him was a ***besserwisser*** . . . ?)

Are you yourself a ***nudnik*** or a ***besserwisser***? Ponder it in your prayers.

JM

A letter

On a retreat once, I got fed up with the usual misery-me prayers, pleas and petitions. Instead I wrote a letter to myself as a child. It was the wisest, saddest letter I've ever written.

Later on I discovered this 'Letter from a Girl to Her Own Old Age' written by Alice Meynell, a pious turn-of-the-century writer not much read now. (I had to learn a poem of her's by heart once. It went 'She is the lady of my delight, a shepherdess of sheep' – ugh!) No wonder the force and honesty of her 'Letter' left me gob-smacked!

A Letter From A Girl To Her Own Old Age
Listen, and when thy hand this paper presses,
O time-worn woman, think of her who blesses
What thy thin fingers touch, with her caresses.

O mother, for the weight of years that break thee!
O daughter, for slow time must yet awake thee,
And from the changes of my heart must make thee!

O fainting traveller, morn is grey in heaven.
Dost thou remember how the clouds were driven?
And are they calm about the fall of even?

Pause near the ending of thy long migration,
For this one sudden hour of desolation
Appeals to one hour of thy meditation.

Suffer, O silent one, that I remind thee
Of the great hills that stormed the sky behind thee,
Of the wild winds of power that have resigned thee.

Know that the mournful plain where thou must wander
Is but a grey and silent world, but ponder
The misty mountains of the morning yonder.

Listen: – the mountain winds with rain were fretting,
And sudden gleams the mountain-tops besetting.
I cannot let thee fade to death, forgetting.

What part of this wild heart of mine I know not
Will follow with thee where the great winds blow not,
And where the young flowers of the mountain grow not.

Yet let my letter with my lost thoughts in it
Tell what the way was when thou didst begin it,
And win with thee the goal when thou shalt win it.

Oh, in some hour of thine my thoughts shall guide thee.
Suddenly, though time, darkness, silence, hide thee,
This wind from thy lost country flits beside thee,

Telling thee: all thy memories moved the maiden,
With thy regrets was morning over-shaden,
With sorrow, thou hast left, her life was laden.

But whither shall my thoughts turn to pursue thee?
Life changes, and the years and days renew thee.
Oh, Nature brings my straying heart unto thee.

Her winds will join us, with their constant kisses
Upon the evening as the morning tresses,
Her summers breathe the same unchanging blisses.

And we, so altered in our shifting phases,
Track one another 'mid the many mazes
By the eternal child-breath of the daisies.

I have not writ this letter of divining
To make a glory of thy silent pining,
A triumph of thy mute and strange declining.

Only one youth, and the bright life was shrouded.
Only one morning, and the day was clouded.
And one old age with all regrets is crowded.

O hush, O hush! Thy tears my words are steeping.
O hush, hush, hush! So full, the fount of weeping?
Poor eyes, so quickly moved, so near to sleeping?

Pardon the girl; such strange desires beset her.
Poor woman, lay aside the mournful letter
That breaks thy heart; the one who wrote, forget her:

The one who now thy faded features guesses,
With filial fingers thy great hair caresses,
With morning tears thy mournful twilight blesses.

Tip: try writing your own letter. It may help you to see your life too in the light of eternity. LB

Pearl Bailey

Religion and 'show business' are too much alike for comfort. Sometimes the clergy fulminate about the sinful excesses of the other, but there is an awful lot of theatre about religious rituals and services; it's just that it is often not very good theatre. Perhaps on some level they are competing – with the emotional odds heavily stacked in favour of the actor. Clergy who become performers can sometimes go astray. But showbiz people who get into religion have to watch how they use their power.

Someone who ventured into religion from the world of theatre, cabaret and cinema was the magnificent Pearl Bailey. After a serious heart attack she studied theology at Georgetown University. So when she came to London to perform in cabaret she took courses with us at Leo Baeck College.

We studied the Book of Isaiah together and Pearl got very enthusiastic about the prophet and his 'song' in chapter 5.

> Let me sing of my beloved,
> A song of my beloved about his vineyard.
> My beloved had a vineyard in a very fruitful hill.
> He digged it, cleared it of stones
> And planted it with the choicest vine,
> And built a tower in the midst of it,
> And also hewed out a vat.
> And he hoped to bring forth grapes
> but it brought forth rotten grapes!
>
> And now, inhabitants of Judah and men of Jerusalem,
> Please judge between me and my vineyard.
> What more should I have done for my vineyard
> That I did not do?
> Why when I hoped it would bring forth grapes
> Did it bring forth rotten grapes?

His technique, she explained, was just like her cabaret act. The first song has to grab their attention, then you talk with them a bit, next comes a slow number, then hit them with something fast and so on. I learnt much from her about the prophets.

She was a warm-hearted and generous person and taught me a lot about caring. When you perform, she explained, you have to pay as much attention to the band as to the audience – or else they lose interest and play up! That's also a challenge to religious teachers – to respect the tradition behind you while respecting the reality of the people in front of you. JM

8 JANUARY

The skull

When I was reading about massacres in the morning newspapers, this remark from two thousand years ago floated into my mind – like the skull.

> When Hillel saw a skull floating on the surface of the water, he said: 'Because you drowned others, they drowned you, and in the end those who drowned you shall themselves be drowned.'
> (*Sayings of the Fathers 2:7*)

How to stop the dreadful cycle?
(Hillel was a Jewish teacher who lived just before the time of Jesus.)
LB

9 JANUARY

Abraham Ibn Ezra

As Lionel and I worked together on various Jewish prayerbooks, we found ourselves confronted with the classical mediaeval poems. They were composed in Hebrew by the Jewish poets of their time to give each of the festival services its own distinctive character. But they often became terribly complicated and convoluted, using Biblical verses and allusions that only an expert could understand. (Something like trying to pray the clues of the Times crossword puzzle.) In the end we took a rather cavalier attitude to them – either they still spoke in some way to us and our own spiritual situation and needs or we should simply leave them out. (Lionel was tougher than I about this at first, but in time I also became quite adept with a blue pencil – no pun intended.)

From time to time I felt pangs of guilt at treating these 'spiritual treasures' in such a casual way. So I was relieved to discover the following passage by the great Spanish mediaeval Jewish thinker, poet, philosopher, physician, grammarian, Bible commentator etc, etc, Abraham Ibn Ezra (1089–1140) – who was never shy about giving his opinion on the writings of his colleagues.

> Since God's glory fills every place, but none of us can watch our behaviour in every place, we need to fix a place where we pray and honour God. Actually, we should really thank and praise God at every moment, for God's mercy is with us every second of our lives! But since we are always busy with worldly affairs, we need to set aside regular times for prayer . . .
>
> Now when we pray we have to watch what we say and remember in our hearts that we stand before a Sovereign who has the power of life and death over us. So it is forbidden to insert into our prayers poems whose basic meaning we do not understand! And we should not just rely on the good intentions of the author, because there is no one who does not sin!

Switching on our hearts does not mean we have to switch off our minds. JM

10 JANUARY

The body

Pious people forget God created the body as well as the mind, and insult it, calling it an ass, a donkey, a mere shell. But the body has its own wisdom and goodness, less subtle but more straightforward than the soul's. If someone falls, my body instinctively bends forward in support, and it tightens up and cringes when I'm ashamed of myself.

William Blake (1757–1827) was a glorious English happy mystic who had no truck with such disdain. My own body is not beautiful, but these lines help me to like it:

> To Mercy, Pity, Peace, and Love
> All pray in their distress;
> And to these virtues of delight
> Return their thankfulness.
>
> For Mercy, Pity, Peace, and Love
> Is God, our father dear,
> And Mercy, Pity, Peace, and Love
> Is Man, his child and care.

For Mercy has a human heart,
Pity, a human face,
And Love, the human form divine,
And Peace, the human dress.

Then every man of every clime
That prays in his distress,
Prays to the human form divine.
Love, Mercy, Pity, Peace.

And all must love the human form
In heathen, turk or jew.
Where Mercy, Love and Pity dwell
There God is dwelling too. LB

Bad prayer

This is what happens when we make God in our own image. We project our own prejudices onto the cosmos and worship ourselves. The prayer of Betjeman's Society Lady is the only one I know to equal the verses below. Both poems are very funny. They have to be, otherwise we couldn't take it. (See 'Good prayer', 18 August)

From *Holy Willie's Prayer*

O Thou, that in the heavens does dwell,
Wha, as it pleases best Thysel',
Sends ane to heaven an' ten to hell,
  A' for thy glory,
And no for onie guid or ill
  They've done afore Thee!

I bless and praise Thy matchless might,
When thousands Thou hast left in night
That I am here afore Thy sight,
  For gifts an' grace
A burning and a shining light
  To a' this place.

What was I, or my generation,
That I should get sic exaltation,

I wha deserv'd most just damnation
   For broken laws,
Sax thousand years ere my creation,
   Thro' Adam's cause.

When from my mither's womb I fell,
Thou might hae plung'd me deep in hell,
To gnash my gooms, and weep and wail,
   In burnin' lakes,
Where damnèd devils roar and yell
   Chain'd to their stakes.

Yet I am here a chosen sample,
To show thy grace is great and ample;
I'm here a pillar o' Thy temple,
   Strong as a rock,
A guide, a buckler, and example,
   To a' Thy flock.

O Lord, Thou kens what zeal I bear,
When drinkers drink, an' swearers swear,
An' singing here, an' dancing there,
   Wi' great and sma';
For I am keepit by Thy fear
   Free frae them a'.

But yet, O Lord! confess I must
At time I'm fash'd wi' fleshly lust:
An' sometimes, too, in warldly trust,
   Vile self gets in;
But Thou remembers we are dust,
   Defil'd wi' sin.

O Lord! yestreen, Thou kens, wi' Meg–
Thy pardon I sincerely beg;
O! may't ne'er be a livin plague
   To my dishonour,
An' I'll ne'er lift a lawless leg
   Again upon her.

* * * * * *

But Lord, remember me an' mine
Wi' mercies temporal and divine,
That I for grace an' gear may shine,
  Excell'd by nane,
And a' the glory shall be thine,
  Amen, Amen!

12 JANUARY

That's love

I don't want Your Paradise and I don't want the world to come.
I only want You.

A saying of Shneur Zalman of Ladi (1745–1813). LB

13 JANUARY

On prejudice

I invited Professor Michael Billig to lecture for me at a Jewish-Christian-Muslim student conference on 'Psychological Aspects of Fascism and Prejudice'. The following makes a lot of sense as we try to come to grips with creating a pluralistic society.

> There is nothing inevitable about human prejudice. There is no biological gene which stipulates that groups should harbour distrust against 'others'. If there is pessimism, it is because the conditions which have created the movement of populations are exactly those which politicians can exploit by using nationalist messages to appeal to popular insecurities.
>
> On the other hand, these conditions also create other possibilities. Instead of fear of 'otherness', there is the possibility of celebrating difference. Few political leaders have the courage to welcome immigration as a positive force in the contemporary world. Far from being a social problem to be avoided, immigration can be seen as a benefit which contains the possibility of cultural innovation. Culture should not be seen as something static, which is threatened by exposure to difference; instead it could be argued that culture stagnates if excluded from difference.
>
> Thus, groups which bring together people from different

religions can symbolize a more hopeful future. The precondition is not that groups should come together in order to learn about 'the other', as if the other were an interesting anthropological specimen. Instead, there should be a willingness to accept that, in learning from others, oneself changes. What might have seemed alien becomes familiar – and that otherness, which has been learnt, becomes part of oneself. This is the very condition which terrifies the authoritarian personality – the acceptance of one's own otherness. However, this acceptance is all the more pressing if tolerance is to prevail over the psychological forces of bigotry; and if understanding, acceptance and hope are to conquer fear. JM

14 JANUARY

The wireless

M. Louise Haskins was a very minor poetess, but George VI who was no intellectual liked her, and to everyone's surprise, her words steadied a whole nation in its darkest hour.

We listened to him quoting them in the dark war winter. We sat in a silent semi-circle, round the old valve wireless, waiting for it to warm up, to strengthen us for what we would soon have to face. We had to face it sooner than we thought, for in the following year France fell, and we were alone.

The Gate Of The Year
And I said to the man who stood at the gate of the year:
'Give me a light, that I may tread safely into the unknown!'
And he replied:
'Go out into the darkness and put your hand into the Hand of God.
That shall be to you better than light and safer than a known way.'
LB

15 JANUARY

Fear of God

Rabbi Samuel went to Rome at a time when the queen lost her bracelet. He happened to find it. Meanwhile a crier went around the kingdom announcing: 'Whoever brings back the queen's bracelet within thirty days will receive a great reward. But if the bracelet is found on him after the thirty days, his head will be cut off!' Rabbi Samuel did not return it within the thirty days, but a day later brought it back to the queen. She asked him: 'Weren't you in the kingdom?' He replied: 'Yes.' 'So did you not hear the proclamation?' He answered: 'Yes.' She asked: 'What did the crier say?' He told her the crier's words. So she asked: 'Then why did you not return it within thirty days?' He replied: 'So that you would not say that I feared *you*, but I returned it because I feared God.' 'Blessed be the God of the Jews!' she said. (*Yerushalmi Baba Metzia 11 par 5 f 8c line 35*)

It's a great story, but I'm not sure I'd want to take the same kind of risk as Rabbi Samuel. JM

16 JANUARY

Priorities

Rabbi Yochanan ben Zakkai said 'If you've got a plant in your hand when people announce that the Messiah's come, plant it first before you welcome him.' LB

17 JANUARY

Keeping the peace

There's a silly joke about a Jew being stopped by someone in Belfast and being asked: are you a Catholic or a Protestant? 'I'm a Jew!' came the bewildered answer. 'Yes, but are you a Catholic Jew or a Protestant Jew?'

I came a little closer to understanding Northern Ireland when I spoke at a conference on 'Religion and Conflict' in Armagh. Being stopped by military patrols in the street (there had been a murder the night before) was disturbing – though it reminded me of travelling in some parts of Israel.

I had the fortune to meet Brendan McAllister who sent me this powerful piece that could apply to a conflict situation almost anywhere in the world.

> We have a host of professionals to service our Troubles. Their experience has made some of them the envy of colleagues across the world. We have a comprehensive service for every category of citizen-victim.

You've got a bullet in the head? We've got a neurosurgery unit in the Royal Victoria Hospital. Those boys know a thing or two.

You've been kneecapped? We've got bones and legs specialists in Musgrave Park Hospital.

You've got a dead body? We've got Mobile Support Units – quick response teams of police; they can be there within minutes. Forensic officers with white boiler suits, white chalk and white tape. We can divert traffic for a couple of hours until one of our black-suited undertakers can come and remove the body in a black zip-up bag and put it in the back of a black van. If you're travelling, listen to the car radio for the latest traffic information. A disc jockey will tell you when the road is clear. And for the scene of the crime? We've got bouquets of flowers. You've got anger and frustration? We've got protest marches, pickets and peace demonstrations.

You've got a suspect? We've got Emergency Provisions and Powers to stop, search, arrest and detain.

You've got an offender? We've got the best prisons in Britain with two prison officers for every prisoner. We've got lengthy periods on remand, non-jury courts, no right to remain silent and we have longer sentences.

You've got pain? Is all this pressure getting too much for you? We've got plenty of drink, cigarettes and nerve tablets. You need a distraction? We've soap operas on the television right after the news.

You need an escape? We've got shopping centres with Christmas and presents and Easter and eggs.

I could go on, couldn't I? Though don't get me wrong. I do not seek to condemn or disapprove. Without most of these responses, things would be much worse here, but is our attitude to peace more to do with peacekeeping than peacemaking? And does the peace we tend to keep ensure a certain harmony and order which simply helps us to live with our Troubles, not bring them to an end?

Are our peace actions more about the keeping of order than the making of peace? JM

18 JANUARY

The hair

In the world to come God will slaughter the evil impulse in the presence of both the good and the bad. To the good it will look like a high mountain, and to the bad like a mere hair and both will weep. The former will exclaim, 'How did we ever overcome such a high mountain?' And the latter, 'Why couldn't we overcome a mere hair like this?' *Succah* LB

19 JANUARY

The Devil and St Moling

This tale was told by Fr Paul Murray O.P. at a Bible study week in Germany. Himself a poet and a great interpreter of poetry (see his poem on 30 January) Fr Murray opened up for us the world of Irish poetry, the tales of Mad Sweeney, the exiled king forced to fly around as a bird till saved by St Moling, the 7th century priest and poet.

Once the Devil came to St Moling and asked for a blessing. St Moling suggested to him that he should read the Holy Books. 'I have' replied the Devil, 'but it's done me no good.'

'Then kneel and say your prayers.'

'I cannot' said the Devil, 'my knees are backwards and I cannot kneel. Still, if you cannot bless me, then curse me!'

St Moling replied: 'No, I will not curse you. But why do you ask?'

Answered the Devil: 'So that the curse would be on your lips!' JM

20 JANUARY

Dead dog

Some scholars came upon a dead dog. The disciples exclaimed, 'How revolting its breath!' But their teacher said: 'Yet how white its teeth!' LB

21 JANUARY

The sins of the clergy

Sorry, it is not those kinds of sins. Though one recalls the joke about the preacher who lost his bicycle. When he came to the part of the service where he read the Ten Commandments and got to the one about not commiting adultery he suddenly remembered where he'd left it.

No, these are different kinds of sins, as described by the Rev Simeon Singer, the great Anglo-Jewish Victorian preacher whose advice to clergy on 'Preaching' can be found in our section of that name.

While addressing potential rabbis on January 17, 1904, he described two kinds of sins of those who conduct Jewish services, but the lessons seem to be universal:

> It is a frequent complaint that clergymen are not always treated with the respect due to their calling. But what if it should be found that they themselves fail to treat their calling with the respect due to it? Can they complain if those whom they are supposed to instruct not only learn from them, but better the instruction? Take the performance of the sacred offices of the synagogue. These admit of two vicious extremes, though which of the two is more fatal to clerical dignity – not to speak of higher and more important interests – I am not prepared to decide.
>
> There is perfunctoriness at the one end. A man is soon found out whose idea of service in the sanctuary is something to be got through with as little preparation as possible beforehand, and with as little cost as possible of thought during the actual process . . .
>
> And, as with the offices of prayer and praise, so with the responsible task of preaching. All perfunctoriness in this sacred work; all inadequate, slovenly, indolent preparation for preaching; all listless, lifeless, soulless, senseless sermons, will have to be paid for in the loss of the esteem of your hearers. Vain is it to complain of this. We reap as we have sown.
>
> But there is the other vicious extreme, and the mischief it does is not easily calculated. Is it surprising that clergymen should fail to secure the respect of those whose respect is worth having, if they make the sanctuary and the Divine service the place and the occasion of personal display? All 'showing off' in voice and manner, all histrionic tricks, all ostentation and affectation, all simulated or artificially stimulated emotion, are an abomination in the sight of those who know and can judge. To whom, one is often forced to ask, does the . . . preacher address his prayers in synagogue – to God or to the congregation? That question was answered in an account, of which I have heard, of a great religious meeting held in Boston, some time ago. The reporter, by a touch of inspiration, described the prayer offered up by the Rev Dr Blank as 'one of the most beautiful and effective prayers ever delivered to a Boston audience.' Every form of display argues unreality, and unreality, however, disguised, leaves the heart unconvinced, and, need one say, unconverted. When Rabbi Zera was appointed to his sacred office, they greeted him with snatches of a bridal song: 'No cosmetics, no rouge, no hair-curling, but yet what a graceful gazelle!' JM

22 JANUARY

Dinners

Christians give thanks before a meal, and Jews, less trusting, after. Scripture says 'Thou shalt eat and be satisfied and bless the Lord, thy God.' (Deuteronomy 8:10) in that order.

I was taught this grace by a toastmaster more magnificent in manner than any cleric. He told me it came from Lancashire and theologically speaking, I think it says it all.

May we who are sinners
deserve our dinners!

No one seems to know who wrote it. LB

23 JANUARY

A little of what you fancy

'A little of what you fancy does you good.'

My maternal grandmother sang songs to suit all tastes. 'O for the wings of a dove' might be followed by music hall ditties, the most memorable of which was this one – originally sung by Marie Lloyd, whose naughty nods and winks on stage added to the fun and ensured she was never invited to appear at the Royal Command Performances. I like her East End down-to-earth advice. (*The Rev Malcolm Johnson,* Master of the Royal Foundation of St Katharine.)

People who don't get a bit of what they fancy become very nasty – unless they're saints. And not many of us are. LB

24 JANUARY

The gibbet

François Villon, a criminal and a poet, wrote this prayer in 15th century Paris. It is spoken by the skeleton of an executed criminal, swaying on a gibbet. Villon himself escaped the death penalty and was banished, but no one knows his end.

As a small child I used to wander the streets of London's East End with my gang, while my parents were looking for work. Some of the gang ended up in reformatory, but I was spared, being infantile rather than juvenile. It was a close thing. There but for the grace of God go I. It can be a matter of luck whether you end in gaol or on the honours list!

> You brother human beings, who live after us
> Don't harden your hearts against us
> Because if you take pity on us
> God might take more pity on you.
>
> You see us swaying, five or six,
> As for our flesh which we nourished so much
> It's coming away in powder and pieces.
> So don't mock our fate
> And ask God to pardon us and you together.

You see not every person is well balanced and sane . . .
('Get on, get honest, get honoured.' – JM) LB

25 JANUARY

The punishment of Moses

When the people asked for water in the wilderness, God told Moses to speak to a rock and water would flow from it. But in his impatience Moses struck the rock instead – the water flowed but as a punishment for his disobedience Moses was not allowed to enter the promised land.

But why such a harsh fate for such a minor action?

I like the explanation given once by Werner Pelz – that Moses' death was actually a blessing. He died while still full of vision and purpose with tasks still to be accomplished. What better fate than to die in harness. A variation on this idea points out how miserable he might have been if he had entered the land and had to cope with immigration officials, housing agencies, welfare officers and the rest of the bureaucracy.

I heard the following explanation from a friend who had once discussed the story with her religious teacher. He told the story of a great religious master who was told that he was about to die. He asked to see Paradise and Hell. He was so horrified at the sufferings that he saw in Hell that he told the angel of death that he refused to enter

Paradise unless he could take with him all the people in Hell. There ensued a great discussion in Heaven and it was finally agreed that this could happen on one condition. His life would be researched to see if he had ever refused anyone anything. The research was conducted and it seems that he had indeed never refused anyone anything so he entered Paradise and took all the souls from Hell with him. (My friend added that Hell was soon replenished!)

She realised that from his concern with others it was clear that he could not enter Paradise – because Paradise would not be Paradise for him while others still remained in Hell. And that was also the reason that Moses had to stay behind in exile. JM

26 JANUARY

I, too, will write and record

This piece, by our colleague Rabbi Alexandra Wright, speaks for itself:

> London, January 26, 1989 – Today I conduct the funeral of a seventy-three-year-old man. Let us call him Vincenz. I have never met him, though I can tell you the events of his life and even what he looked like. The pictures show a tall, broad-shouldered man and a face that betrays just the suggestion of a smile at the edge of his mouth. I recite the *tzidduk ha-din* – 'You are righteous, O God our Rock, and all Your ways are just . . .' His widow weeps. I read slowly and steadily: 'You are a faithful God, righteous and just and without iniquity . . .'
>
> Riga, 7–9 December, 1941 – A three day raid on the Riga ghetto kills 25,000 Jews, among them the Jewish historian, Simon Dubnow, whose last words are remembered: *'Schreibt und farschreibt'* – 'Write and record!' Among those deported from the ghetto is Vincenz. His destination is Buchenwald. With the deportees is a young boy of twelve years whose name is Josef. Vincenz has lived in Riga all his life. His parents, three sisters and two brothers are among the 40,000 Jewish inhabitants living there before the outbreak of the Second World War. Only one sister survives the war with him. Whatever it is that binds their destinies together, dictates their deaths to occur within one week of each other.
>
> London, 25 January, 1989 – Vincenz's widow is signing forms. She has been showing me photographs of holidays, friends, Vincenz

last year, two years ago, five years ago. This is Vincenz in Riga, fifty-two years ago. He is twenty-one, very good looking. Next to him stands his bride. Perhaps not more than nineteen. 'They were very young' says the widow. She hands me a slightly battered photograph album. The forms are waiting to be signed. We return to the forms and she signs. I open the photograph album. I feel like a voyeur. Page by page, I identify the sisters and brothers. It is 1937, Riga. There are many pictures – little black and white pictures of Vincenz with his dark-haired bride and her wide brown eyes. So very happy. I move on. There is a baby, I see her growing into a toddler, then as a little three-year-old. The photographs come to an abrupt end and the rest of the black pages are empty. The widow tells me that the child and her mother were both shot.

30 January, 1989 – I arrive at my desk on Monday morning to find a rather scruffy little note to me from someone whose name I can't read. 'Urgent' underlined twice. 'Please phone me tonight.' I ring that evening. It is Josef, who survived Buchenwald with Vincenz. Why wasn't he told about the funeral? Did I know Vincenz? Did I know about Riga and Buchenwald? Did I know what happened? And what did I say in my address?

What did I say? I wrote and recorded as much as I could. Because Vincenz never spoke. How could he? What would he say that would be rational, compatible somehow with where he was now? I said that I did not know how much he would have wanted us to rehearse the events of his life. I wanted to respect that. But I said that we, the generation who are left, need to hear and tell what happened. This is how I remember. Josef will come and tell me his story and Vincenz's story and I will remember and tell it as I am telling you now.

True, it is not my story. It is not even my parents' story. So let Josef tell it. Or Vincenz's widow who survives him childless, because Vincenz could not bear to have another child after the loss of his first family.

And then when they have told and died, there will be silence and no one will ever need to hear it again. And there will be none to tell it to your children or your children's children. And yet . . .

They told the story long ago of a people debased and humiliated, slaves to Egyptian Pharaohs, 'You shall tell your children . . .' We have not forgotten Egypt's taskmasters, nor the bitterness of slavery. *Schreibt und farschreibt.* It has been written and it is recorded. And I too, will write and record what I hear from the lips of those who knew. Even though I do not understand. 'Who can understand the secret of Your ways? God our Rock, the perfect God, slow to anger and full of love, have compassion and pity upon parents and children . . .' Slowly, we will continue to read together and so piece together the shards of broken lives, for in the telling and retelling, there is the healing and perhaps the understanding. JM

27 JANUARY

Playing God

Sometimes religious people forget they're in sales not in management and are tempted to play God in other people's lives. For some years I administered religious divorces to my corner of the Jewish community. This poem by Robert Browning gave me pause.

A Light Woman
So far as our story approaches the end,
  Which do you pity the most of us three?
My friend, or the mistress of my friend
  With her wanton eyes, or me?

My friend was already too good to lose,
  And seemed in the way of improvement yet,
When she crossed his path with her hunting-noose
  And over him drew her net.

When I saw him tangled in her toils,
  A shame, said I, if she adds just him
To her nine-and-ninety other spoils,
  The hundredth for a whim!

And before my friend be wholly hers,
  How easy to prove to him, I said,
And eagle's the game her pride prefers,
  Though she snaps at a wren instead!

So I gave her eyes my own eyes to take,
  My hand sought hers as in earnest need,
And round she turned for my noble sake,
  And gave me herself indeed.

The eagle am I, with my fame in the world,
  The wren is he, with his maiden face.
You look away and your lip is curled?
  Patience, a moment's space!

For see, my friend goes shaking and white;
  He eyes me as the basilisk:
I have turned, it appears, his day to night,
  Eclipsing his sun's disk.

And I did it, he thinks, as a very thief:
  'Though I love her – that, he comprehends –
'One should master one's passions, (love, in chief)
  'And be loyal to one's friends!'

And she, – she lies in my hand as tame
  As a pear late basking over a wall;
Just a touch to try and off it came;
  'Tis mine, – can I let it fall?

With no mind to eat it, that's the worst!
  Were it thrown in the road, would the case assist?
'Twas quenching a dozen blue-flies' thirst
  When I gave its stalk a twist.

And I, – what I seem to my friend, you see:
  What I soon shall seem to his love, you guess:
What I seem to myself, do you ask of me?
  No hero, I confess.

'Tis an awkward thing to play with souls,
  And matter enough to save one's own:
Yet think of my friend, and the burning coals
  He played with for bits of stone!

One likes to show the truth for the truth;
  That the woman was light is very true:
But suppose she says, – Never mind that youth!
  What wrong have I done to you?

Well, any how, here the story stays,
  So far at least as I understand;
And, Robert Browning, you writer of plays,
  Here's a subject made to your hand! LB

28 JANUARY

Bashir's diary

Bashir is a convert to Islam. Born in Europe his interest in Islam was kindled in his teens which led him to the Middle East where he sat at the feet of a Sufi master. He has great presence and humour. You can tell the season by the size of his beard and his mane of white hair since he only cuts them once a year. He has great tales to tell about his experiences working with sheep and camels. Beneath the humour is a great seriousness and commitment to improving the situation of the Muslim minorities in Europe.

He tends to speak about himself in the third person and told me that I could quote the following anecdote:

> Bashir has a diary till the year 2000. Someone asked him 'Bashir, why do you need a diary that goes so far ahead? What if you die before the year 2000, the diary will be of no use!'
>
> He replied: 'If I die there is certainly no problem. It's if I don't die that I need a diary!' JM

29 JANUARY

Integrity

For me it's the integrity of Dr Johnson which shines through the pages of Boswell's biography – more than his wit or his judgments. It's his loyalty to his damp wife Titty, to a stray cat, to the black servant he adopted as a son, to the flotsam he housed, so that he dreaded going home.

He was a sensitive man who inhabited the body of an ogre. This last prayer of his is without sentimentality or self-pity, cant or self-indulgence. It's the prayer of a gentleman.

> Almighty and most merciful Father, I am now, as to human eyes it seems, about to commemorate, for the last time, the death of thy Son Jesus Christ our Saviour and Redeemer. Grant, O Lord, that my whole hope and confidence may be in his merits, and thy mercy; enforce and accept my imperfect repentance; make this commemoration available to the confirmation of my faith, the establishment of my hope, and the enlargement of my charity; and make the death of thy Son Jesus Christ effectual to my redemption. Have mercy upon me, and pardon the multitude of my offences. Bless my friends; have

mercy upon all men. Support me, by the grace of thy Holy Spirit, in the days of weakness, and at the hour of death; and receive me, at my death, to everlasting happiness, for the sake of Jesus Christ. Amen.
LB

30 JANUARY

The passion of a priest

I met Father Paul Murray at the annual Jewish Christian Bible Week that I organize in Germany. He had been invited to speak on the poetry of exile; we'd fixed it up on a quick phone call to Ireland some months before and given him the dates – and then somehow because of crossed wires at our end no confirmation or follow-up letter was sent. Three weeks before the conference I began to get panicky and tried to reach him in Ireland, only to learn that he was in Rome. Phone calls to Rome missed him and he got in touch as soon as he was back in Ireland. He agreed the dates and the travel arrangements. On the Sunday the message came from Heathrow that his ticket had not arrived, and that he had missed the group flight. After complicated transactions with credit cards he managed to get on the next flight. We figured he'd finally arrive by about midnight, but still no sign. So we put out a series of notes and front-door keys so that he could find my room when he arrived. His plane had been delayed for four hours and we finally met at two in the morning.

There is an old Jewish superstition that when things go wrong in this kind of way it means that something really important is in the offing and that Satan is interfering! Paul's lecture was marvellous and so was his contribution to the study week. He introduced us to his own poems, including the following.

A Note On Human Passion
Sacred or profane
– it does no matter –
one must not anaesthetize
or dull the pain
but instead sustain
the splintered heart's
helpless yet terrifying
and sharp desire
never to be healed
of the wound of living. JM

My father

Dr Johnson's father was a failed bookseller. Mine was for many years an unemployed master tailor. Both fathers died before their sons could say sorry.

Dr Johnson made atonement in this incident.

> Just before the supper-hour, the door opened, and the Doctor stalked into the room. A solemn silence of a few minutes ensued, nobody daring to inquire the cause of his absence, which was at length relieved by Johnson addressing the lady of the house in the following manner: 'Madam, I beg your pardon for the abruptness of my departure from your house this morning, but I was constrained to it by my conscience. Fifty years ago, Madam, on this day, I committed a breach of filial piety, which has ever since lain heavy on my mind, and has not till this day been expiated. My father, you recollect, was a bookseller, and had long been in the habit of attending Uttoxeter market, and opening a stall for the sale of his books during that day. Confined to his bed by indisposition, he requested me, this time fifty years ago, to visit the market, and attend the stall in his place. But, Madam, my pride prevented me from doing my duty, and I gave my father a refusal. To do away the sin of this disobedience, I this day went in a postchaise to Uttoxeter, and going into the market at the time of high business, uncovered my head, and stood with it bare an hour before the stall which my father had formerly used, exposed to the sneers of the standers-by and the inclemency of the weather; a penance by which I trust I have propitiated heaven for this only instance, I believe, of contumacy towards my father.'

After I read it, I stood in the market where my father tried to sell ice cream in the rain (to support me) and asked his pardon, wherever he is.
LB

FEBRUARY

1 FEBRUARY

The meal

I sat in a hotel room, stranded by 'flu in a small town in Germany. I read this poem and it transformed my loneliness into solitude. If you believe in God you're never alone (though sometimes you would like to be).

It's the heart of religion and the greatest mystical poem in the English language. This is not just my opinion. Simone Weil thought so too. So did my friend Sister Louis Gabriel also known as Dr Charlotte Klein. (You will meet both ladies in these pages.)

Love bade me welcome: yet my soul drew back,
  Guiltie of dust and sinne.
But quick-ey'd Love, observing me grow slack
  From my first entrance in,
Drew nearer to me, sweetly questioning
  If I lack'd any thing.

'A guest,' I answer'd, 'worthy to be here':
  Love said, 'You shall be he.'
'I the unkinde, ungratefull? Ah, my deare,
  I cannot look on thee.'
Love took my hand, and smiling did reply,
  'Who made the eyes but I?'

'Truth Lord, but I have marr'd them: let my shame
  Go where it doth deserve.'
'And know you not,' sayes Love, 'who bore the blame?'
  'My deare, then I will serve.'
'You must sit down,' sayes Love, 'and taste my meat':
  So I did sit and eat. (*George Herbert*) LB

2 FEBRUARY

Suicide pact

I did not know him well. We met perhaps half-a-dozen times. I had heard much about him in advance. A young Russian Jew who had left the Soviet Union to settle in Israel. He had mastered Hebrew and made such a fine impression that he was invited to return to Russia to help the Jewish community develop in this new freedom. Suddenly the news came of his death in a suicide pact in a hotel in Israel. The woman with him was not his wife.

When someone dies at their own hand, we experience many conflicting emotions: shock at this finality and the brutality of the act; pain and a deep sense of bewilderment. But maybe anger too. Partly from guilt – did we fail to be there when we were needed? In other circumstances might there have been a different result? But we may also feel that we have been abandoned unfairly, even betrayed. A conversation has been broken off in mid-sentence, a door shut in our face, a relationship suddenly ended, and we have had no chance to reply, to say our piece, to offer our help or ask why. Or even to say goodbye.

It is as if some of the last emotions of one who dies by their own hand, the unresolved feelings that invaded them, are left behind for us to deal with, even though they do not rightfully belong to us.

We do not really know anyone else. We can only mourn the life of someone that has ended too soon, in too brutal a way, and in a mystery. My friend contained within himself the spirit of the new Jewish world emerging from the former Soviet Union, but also all its confusions and contradictions, its hopes and its tensions. He made his own contribution to the rebirth of all those who have emerged from a dark and bitter past. Perhaps some of that darkness clung to him and in the end it dragged him down – too soon! JM

3 FEBRUARY

Wit

Judaism is redeemed by its jokes and the Church of England by its wit. They puncture the false pride of both and rescue them from their pretensions. I was told this story of a deceased Bishop of London.

Montgomery Campbell, the new Bishop of London, came to take possession of his cathedral, accompanied by his verger. In accordance with tradition the latter knocked at the door demanding admission. Nothing happened. Again he knocked, and at last a deaf, doddery canon opened up. 'Ah' said the new Bishop sweetly, surveying his geriatric clergy, 'the See brings forth its dead!'

Now this is not a nice remark, but in high religious circles any wit which cuts through the bland banalities or platitudes is welcome. And I'm grateful to the Anglicans who have lots of it! LB

The passionate jew

Most modern rabbis are pretty conventional, so I was fascinated to discover an extraordinary character called Izak Goller. He was born in Lithuania in 1891 and was taken as a child to England. He served in congregations in Manchester and London before arriving in Liverpool. The Encyclopedia explains that 'because of his advanced social views' he was dismissed in 1926 and promptly created his own Zionist-oriented synagogue in the same city. What these 'advanced social views' are, is not clear. Certainly Zionism was not a popular cause in the twenties, but in addition to his rabbinic work, he was a poet, dramatist, writer and artist, categories that could well have confused and unnerved his congregants. They cannot have taken too kindly either to a poem that begins:

> Oh God, help me!
> For I have fallen into the hands of the righteous
> And the sons of the pious have encompassed me.
> Their gentle hands are choking my life from me,
> Their pinky lips glow black with my blood.

His book of poems, 'The Passionate Jew and Cobbles of the God-Road', contains many passionate love lyrics, some addressed to God but by no means all. A poem that begins: 'I am dying of love of you,/ My darling, my sin!' may well have raised a few pious eyebrows. In fact his combination of earthly and divine love, mixed in with poems on the excitement and pain of creativity itself, is not so far from the writings of the great mediaeval Jewish poets of Muslim Spain. Perhaps Goller was simply born in the wrong century.

In his preface he writes: The Author hopes that God will have more mercy on him than the Critic.

> *The Wail of the Ego*
> Leave them alone, God! Leave them alone!
>   They are not worthy of Thee.
> They prison Thy spirit in dungeon of stone,
>   And dare not think to Thee.
>   Better the madman blasphemingly flinging his burden
>   of pain at Thee.

Leave them alone, God! Leave them alone!
  And turn Thy face to me.
Deep in my womb have I buried my throne
  To lure Thee nearer to me,
  Breaking with poems the pale apparitions that sucked
    Thy sap from me!

Leave them alone God! Leave them alone!
  Kill me or make me free!
Kiss me or lash me – nor heed my moan,
  So Thou are proven to me!
  Mad with the rattle of fugitive battle I hurl my self at
    Thee. JM

5 FEBRUARY

A lost vision

Beneath the debris of Stalinism, the palaces of culture, the gulags, the personality cult, the rigged trials, a few nuggets still remind us that there was once a vision of justice, but it was lost.

> 'From each according to his ability, to each according to his need.' (*Karl Marx*)

This sentence is still morally right. LB

6 FEBRUARY

A guide

Janusz Korczak, who was born Henryk Goldszmidt, was famous in his native Poland as an author, social worker and pioneer in children's education. He was head of the Jewish orphanage in the Warsaw Ghetto and despite the chance of a last-minute personal reprieve, accompanied some two hundred orphans in his care on their journey to the concentration camp where he died with them. This little passage is just a hint of the sensitivity with which he understood the realities of the world of the child.

> The child must be seen as a foreigner who does not understand the language of the street plan, who is ignorant of the laws and customs.

Occasionally he likes to go sightseeing on his own; and when up against some difficulty, asks for information and advice. Wanted – a guide to answer questions politely. JM

7 FEBRUARY

Feet

'Even if we cannot give up our life for our brother, we can at least wash his feet.'

From a sermon of *Father Livinus* which I heard at the Discalced Carmelite Priory in Oxford. LB

8 FEBRUARY

The singer not the song

It does seem very unfair. There are people who can sing passably well, or at least hold a tune. And there are those who are vocally challenged, otherwise known as tone deaf. They seem to be divided between those who are tone deaf and know it, so they generously resist the temptation to sing in public. And those who don't know it (or know it and don't care), so they sing along in public at every opportunity. Part of me, the democratic, generous and compassionate part, welcomes their contribution. Part of me winces and tries to move my seat. There was a time at my rabbinic college when we had a good five such students at the same time, whose contribution to the daily service was unbelievably, nay awesomely, horrible. Sitting amongst them, trying to hold a tune, was an excruciating experience, especially when stuck between the two who thought they could overcome what they lacked in accuracy by increased volume.

Interestingly, at least two of them improved greatly with some coaching, and people with much more severe handicaps have been trained to make a highly effective choir. As so often it is an example of transforming a weakness into a strength, with patience, imagination and a lot of hard work.

A little tongue in cheek, I put the following quotation in front of the song anthology of one of the prayerbooks that Lionel and I edited. It was written by Menachem de Lonzano who lived between 1550 and 1624. He was probably born in Constantinople and emigrated to

Jerusalem, then moved to Safed, the centre of Jewish mystical fervour.

Judging by this passage he must have been a generous-hearted man – or maybe he was also a bit audibly challenged.

> Those whose voice is bad and unpleasant, and who cannot perform hymns and songs according to their tunes and who cannot remember melodies, even to people like this it is allotted to raise their voice. JM

9 FEBRUARY

A warning to theologians

'Don't talk about God, talk *to* Him!'
(*St Rose of Lima*. 1586–1617) LB

10 FEBRUARY

Free speech

Judah Loew ben Bezalel (1525–1609) is better known as the Maharal of Prague, the city where he served as chief rabbi for much of his life. He was a scholar, moralist, educator and mathematician. Ironically, people hardly remember him for his learning but instead because his name is linked with the famous Golem of Prague. Legend tells that he created from dust a human figure that came to life when he placed in its mouth the name of God. The Golem protected the Jewish community, though like the monster created centuries later by a certain Dr Frankenstein, it also ran amok.

The following passage about religious integrity is a challenge to every suppressive regime, to every committee that shivers at the thought of a dissident opinion being expressed and to every religious community that demands total uncritical loyalty to the party line:

> Even if what someone says is directed against your religion or faith, do not tell them not to speak or suppress their words. Otherwise there will be no clarification in religion. In fact, you should tell such people to say whatever they want . . . and not give them the excuse that they would have said more if they had been given the opportunity . . .
>
> My views are the opposite of what some people think. They

believe that when it is forbidden to speak against religion, religion is strengthened . . . But this is simply not so. By suppressing the opinions of those who are opposed to religion, you actually undermine religion and weaken it. It is far better to go looking for them and study them . . . For anyone of character who wants to wrestle with someone else and show their own strength will be eager to make sure that their opponent has every advantage so as to show off their own real powers . . . But what strength do you show when you forbid your opponents to defend themselves and fight against you? JM

11 FEBRUARY

Consolations of religion

Simone Weil irritated Catholics because she never fell into the baptismal font – and Jews, too, because she was a self-hating Jewess. She wore out Trotsky, and I want to hurl her books out of the window. But if I did, I would have to hunt for them again, because they are ruthless and go to the heart of modern religious problems.

I must have met her at the National Gallery lunchtime concerts during the war. It is the most important might-have-been of my life. She died in 1944, some say from anorexia, some from fatigue, some from misguided saintliness because she would eat the rations of occupied France. For me she is the greatest thinker to come out of those terrible times.

One of these falsehoods is the false gods which are given the name of God. We may believe we are thinking about God when what we really love is certain people who have talked to us about him, or a certain social atmosphere, or certain ways of living, or a certain calm of soul, a certain source of joyful feeling, hope, comfort, or consolation. In such cases the mediocre part of the soul is perfectly safe; even prayer is no threat to it. LB

12 FEBRUARY

A bookmark in a synagogue prayerbook

Sometimes the words of an older, seemingly more innocent age, still ring true for us today. The piety is the same, but it is less knowing or less evasive. I do not know who wrote the following passage. It comes from a bookmark that was placed in the prayerbook of the Bradford Synagogue, one of the first reform synagogues created in Britain in the middle of the nineteenth century. The message is no less appropriate today.

Gentle words to the worshipper
As thou comest in, pray, do thou remember that, though no words may yet be spoken aloud, worship hath already begun. Therefore, at once apply thine heart to God. Converse not with thy neighbour; and make no sound or movement that might disturb the sacred air of devotion. Throughout the service, as far as may be possible, enter thou with all thine heart, into the fellowship of prayer. Where, according to custom, words are sung or spoken aloud by the congregation, do thou join with all that are assembled. And continuously, let thy thought be united in divine supplication and praise with that of the holy congregation, until, with reverent heart and chastened spirit, thou shalt depart in peace. God bless our worship. JM

13 FEBRUARY

Gentility

I was given *Cranford* as a Sunday School prize. Perhaps the authorities didn't realize Mrs Gaskell was a Unitarian, not an orthodox Christian. So much goodness and affection permeate the pages of her novel it has become a sort of scripture for me. It makes goodness real – I can touch it and smell it and love it. It's the real thing.

It tells the story of some elderly ladies making ends meet as the industrial revolution gets under way. (Cranford was Knutsford in Cheshire, caught in the tentacles of giant Manchester.) Miss Matty has lost her little competence in one of the bank failures so common at that time, and the other ladies rally round with exquisite tact.

On coming downstairs I found Mrs Forrester waiting for me at the entrance to the dining parlour; she drew me in, and when the door was shut, she tried two or three times to begin on some subject, which was so unapproachable apparently, that I began to despair of our ever getting to a clear understanding. At last out it came; the poor old lady trembling all the time as if it were a great crime which she was exposing to daylight, in telling me how very, very little she had to live upon; a confession which she was brought to make from a dread lest we should think that the small contribution named in her paper bore any proportion to her love and regard for Miss Matty. And yet that sum which she so eagerly relinquished was, in truth, more than a twentieth part of what she had to live upon, and keep house, and a little serving-maid, all as became one born a Tyrrell. And when the whole income does not nearly amount to a hundred pounds, to give up a twentieth of it will necessitate many careful economics, and many pieces of self-denial – small and insignificant in the world's account, but bearing a different value in another account-book that I have heard of. She did so wish she was rich, she said; and this wish she kept repeating, with no thought of herself in it, only with a longing, yearning desire to be able to heap up Miss Matty's measure of comforts. LB

14 FEBRUARY

Almost first love

She wasn't quite my first love – and at age twenty-seven it came a bit late in the day. But it was the first one where all the yearning and pain of separation and confusion and longing and doubt and regret and loss came together. I had the loan of a flat in the South of France in November and asked her to join me. She was even more uncertain than I was – so our two insecurities made life very difficult. But off I went not knowing if she would come. On the day her train was due, if she was coming at all, I went to the station to meet her. She was not there. I trudged off back to the flat – and there she was in the street, having caught an earlier connection. It was a scene straight out of the movies. Living together for those few days did not make it any easier, though it made me feel very grown up.

Not long after we came back to England she returned home. I visited once – very awkward. But every couple of years we still drop a line to each other or phone. One of her watercolours hangs in my front hall.

Still in France I wrote her a song and I like to sing it from time to time, because the tune is sweet and the words surprisingly true.

Elisa's Blue

Clouds upon a sunny afternoon,
Worrying the restless autumn sea.
Something strange and new,
What is there to do?
Elisa's blue.

Hidden where my words can never reach.
Locked up in a world all of her own.
Is it something bad?
A private dream she's had?
Elisa's sad.

Riddles of the way that two must share.
What was it that might have caused her pain?
Still you will not find
It staying on her mind,
Elisa's kind.

This funny little tune is all I know
To tickle all the darker clouds away.
Still it's worth a trial
To see for just a while
Elisa's smile. JM

15 FEBRUARY

Marcus Aurelius

Christians and Jews have never liked him much because he was an agnostic and a stoic. But I do because I also don't deny my doubts. He was a Roman emperor who lived in the saddle, trying to keep the Empire (i.e. civilization) together. On the hoof, so to speak, he kept a notebook, and it provides still the irreducible basis for the good life.

'If God exists follow him; if He doesn't, be like a god yourself!' What more can one say? LB

16 FEBRUARY

Nostalgia

Two years after parting from the girl who was my 'almost' first love (see 14 February) I received a letter from her. And another song came unbidden. How quickly the sweet pain of past love turns into nostalgia, and how seductive the thoughts of what might have been.

On A Morning Like Today
On a morning like today
When the sun is climbing high upon the hill
And I remember how it was and how it could be still.

With your letter in my hand
Moved by words as I have never been before
I cannot help but dance for joy at meeting you once more.

And I want to capture sounds,
Gather for you all the blueness of the skies
And share the colours and the shapes that leap before my eyes.

For a strange enchanted hour
Caught between familiar smiles upon your face
And all the timeless pain and mystery that fill this place.

Slowly walk back into town,
Growing restless and then once more ill at ease
To hear the sound of laughter floating on the evening breeze. JM

17 FEBRUARY

Lockout

As so many places are bolted and barred because of vandalism and high insurance premiums, it's worth taking a tip from Marcus Aurelius.

> People look for retreats in the country or by the sea – you probably sigh for one yourself. But this is a popular illusion, because you can retreat from noise and worry whenever you like inside yourself, in your own soul. Use it.

Covering your head with an almost clean table-cloth can turn your kitchen into a contemplative retreat. LB

The golden agers

It was my first sabbatical and I was offered a place at Tel Aviv University. A friend lent me a flat in the seaside suburb of Herzliya and I settled down to study and write. I got involved with a colony of expat. South Africans, most of whom had got out on political grounds. I was invited to join their regular Saturday morning routine of an early morning walk on the beach before breakfast. It was hardly the traditional Jewish way of celebrating the Sabbath – in Jerusalem I'd have been taken by a similar group to synagogue. But it was great fun and inspired the following tribute:

Four abreast we stride the beach
the dawn patrol of the golden agers.
Seventeen minutes briskly
skirting the soft sand
nimbly over the sewage outlet
breathing in the vistas of sky and sea
in measured gasps.

Past the back of the high rise blocks
the first deckchairs
a sudden nest of children
the glazed intensity of oncoming peers
chugging through our ragged ranks.

The return is leisurely
pausing to enjoy the *hamsin* calm of the sea
pale shades of blue
fading into grey
brushed by the faintest purple haze
a subtle gift of urban fumes
caressing the margin of sea and sky.

Sand brushed off, sandals on
await the womenfolk drifting behind
home to breakfast fritters – unsweetened
coffee – no sugar
Sabbath day ritual in the holy land
counting our blessings of the morning
offering up calories of praise.
(Tel Aviv 5.11.90) JM

19 FEBRUARY

The same woman

Lot's of people say they're sorry, but do they mean it? The Talmud is exact.

> Who is truly repentant? Rabbi Judah said: A man who does not repeat the sin when the same opportunity occurs again. He added: 'The same woman, the same time, the same place.' (*Yoma 86a*) LB

20 FEBRUARY

Bag lady

I don't know if she is a kindred spirit, but she got under my skin enough to write a poem about her. I still can't decide if I'm being detached about her or sympathetic or unkind. She certainly had style:

> There aren't enough bag ladies in Jerusalem
> that they have to import them
> from Brooklyn?
>
> She harangued us for an hour
> a table at a time,
> between screaming at the waitress
> for poisoning her food.
>
> Here two years,
> she told us of cities and countries she'd seen,
> how her old neighbourhood had changed,
> how her mother taught her Yiddish,
> and her father's advice
> always to speak with appreciation
> of places she'd just left.
>
> When she'd emptied the café
> despite hiding behind my papers
> it was my turn.
> But suddenly she was precise:
> 'I can tell you're busy,
> just listen to this,
> I won't take long.'

So I heard about the clever barman
on the second floor of a bus station in New York
who let her drink a beer on a hot day
between buses
in the early afternoon
though single women didn't drink in such places.
Saved her life.

'That's it!'
She stopped.
It took ten minutes of false starts
and pottering about
and gathering her possessions
and paying her bill
and muttered commentary
till she clumped out,
her life saved again
on another warm afternoon, between stops.
(Jerusalem, December, 1990) JM

21 FEBRUARY

Scripture – the unauthorized version

The Bible just tells the story – the children of Israel having escaped from Egypt now face the waters of the Sea of Reeds. With Pharaoh's army behind them and the sea ahead all seems lost. Moses raises his rod, God made the sea part, 'and the children of Israel went down into the sea' (Exodus 14:22).

The rabbis were never happy with leaving it all up to God; we have to do something as well. So they discussed who was the first to brave the waters of the sea – and came up with the authorized and unauthorized versions.

> Rabbi Meir said: When the tribes of Israel stood by the sea, one said: 'I will go down to the sea first!' and the other said: 'I will go down to the sea first!' While they were standing and arguing, the tribe of Benjamin jumped up and went down into the sea first . . .
>
> Rabbi Judah said: When the Israelites stood at the sea, one said: 'I'm not going down to the sea first!' and the other said: 'I'm not going down to the sea first!' While they were debating the matter, Nachshon son of Aminadav jumped up, went down to the sea and fell in. (*Mechilta Beshallah to Exodus 14*) LB

Lazy student

22 FEBRUARY

Students have a reputation for being lazy, which is unfair but it goes back a long way. The Book of Proverbs hinted at it over three thousand years ago, and the rabbis added their views a thousand years later.

> Solomon said seven things about the lazybones in the Book of Proverbs. They said to the lazybones: 'Your teacher is in the city, go and study the Teaching (Torah) with him'. But he answered them and said: 'I am afraid that there might be a lion on the way!', as it says in Proverbs 26:13, 'The lazy person said, there is a lion on the way!' They said to him: 'Look, your teacher is in the middle of the city, get up and go to him!' He replied: 'I'm afraid there may be a lion in the middle of the roads,' as it says, (ibid) 'there is a lion between the roads!' They said to him: 'Look, he's living next door!' He answered: 'The lion is just outside!', as it says (Proverbs 22:13) 'The lazybones said there's a lion outside!' They said to him: 'Your teacher's in your house!' He replied: 'What if I go and find the door locked, should I keep going backwards and forwards?!' They said to him: 'It is open!' How do we know this; it is from the verse which says (Proverbs 26:14): 'The door is turning on its hinges, but the lazybones is in his bed!'
>
> In the end when he runs out of excuses, he says: 'Whether the door is open or locked, I want to sleep a bit more!' How do we know this? It is from the verse (Proverbs 6:9): 'How long will you lie in bed, lazybones?!' He wakes up on the morning and they put food before him, but he is too lazy to put it in his mouth. How do we know this? From where it says (Proverbs 26:15), 'The lazybones buries his hand in the plate and is too lazy to bring it back to his mouth.' (*Deuteronomy Rabbah 8:6*) JM

When should a rabbi retire

23 FEBRUARY

Rabbi André Ungar was a minister when I was a student. He had come to England from Budapest just after the war. I learnt a lot from him. He was not only the most sophisticated rabbi I had ever met but also the gentlest, with no rancour. He has been with the same congregation in

America now for over thirty years, a remarkable feat in a restless society.

> As a very young rabbi I accompanied my senior colleague, Harold Reinhart, to a funeral . . . the very first I ever attended. It was a truly tragic affair: a young man killed in an accident, leaving wife, parents and small children behild. I was overwhelmed by the family's grief, full of bewilderment, outrage, pity, the old theological questions.
>
> Driving home, Rabbi Reinhart and I sat silently in the car. After a while, I heard myself blurt out in embarrassment, 'I suppose after a time you get used to this sort of thing.' He looked over at me, frowned, and whispered, 'André, the day you get used to it, get the hell out of the rabbinate.'
>
> I never forgot his words.
>
> I never did get used to it. LB

24 FEBRUARY

Having a good time

Judaism has an ascetic streak, but manages to keep it pretty firmly under control. Even someone as solemn as Maimonides, who prefers the 'golden mean', is pretty cautious about denying oneself legitimate pleasures.

> You might say, since jealousy, passion and love of honour can bring disaster on us we should therefore go to the opposite extreme and say: 'I will avoid meat and wine or marriage or a beautiful house or fashionable clothes . . . This is an unacceptable way and forbidden! Whoever follows such a way is a sinner! . . . Are there not enough prohibitions in the Torah that you go looking for extra ones? (*Mishneh Torah, Deot 3:1,2*)

The Talmud puts it even more simply: We will have to give an account to God for all the good things that our eyes saw but which we refused to enjoy. (*Yemshalmi, Kiddushin II, 65*) JM

25 FEBRUARY

Surprise, surprise – that's life

It's not enough for me to know the theology of my colleagues. I also want to know the lives on which their theology and attitudes are based. I do not trust disembodied truth. So much of life is made up of small personal things which never hit the headlines.

> A million years ago, one Friday evening, I was standing in my pulpit. I looked out over my tiny congregation.
>
> Some of the people I knew well, others slightly, some not at all. And then there was a young woman with a slightly supercilious smile. Now where the dickens did I know her from? Beyond a doubt, I knew her. But I couldn't think of her name, or where I had met her. Maybe she had attended a talk I gave. Perhaps she had once been a student of mine. Shame on me for my prematurely senile forgetfulness. What was absolutely certain was that I knew her.
>
> After the service was over, I asked her. There was a gently condescending, pitying tone in her voice as she said, 'No. You couldn't know me. I've just got back from India.' Before that, it was Texas, and Illinois, *terrae incognitae* as far as I was concerned.
>
> I blushed with shame. God, of all the trite, dull, dumb lines! I meant it in utter earnest. I made a fool of myself, totally, irreparably. Five weeks later we were married.
>
> We've just celebrated our thirtieth anniversary.
>
> (*Rabbi André Ungar*) LB

26 FEBRUARY

A tough teacher

One of my teachers once pointed out: 'Where in the Bible does it say you have to be nice?!' Honest, just, religious – yes; but 'niceness' is a very special kind of characteristic. I remember this question whenever I come across the name of Akavya ben Mehalalel. He was one of the pioneering figures from the beginning of the Rabbinic period. Only some of his teachings have come down to us, and they are somewhat obscure points on Jewish law. But clearly he was a tough-minded, independent kind of thinker with little room in his make-up for sentimentality. He is responsible for the saying:

> Reflect on three things and you won't come into the power of sin. Know where you come from and where you are going and before whom you will one day have to give an account and reckoning [for your actions]. Where do you come from? A putrefying drop. Where are you going? To a place of dust, worms and maggots! And before whom will you have to give an account and reckoning? Before the King above the kings of kings, the Holy One of blessing! (*Sayings of the Fathers* 3:1)

It is a pretty stark philosophy, but he was obviously very consistent in his religious views and his own peculiar kind of integrity. He was almost excommunicated by the Rabbis for holding four views that were in complete opposition to the other Rabbis. But before he died he told his son not to continue to teach these views. So his son asked him why he did not withdraw them himself? Akavya answered:

> I heard these views from a majority, and my opponents heard the opposite views from a majority. So I stuck to the law as I had heard it, and they did likewise. But you have heard these legal views only from me, while you have heard the opposite view from the majority. So for yourself you should abide by Jewish law and follow the majority opinion. (*Eduyot 5:7*)

But if this let his son off the hook, another story about Akavya shows just how strict and consistent he could be. His son asked him to recommend him to his colleagues, but Akavya refused. When the son asked his father whether he had found something wrong in him that made him refuse to recommend him, Akavya said 'No!'. But added:

> Your own deeds will draw people to you and your own deeds will drive them away from you! (ibid) JM

27 FEBRUARY

Warning

'Don't stare long into the abyss, lest it begin to stare into you.' (*Nietzsche*) Have a cup of tea instead!

PS. I came across this in adolescence, a long time ago. If it wasn't Nietzsche it must have been Schopenhauer or someone even darker and darker. LB

28 FEBRUARY

Soul food

It is hard to get into the mindset of earlier generations. We all face the same problems in life, but different cultures express them in different ways. So when we read 'classic' texts from the past we have to do a very special kind of translation to appreciate them today.

In the eighteenth century a Jewish scholar from Italy, Moses Hayyim Luzzatto, made an all too brief but dramatic impact on Hebrew literature. He wrote brilliant poetry of a quite new sort, commentaries on traditional Jewish texts and a major book on Jewish ethics, *Mesillat Yesharim, The Path of the Upright*. He was devoted to mysticism, which led to some of his writings being banned. At the age of forty, when, according to Jewish tradition, one should only *begin* to study the mystical tradition, he set off on a journey to Palestine – perhaps convinced that he was himself the promised Messiah. Only to die there that same year.

His search for spiritual perfection, and the style in which he wrote, can still speak to us today. The following seems particularly appropriate in a diet-conscious age:

> The pleasures of eating are the most immediate and intense. But is there any experience that is so shortlived and limited? For it only lasts for as long as the food enters the gullet, and by the time it reaches the stomach its memory is forgotten as if it had never been. And if we eat enough, whether fatted capons or simple bread, we are satisfied.
>
> Moreover, if we consider all the many illnesses that we could suffer from gorging ourselves, and not least the feeling of oppressive heaviness and the gases that dull our minds, how much more should we be concerned about eating. For all these reasons, we should not seek enjoyment in this, for the good we derive is not really good and the evils are evil indeed! JM

29 FEBRUARY

Leapyear

What would be the right thought for 29 February?

We are so used to adding an extra day every four years that we rather take it for granted. But it must have taken an incredible amount of careful mathematics to get it right. The Rabbis did it a bit differently. They measured time by lunar months of twenty-eight days – though they were not the first to realize that the lunar month was actually twenty-eight days and a bit. Since 'thirty days hath September, etc', it is pretty obvious that their year will be out of sync with our reckoning which is based on the solar year. In fact the Jewish festivals 'retreat' backwards relative to our counting by a week per year. (My father told me that his teacher in Glace Bay, Nova Scotia could never understand why he had a different date for his birthday each year.) But the Rabbis had their own way of catching up with the solar year. Instead of an extra *day* every four years they simply added an extra *month* to get back on schedule – which is why every four years Easter and Passover coincide. (It gets a lot more complicated than that but I get lost.)

In the end I thought of a verse from a Psalm which seems the most appropriate for this strange day that is sometimes there and sometimes not. The key word is the Hebrew verb *manah* which means something like to 'count' or to 'measure'. Psalm 90 is quite a solemn one about the brevity of our life and our nearness or distance from God at different stages. So this verb gives real weight to verse 12. Literally translated it would read, 'To count/measure our days, so make [us] know, and we will bring a heart of wisdom.' But the sense is probably the following – though it applies to the rest of the year as well: Teach us how to measure our days so that we get ourselves a wise heart. JM

MARCH

1 MARCH

The real struggle

Boethius was the last Roman and minister to that sophisticated barbarian Theodoric (who murdered him). He wrote in prison:

> 'Why this war in the nature of things!
> This unending struggle between one truth and another.'

That's the rub! The struggle between truth and lies is so much easier to handle. LB

2 MARCH

A quiet night at the Bal Paré

Some friends in Germany invited me out for the evening. It seemed like fun to visit an old-fashioned dancing club. I remembered my first trip to Berlin thirty years ago and a trip to the Resi (Residenz Palast), the dancing club that had telephones on the tables. One of us, for fun, and with his fiancée's slightly grudging approval, tried to ring a number but got a crossed line. Instead of the sweet young thing he had wanted, a slightly more mature woman answered the phone. Ever the gentleman he invited her to dance. As he was rising to go to meet her, she rang back to our table. 'Don't worry', she reassured him, 'I have plenty of money!'

The Bal Paré has no telephones, just a nice 'Stimmung' for the older crowd:

> A quiet night at the Bal Paré.
> The DJ seems his usual cheery self
> perched in his organ loft above the bar.
> The usual medley of five –
> *umpapa umpapa*
> slow, becoming fast
> with the odd waltz in between.
> 'Tanz mit mir Corinna.'
> 'You're my heart, you're my soul.'
> 'Einfach da zu sein.'
> 'Sempré, sempré tu.'
> Sometimes quite suggestive

in a jolly sort of way:
'Erst ein Capuccino
dann ein bisschen Vino
und dann du!'

It's a nicer place than some.
Fewer expectations,
not the urgency of the disco set.
A different sort of display:
the art of the quick-step
breathtaking turns
hip-hip-hopping on tippy-tip-toe,
bodies a little past their prime
but what style!

For the 'green widows'
a night away from the telly
at a place where a woman may come alone.
A chat with the girls
joke about the men
enjoy a dance
who knows . . .
For the ageing 'swingers',
a break from the bed-sit
little risk of refusal for at least one medley
a few moments of closeness
and, after all, who knows . . .

At the turn of the hour the women may invite
but seldom do.
Older traditions prevail
proprieties are still observed
even on a quiet night
at the Bal Paré. JM

3 MARCH

The cemetery

When you go to a cemetery to visit your parents' graves, converse with them. Tell them silently what you didn't dare when they were alive. They can reply, because our dead parents still live in us, they are part of us.

An idea that came to me during a therapy session. LB

4 MARCH

Portrait

Most cells of our body are in a constant state of change and renewal. We replace ourselves at regular intervals. So we really are not the same person today as yesterday.

When I first went to Jerusalem I needed a passport photo. There was a little shop in Zion Square and the elderly proprietor made sure I looked appropriately smart for the occasion. Some months later I found that he had put my photo in his display cabinet. So whenever I returned to Jerusalem over the years I went to see if I was still there. And indeed I survived for over twenty years, though gradually got surrounded by photos of dark-bearded Orthodox Jews who were increasingly settling in the city. Whether they would have pushed me out I will never know – suddenly the shop was closed, probably on the death of the elderly owner.

The last time I saw myself was in 1989, which inspired the following poem:

He is still in the show-window off Jaffa.
That sixties face
marooned among the black hats of the eighties
encroaching fast.

Dark curly beard
hair already receding at twenty-five.
I'd forgotten the eyes were so intense.
What was he seeing so clearly
that young man
growing into Jerusalem
half-a-lifetime ago?

Today the greying hair and beard are cropped
executive style.
Glasses all the time,
bifocals soon.

Are the eyes as intense?
Would he be picked again
from a thousand portraits
to sit in that window?

A different face
in a different Jerusalem. JM

5 MARCH

Your own funeral

Like many people I used to indulge in self-pity by anticipating the nice things said about me at my own funeral. (We really didn't treat him right, etc etc . . .)

Dean Swift (1667–1745) cured me (almost) of this self-indulgence.

My female friends whose tender hearts
have better learnt to act their parts,
receive the news in doleful dumps.
'The Dean is dead! Pray what is trumps?' LB

6 MARCH

Happy lady

1967 was an incredible year for me. Having finished my house jobs as a fledgling doctor I headed off to Jerusalem to study Hebrew as a preparation for entering Rabbinic studies in the autumn. And suddenly burst into blossom, intoxicated by the place and the people I met, and also into song.

I saw out the Six-Day War as a volunteer doctor in Hadassah hospital. They looked at my medical credentials and experience and put me in the delivery room – so I spent the war doing a few episiotomy repairs.

One of the first people I met was Leah, an American who had settled in Israel many years before. She was an artist and involved with dance and all sorts of different kinds of creativity. She and Moshe lived in an amazing house, the stable of a former Turkish prison, with a high domed ceiling to the main living room.

Their front door was a large glass window, in those innocent days permanently unlocked, that slid open into a little enclosed garden leading into a park. As you stepped into the main living room you climbed over a row of children's books. Leah had seen that many of the local children had no books available, so she created her own private lending library. The children could just come and take one as they wished, and when they returned it, take another. It was part of the enchantment of that house, garden and family. I rather idealized them – never very fair on people who have to lead flesh and blood lives. But I wrote a song about the 'happy lady'.

Chorus:
Happy lady dance
Happy lady sing
Happy lady share the joy you bring.
If you take a chance
Younger you can grow
Lady loves the joy she helps to sow.

Weary is the road we find
Beginning to rust and to go blind.
Jealous of the day
That slipped away
Remembering the child we left behind.
　Happy lady dance . . .

If you've not yet given in
Climb into a second skin
Take a tune that's sweet
Teach it to your feet
Let the rhythm's spell begin.
　Happy lady dance . . .

Clumsy seconds quickly fade
Never more need be afraid
When the music plays
See the colours blaze
In the sudden sunshine where you strayed.
　Happy lady dance . . .　JM

A badge

I was a gauche student and André Ungar was already a minister – courteous, kind, amused and amusing, as only a Hungarian can be. I first saw him calmly absorbed in a book of philosophy while bad-mannered children raged around him.

Here is how he experienced the Nazi persecutions. I have, alas, too much hate and anger in me to see such a badge as beautiful.

> When the Nazis occupied my beloved native Budapest, posters appeared all over town ordering all Jews to wear yellow stars. Most Jews were utterly terrified at this edict: they regarded it as humiliating, medieval, hateful, ominous. And it was indeed one logical step in a deathly process of extermination.
>
> But being young and therefore both bright and unutterably stupid, I caught myself reacting in a very different way. To me, it was a gift, a grace, a blessing. To be permitted – no, commanded – to show publicly that I was a Jew, was an occasion of profound pride and pleasure. A golden Star of David over my heart . . . why, whatever some idiots may have thought, it was an honour, a privilege, a heart-felt delight. God knew, and so did I, and so did decent people everywhere, that such an identification was a medal of valour, to be cherished and prized.
>
> A little bit less charitably, it also gave me a thrill to see self-hating and self-denying and even baptized Jews, forced to carry this badge of self-identification. Serve them bloody well right! What their own conscience failed to make them do, the Germans succeeded in accomplishing.
>
> And then there was the sheer aesthetics of it. Suddenly the blustery Budapest spring blossomed with hundreds of thousands of golden daffodils.
>
> Later, the nightmares began. But on that first day, to one crazy Magyar kid, it was a thing of beauty and glory. LB

Musician

There is a very special British type – the hobbyist, the gifted amateur, who does what he or she does, with a seriousness, commitment, love and total altruism. Because it is fun, or 'nice' or just 'what one does', it is a hobby that somehow defines a whole way of life.

I only know him as 'Neville'. The poem was written in the Victoria Bodega, Mahon, Minorca on the 26th of March 1980.

The Best
Neville, Neville,
I envy you the night you stood in
for George Shearing
for two sets at a jam session
in London in the fifties
even though you were only
a semi-pro.
'Playing with the best
brings out the best in you!'

The British colony's own
resident
pensioned
semi-pro
mainstream
jazz band.
'Charity performances
every Monday night'.

You're looking forward to July
when George Chisholm comes
for two weeks.
'He must think we're good
to want to play with us again.'

Thanks for letting me sit in
on harmonica
for two numbers, Neville.
I hope I'll remember it
thirty years from now
that night at the Casino Bar, San Clemente
in the eighties.

Playing with the best
brings out the best in you. JM

9 MARCH

Guts

A lot of religion is pathetic or bathetic, time-serving or timid. But not Emily Bronte's. That lonely Yorkshire lass had guts.

No coward soul is mine,
No trembler in the world's storm-troubled sphere:
I see Heaven's glories shine,
And faith shines equal, arming me from fear.

O God within my breast,
Almighty, ever-present Deity!
Life – that in me has rest,
As I – undying Life – have power in Thee!

Vain are the thousand creeds
That move men's hearts: unutterably vain;
Worthless as withered weeds,
Or idlest froth amid the boundless main.

To waken doubt in one
Holding so fast by thine infinity;
So surely anchor'd on
The steadfast rock of immortality.

With wide-embracing love
Thy Spirit animates eternal years,
Pervades and broods above,
Changes, sustains, dissolves, creates and rears.

Though earth and man were gone,
And suns and universes ceased to be,
And Thou were left alone,
Every existence would exist in Thee.

There is not room for Death,
Nor atom that his might could render void:
Thou – THOU art Being and Breath,
And what THOU art may never be destroy'd. LB

Biblical cabaret

Biblical prophets seem to have been a pretty serious and glum lot – forever raging against the sins of the people. But once in a while they surprise us when we get to know their style. Isaiah turns up some passages that would not be out of place in a satirical cabaret – somewhere in Berlin in the thirties.

For example, there's a little dialogue he writes that would fit into any post-Watergate scenario when people who would normally be queuing up to be in charge of the country suddenly don't want to know.

A man will grab his brother in their father's house: 'You've got a robe, *you* be our leader! This ruin (Isaiah's pun on 'reign') can be in *your* hands!' But he will reply on that day: 'I can't patch it up. And there's no food in my house – and no robe! Don't make me leader of the people.' (*Isaiah 3:6–7*)

He parodies official bulletins issued by the government. The original must have read something like:

'We have reached an agreement with W and signed a treaty with X, when the invasion comes it will not affect us, for we have made Y our refuge and in Z we are concealed.'

Isaiah's version comes out as:

'We have reached an agreement with death and signed a treaty with hell, when the invasion comes it will not affect us for we have made lies our refuge and in falsehood we are concealed.' (*Isaiah 28:15*)

But my favourite piece is a little ditty that, if Isaiah did not make up himself, he must have heard in some pub in Jerusalem about 700 BC. He is talking about the city of Tyre, a great merchant city, that has been out of business for some time but is now picking up business and trade again. How else describe it but as a lady of the streets back in town and looking for clients – a role ready made for Marlene Dietrich:

Pick up your harp,
go round the town,
forgotten whore.
Play it well,
sing lots of songs,
to be recalled once more.
(*Isaiah 23:16*)

Next year – 'Isaiah – The Musical'! JM

11 MARCH

Sheer delight

The Fish's Nightsong of Christian Morgenstern (1871–1914) is good to read when you've read too much Nietzsche, stared into the abyss and are beginning to take life far too heavy. No translation needed! LB

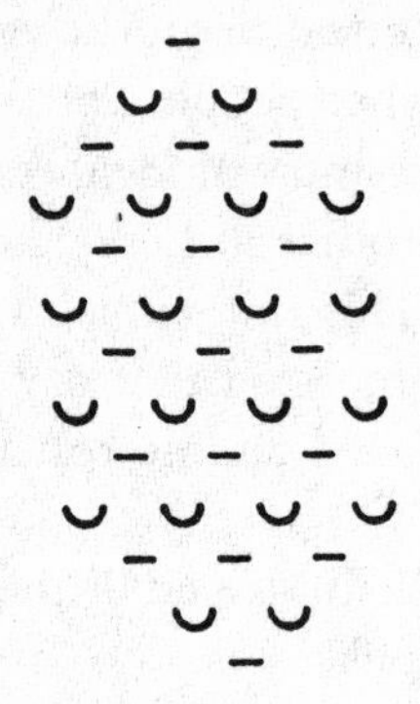

12 MARCH

Arguing with God

One of the surprising aspects of Jewish tradition is the number of Rabbinic stories about arguments with God. All right, Jews like a good argument – but to take on God displays a kind of familiarity that would appear to be scandalous in any other tradition.

When the children of Israel left Egypt and wandered in the desert they came to Mt Sinai. Moses went up the mountain to obtain from God the Ten Commandments – the constitution of the new society he was trying to create. But he took so long getting it that the people feared he was dead, that they were abandoned, and persuaded Moses' brother Aaron to make a 'golden calf' they could worship, like the idols they had just left behind in Egypt. When Moses came down the mountain, he was so furious at this betrayal that he smashed the tablets with the Ten Commandments.

But even though he was angry with the people, he was somehow stuck with them and duty bound to defend them to God. The Rabbis put the following argument into Moses' mouth (*Exodus Rabbah 43:6*):

> Moses said: Master of the world, they try to help you and you are angry with them? This calf they made will be a help for You. You

bring up the sun and he the moon; You the stars and he the planets; You bring down the dew and he will blow the winds; You bring down the rains and he will grow the plants.

God said: Moses! Are you mistaken like the rest of them? There is no reality in this calf!

Moses replied: If that is the case, why are you angry with your children?! JM

13 MARCH

Loyalty

1956 was a year of great unrest in Bahrain. Arab unrest follows its own peculiar pattern: from men, a hoarse, excited shouting; from women, frantic ululation. An Arab expert may be able to tell when the situation is likely to become ugly. I was no expert, but at that time I was living in a purely Arab quarter of Muharraq, in a narrow street opposite a Mosque. Five times a day, an ancient *muezzin* would climb the minaret to issue a quavering call to prayer. At my roof level, he was barely thirty yards away. I used to race up on to the roof to watch him broadcasting the message that there was only one God and that Mohammed was His Prophet. 'Quite so', I would think. 'But this in no way need conflict with our worship of the Lord Jesus'.

I was not alone in the house. A Pathan called Gulzaman was with me. On March 12th, I had adopted him by the simple expedient of being told (by him) that he was my son. No amount of argument would dissuade him, so I didn't think to argue, but accepted the situation with mixed feelings.

Because of so much unrest in the streets, Gulzaman was far from keen on us remaining in Muharraq when we could easily have gone to stay with James Belgrave, son of the Adviser to the Ruler, in the safety of Dufair. But I wouldn't have this. Largely by accident, I had become a friend of Abdul-Aziz Shemlan, of the revolutionary self-styled 'High Executive Committee'. He had assured me that I had no reason to fear the shouting mob, whatever their threats. I had a perverse wish to put him to the test.

Thus things were on March 13th, when I discovered that the battery of my car – an all but defunct Cadillac kindly lent me by Sheikh Sulman, one of the Ruler's cousins – was flat. So I couldn't escape, even had I wanted to. As the telephone was still working, I arranged for someone to come along with a fully-charged battery. When it arrived, two men from the local bicycle shop helped to install it, just as a call to prayer was echoing from the minaret. It was then that trouble started.

The street was suddenly full of men converging on the Mosque. One man gave the car a thump, shouting something unpleasant. Whereupon others began to thump and yet others rushed up to remonstrate with the thumpers. I called out: '*Ana Muharraqi*!' (I'm a Muharraqi), as I retreated inside the house. From the balcony I heard an argument developing: 'Why did you leave your prayers to help the unbeliever?' 'It is my religious duty to help my neighbour!', etc., etc.

Suddenly, Gulzaman was no longer there. Then I realized that he'd gone downstairs and was standing alone outside the street door, a knife, (actually a breadknife) in one hand, whilst with the other he patted the Cadillac. 'Death to the first man who touches this car!', he was shouting. Then, with a threatening flourish, he took up a position at the bottom of the stairs, ready to pounce on any man trying to force a way in.

My heart was pounding with fear for myself and anxiety for him. His eyes were expressing something I'd never known before: fierce beyond belief, yet as blank and shining as pebbles straight from the sea.

What I was privileged to be seeing was the naked face of loyalty; an underrated quality until the moment when it and it alone is what counts in life. I hardly had time to think: 'This is too important ever to be forgotten', before there were scuffles outside and shouts from those in authority. The Police? Not at all. No policeman could have ventured into the narrow alleyways of Muharraq at that moment. They were stewards sent by the High Executive Committee in the nick of time. The mob wavered, then started to disperse. Abdul-Aziz Shemlan had honoured his pledge; we had been saved. The words of 'Onward Christian soldiers!' came to mind, but what I said to Gulzaman was: '*El Hamdu l'Illah*'. At that moment, it seemed more appropriate to praise God in the guise of Allah; for in what way did the One differ from the Other?

It is not entirely fanciful to think that, but for Gulzaman, I might not be alive today. No wonder, then, that he has never ceased to be my son. (*Roderic Owen*) LB

That'll do nicely

Women have a pretty rough time of it in the Hebrew Bible. Mind you, men have to put up with a lot of unpleasantness as well, but women are trapped in a legal system that only recognizes them as someone's daughter or someone else's wife. A woman alone, widowed or orphaned, has to fend for herself as best she can, and often resort to means that are not altogether respectable. The Book of Ruth describes very faithfully, and from the woman's perspective, the difficulties of obtaining some kind of 'security' in this situation – which essentially means finding a husband to look after you and having a son to take on the task in later life.

One woman who literally had to sell herself to get her civil rights was Tamar, whose tale is recorded in Genesis 38. The story is pretty strange. She was married to a man called Er, the son of Judah. When Er died unexpectedly without having offspring, she was automatically married off to his brother, the famous, or infamous Onan, as was the custom. (Childless widows married the next brother in line so that the family name could be preserved.) Onan did not wish to have a child since it would actually be a rival with him to inherit his father's property, so he 'spilled his seed' onto the ground. Though this led to the term 'Onanism' becoming used for masturbation, and a lot of taboos growing up around it, his sin was not the act of masturbation itself but the failure to take his family responsibility and produce a child on behalf of his brother. (A lot of guilt and misery might have been spared young men if they had actually read the story instead of only being told about it!)

Judah has a third son, Shelah, but by now he's a bit worried about the effect Tamar seems to be having on his offspring. So he tells her to go home till Shelah is old enough to marry her, but he has no intention of risking his third son on her.

When time goes by and it is obvious to Tamar that Judah is not going to fulfil his promise, she puts on the clothes of a lady of the street and sits by the road where Judah passes. He has intercourse with her, she becomes pregnant and eventually, when Judah accuses her of adultery (she was officially still 'married' to Onan), she points out that he is the father!

It is all very sordid – especially the part played by Judah who tries to pretend that the woman he slept with was a Temple prostitute and not any old common or garden whore. But the Bible seems to be very much on Tamar's side – and from her child will descend Boaz who marries Ruth who becomes the great-grandmother of King David. Happy end!

But all of this story is incidental to something else that Tamar did that makes her the mother of modern credit card services. Her conversation with Judah goes as follows:

Judah: Let me come unto you.
Tamar: What will you give me for coming unto me?
Judah: I will send you a kid from the flock.
Tamar: Only if you give me a pledge till you send it!
Judah: What pledge shall I give you?
Tamar: Your seal, your cord and the staff in your hand.
(*Genesis 38:16–18*)

Since the 'seal' was effectively his way of identifying himself in any business transaction that he undertook, she actually took his credit card. Which proves that in the method of paying for services, and the sort of services for which credit cards are sometimes used, there really is nothing new under the sun. JM

15 MARCH

An alternative ten

The Ten Commandments are prominently displayed in every synagogue and many churches. I discovered this version in my teens, and it's lodged in my mind ever since. Arthur Hugh Clough (1819–1861) was a Victorian – we underrate their penetration! I would like his version to be displayed on a pious plaque too, but no one would have it – it's too near the bone.

Thou shalt have one God only; who
Would be at the expense of two?
No graven images may be
Worshipped, except the currency:
Swear not at all; for thy curse
Thine enemy is none the worse:
At church on Sunday to attend
Will serve to keep the world thy friend:
Honour thy parents; that is, all
From whom advancement may befall:
Thou shalt not kill; but needst not strive

Officiously to keep alive:
Do not adultery commit;
Advantage rarely comes of it:
Thou shalt not steal; an empty feat,
When it's so lucrative to cheat:
Bear not false witness; let the lie
Have time on its own wings to fly:
Thou shalt not covet; but tradition
Approves all forms of competition.

The sum of all is, thou shalt love,
If any body, God above:
At any rate shall never labour
More than thyself to love thy neighbour. LB

16 MARCH

Sallah Eid

I cannot claim to know too much about Islam, but I do feel close to a number of Muslims with whom I have worked, prayed, studied and laughed over the years. The personal meeting comes first. After that we can begin to look at our similarities and the differences out of mutual respect and curiosity, not simply defensiveness and the need to prove that our own tradition is 'better'.

Sallah Eid was one of the first Muslims I met and perhaps the one who did more than anyone else to bring home to me the faith, importance and simple reality of Islam. So I owe him a lot.

We met in Berlin after the Six Day War at a conference arranged to try to see if the three great monotheistic faiths, Judaism, Christianity and Islam, could find some point of meeting beyond the disastrous political one. During one of the sessions we were asked to explain what it was that had led us to attend this meeting. Sallah told us that he came from Egypt and that his brother had been killed in the Sinai during the Six Day War.

There followed an awkward silence, and, on my part, panic, not knowing what to expect next. All my prejudices came to the fore – about 'Arabs' and 'Muslims', prejudices which belonged in part to my Jewish upbringing and Israel orientation, but even more to a typical Western education that gives an arrogant sense of superiority to the peoples of the Middle East. What would he say next?

Sallah continued. He said that if there was no peace between Egypt and Israel as a result of the War, then his brother had died for nothing. That was why he had come to this conference, to meet with Jews.

In one moment he overturned every stereotype that I had, and I made a personal commitment that I would try to match the courage and generosity of spirit that he had shown. Since then whenever the Jewish-Muslim dialogue has seemed difficult or not worth trying to continue, I thought of Sallah and found the strength to carry on. JM

17 MARCH

The ladder

O world invisible, we view thee,
O world intangible, we touch thee,
O world unknowable, we know thee,
Inapprehensible, we clutch thee!

Does the fish soar to find the ocean,
The eagle plunge to find the air –
That we ask of the stars in motion
If they have rumour of thee there?

Not where the wheeling systems darken,
And our benumbed conceiving soars!
The drift of pinions, would we hearken,
Beats at our own clay-shuttered doors.

The angels keep their ancient places;
Turn but a stone and start a wing!
'Tis ye, 'tis your estrangèd faces,
That miss the many-splendoured thing.

But (when so sad thou canst not sadder)
Cry, and upon thy so sore loss
Shall shine the traffic of Jacob's ladder
Pitched betwixt Heaven and Charing Cross.
(*Francis Thompson* 1859–1907)

Something like that happened to me too, but at King's Cross not Charing Cross, while munching a doughnut to ease my despair. That's when heaven happens. LB

'My cat Jeoffry'

Lionel is a dog person. I have a kind of ambivalent relationship with Sophie, the family cat. She was left with us by a friend during her visits abroad. But as the visits got longer, Sophie got more and more adapted to our home and gradually settled in. She and I have an uneasy truce. I suppose I resent her apparent affection when it is food time – her friendliness is too transparent. But then, how else do you operate when you are so dependent on someone to provide for you? She often ends up on the balcony of my study, yowling piteously to be let in, though she can always come through the back door. There is something calculated about this – displaying the power of the powerless and teaching me liberation theology. Of course this is all projection on my part – or does she really communicate? Only real cat lovers can answer – Sophie and I will continue to argue the point.

But all of this is to introduce another cat who features in a poem, *Jubilate Agno* by Christopher Smart (1722). I would know nothing about this but for a copy given me by a friend, for which much gratitude. The poem is such fun and offers such a marvellous interpretation of Sophie's behaviour that it might persuade me to take her even more seriously.

For I will consider my cat Jeoffry.
For he is the servant of the Living God duly and daily serving him.
For at the first glance of the glory of God in the East he worships in his way.
For is this done by wreathing his body seven times round with elegant quickness.
For then he leaps up to catch the musk, which is the blessing of God upon his prayer.
For he rolls upon prank to work it in.
For having done duty and received blessing he begins to consider himself.
For this he performs in ten degrees.
For first he looks upon his fore-paws to see if they are clean.
For secondly he kicks up behind to clear away there.
For thirdly he works it upon stretch with the fore paws extended.
For fourthly he sharpens his paws by wood.
For fifthly he washes himself.
For Sixthly he rolls upon wash.

For Seventhly he fleas himself, that he may not be interrupted upon
the beat.
For Eighthly he rubs himself against a post.
For Ninthly he looks up for his instructions.
For Tenthly he goes in quest of food.
For having consider'd God and himself he will consider his
neighbour.
For if he meets another cat he will kiss her in kindness.
For when he takes his prey he plays with it to give it a chance.
For one mouse in seven escapes by his dallying.
For when his day's work is done his business more properly begins.
For he keeps the Lord's watch in the night against the adversary.
For he counteracts the powers of darkness by his electrical skin and
glaring eyes.
For he counteracts the Devil, who is death, by brisking about the life.
For in his morning orisons he loves the sun and the sun loves him.
For he is the tribe of Tiger.
For the Cherub Cat is a term of the Angel Tiger.
For he has the subtlety and hissing of a serpent, which in goodness
he suppresses.
For he will not do destruction if he is well-fed, neither will be spit
without provocation.
For he purrs in thankfulness, when God tells him he's a good Cat.

JM

19 MARCH

Another country

I learnt this poem by heart when I was six. I recognized that country instinctively and knew it was home.

My Soul, there is a country
Far beyond the stars,
Where stands a winged sentry
All skilfull in the wars,
There above noise, and danger
Sweet peace sits crown'd with smiles,
And one born in a manger
Commands the beauteous files.
He is thy gracious friend,

And (O my soul awake!)
Did in pure love descend
To die here for thy sake,
If thou canst get but thither,
There grows the flower of peace,
The rose that cannot wither,
Thy fortress, and thy ease;
Leave then thy foolish ranges;
For none can thee secure,
But one, who never changes,
Thy God, thy life, thy cure.
(*Henry Vaughan* 1622–1695) LB

20 MARCH

The zen of surgery

I do not recall much of my medical studies – in fact I have spent half a lifetime trying to forget them. My recurring nightmare was to be in an auditorium when someone was taken ill, and helpful friends would volunteer me to go and help. I assumed that I would indeed be the first person on my feet – but heading for the nearest exit. I do recall one remark from a surgeon on a ward round which summed up his philosophy when it came to looking after patients. 'Masterly inactivity', he said. And paused while we let that sink in. Fair enough, never get panicked into doing unnecessary treatments. And then he added the second half of the equation: 'and catlike observation'. It seems to work when doing most things. JM

21 MARCH

One step

Prayer has never shown me the distant scene – only the next step, and how to get the courage to take it.

Lead, kindly light, amid the encircling gloom,
Lead thou me on;
The night is dark, and I am far from home;
Lead thou me on.
Keep thou my feet; I do not ask to see
The distant scene: one step enough for me.

I was not ever thus, nor prayed that thou
    Shouldst lead me on;
I loved to choose and see my path; but now
    Lead thou me on.
I loved the garish day, and, spite of fears,
Pride ruled my will: remember not past years.

So long thy power hath blessed me, sure it still
    Will lead me on
O'er moor and fen, o'er crag and torrent, till
    The night is gone,
And with the morn those angel faces smile
Which I have loved long since, and lost awhile.
(*John Henry Newman* 1801–1890) LB

22 MARCH

Teacher's pet

The following story does not belong in this book – since it is largely about 'nice' people who we are happy to recognize as friends or teachers. But a book without a few 'baddies' might be very boring.

I will simply introduce him as someone who, quite late in life, had become an academic. But in his earlier years, he told me, he had been a teacher. When he entered a private school on his very first day of teaching, one of his colleagues took him aside to give him some advice. 'I hope you won't mind my telling you this, but I can see that you are rather short, and you will have some difficulties maintaining your authority in the classroom. May I suggest that you do the following thing. On the first time in class, pick on the smallest, most insignificant and innocent child in the room, and accuse him of something, haul him out in front of everyone and beat him! They will hate you, but, by God, they'll respect you!'

He told this tale and smiled at my obvious horror at such an action. Then he concluded, 'So I did it, and it worked!' JM

23 MARCH

Shopping

An ordinary man, a piece of professional cannon fodder in the interminable 'religious' and dynastic wars of the 17th century, became the humble extraordinary Brother Lawrence, a Carmelite lay brother and a cook. I came upon his *'The Practice of the Presence of God'* in the Quaker book shop in Euston Road after missing a train. Missing that train was the best fortune I enjoyed that year. His book made religion so simple.

> That he had been lately sent into Burgundy to buy the provision of wine for the society, which was a very unwelcome task for him, because he had no turn for business and because he was lame, and could not go about the boat but by rolling himself over the casks. That, however, he gave himself no uneasiness about it, nor about the purchase of the wine. That he said to God; *It was His business he was about*, and that he afterwards found it very well performed. That he had been sent into Auvergne the year before upon the same account; that he could not tell how the matter passed, but that it proved very well.
>
> So, likewise, in his business in the kitchen (to which he had naturally a great aversion), there for the love of God, and with prayer upon all occasions for His grace to do his work well, he had found everything easy during fifteen years that he had been employed there.

It helps me in the dilemmas of choice which bewilder me in the supermarket, and in my aversion to unloading the dishwasher. Both activities can be paths to heaven. LB

24 MARCH

I've made up my mind

I still recall the ward rounds with the professor of medicine, a cardiologist. He was nearing retirement, a formidable figure of enormous authority who therefore scared the wits out of me – heaven forbid he should ask a question. So I tended to hide at the back of the little group of medical students who in turn stood behind the registrars, housemen and assorted nurses and physios that made up this strange hospital hierarchy.

But I do remember a story he told about his own days as a medical student. He too had gone on the classical ward round with his professor. This was the days when the blood-pressure machine had only just been invented, and his professor refused to use such a new-fangled contraption. Instead he taught the classical virtues of taking the pulse and the many different, significant measurements you could obtain from careful observation of the rate and rhythm. Not only that, insisted his professor, but a skilled practitioner could get an accurate sense of the blood pressure by careful feeling alone. My own professor must have been something of an iconoclast. He told us that the students decided to test out their master's skills. After the round they visited each patient they had seen and checked his estimate of the blood pressure against the measurement shown by the new machine. In every single case their teacher turned out to be one hundred per cent wrong! I am grateful for that reminder that all authority figures need to be questioned and challenged – and the reminder that not all new things are necessarily bad. JM

25 MARCH

Regret

Lord Alfred Douglas did not play an altogether honourable part in Oscar Wilde's downfall. Too often we hurt the thing we love, and only weep when that thing or person has died. But though the past cannot be undone, it is still not too late to make peace, for those we love still live as voices within us.

The Dead Poet
I dreamed of him last night, I saw his face
All radiant and unshadowed of distress,
And as of old, in music measureless,
I heard his golden voice and marked him trace
Under the common thing the hidden grace,
And conjure wonder out of emptiness,
Till mean things put on beauty like a dress
And all the world was an enchanted place.
And then methought outside a fast locked gate
I mourned the loss of unrecorded words,
Forgotten tales and mysteries half said,
Wonders that might have been articulate,
And voiceless thoughts like murdered singing birds.
And so I woke and knew that he was dead. LB

26 MARCH

The hermeneutics of suspicion

I have a love-hate relationship with the word 'hermeneutics'. It has something to do with the 'interpretation' and the 'study of meaning'. At one time it became very fashionable and the essential 'in-word' for any kind of study of literature. Like all such technical words there is a narrow line between the proper, and helpful, use of the term and a kind of intellectual 'name-dropping'.

I once heard from a Christian colleague a marvellous definition of one particular application of the term, the 'hermeneutics of suspicion'. This means an approach to a text that requires that we question the motivation of the writer, the way in which he or she seeks to manipulate the reader. My friend gave a somewhat more direct example of how the method operated.

'Whenever I hear a speech from a politician I ask myself: why is the bastard lying to me?' JM

27 MARCH

Mad dog

An Elegy on the Death of a Mad Dog

Good people all, of every sort,
  Give ear unto my song,
And if you find it wondrous short,
  It cannot hold you long.

In Islington there was a man
  Of whom the world might say
That still a godly race he ran
  Whene'er he went to pray.

A kind and gentle heart he had,
  To comfort friends and foes;
The naked every day he clad,
  When he put on his clothes.

And in that town a dog was found,
  As many dogs there be,
Both mongrel, puppy, whelp, and hound,
  And curs of low degree.

This dog and man at first were friends;
But when a pique began,
The dog, to gain some private ends,
Went mad, and bit the man.

Around from all the neighbouring streets
The wond'ring neighbours ran,
And swore the dog had lost his wits,
To bite so good a man.

The wound it seemed both sore and sad
To every Christian eye;
And while they swore the dog was mad,
They swore the man would die.

But soon a wonder came to light,
That showed the rogues they lied:
The man recovered of the bite –
The dog it was that died.
(*Oliver Goldsmith* 1730–1774) LB

28 MARCH

Angels

There's a lot of Jewish folklore about angels. But the Rabbis were always careful to limit their powers. Because they were so ethereal they did not really understand the passions, struggles and sufferings of human beings. In fact they rather resented that God paid us so much attention. Perhaps that is why some of the stories insist that they learn their place in the scheme of things.

According to Rabbi Joshua ben Levi, who lived in the 3rd century and was a great interpreter of Biblical passages, a company of angels walk before each human being and announce our coming, like the heralds who precede a king. But what do these angels proclaim? 'Make way for the image of God!' (*Deuteronomy Rabbah Re'eh 4*) JM

29 MARCH

The spirit abhors a vacuum

The Quakers say if you empty your mind, the spirit of God flows in to fill it. I tried it out myself and it was true. Brother Lawrence gave up the pleasures of this world and the joys of another flowed in – to his surprise.

> He told me that God had done him a singular favour in his conversion at the age of eighteen.
>
> That in the winter, seeing a tree stripped of its leaves, and considering that within a little time the leaves would be renewed, and after that the flowers and fruit appear, he received a high view of the providence and power of God, which has never since been effaced from his soul. That this view had perfectly set him loose from the world, and kindled in him such a love for God that he could not tell whether it had increased in above forty years that he had lived since.
>
> That he had been footman to M. Fieubert, the treasurer, and that he was a great awkward fellow who broke everything.
>
> That he had desired to be received into a monastery, thinking that he would there be made to smart for his awkwardness and the faults he should commit, and so he should sacrifice to God his life with its pleasures; but that God had disappointed him, he having met with nothing but satisfaction in that state. LB

30 MARCH

Charity

It is appropriate to give charity before praying. (*Shulchan Aruch*) JM

31 MARCH

Practice makes perfect

> . . . In order to form a habit of conversing with God continually and referring all we do to Him, we must first apply to Him with some diligence; but that after a little care we should find His love inwardly excite us too without any difficulty. (*Brother Lawrence*)

I can attest to the truth of this. I first felt embarrassed and a ninny chatting to someone who wasn't there. Now I wander into empty places of worship (or park benches if they're not open) and hold His hand, as it were, and we converse without words. (A warning! Don't make God too chatty. You're not a ventriloquist and He's not your dummy.) LB

APRIL

Definition of a fool

I heard this definition of a fool from a leading Orthodox thinker of our generation – who has also a great sense of humour.

A fool is someone who says in public what he should only say to his wife in bed; and says to his wife in bed what he should only say in public. JM

Sentiment

Sentiment did not embarrass the Victorians. And sometimes the sentiment is overpowering when it rings true. Eliza Cook was the poetess of the people, her works found in every country cottage and back-to-back beside the Bible and The Pilgrim's Progress. (I found her in a Devon country cottage during the evacuation years.) She is, of course, neglected by critics, but she speaks to me. And the lines recall my grandmother and the few common things I still have of hers, a photo, a pan, a glass dish – no armchair, alas.

The Old Arm Chair
I love it – I love it, and who shall dare
To chide me for loving that old arm chair!
I've treasured it long as a sainted prize –
I've bedewed it with tears, and embalmed it with sighs;
'Tis bound by a thousand bands to my heart,
Not a tie will break, not a link will start.
Would you learn the spell? a mother sat there;
And a sacred thing is that old arm chair.

In childhood's hour I lingered near
The hallowed seat with listening ear;
And gentle words that mother would give,
To fit me to die, and teach me to live.
She told me shame would never betide,
With truth for my creed and God for my guide;
She taught me to lisp my earliest prayer,
As I knelt beside that old arm chair.

I sat and watched her many a day,
When her eyes grew dim and her locks were grey,
And I almost worshipped her when she smiled
And turned from her Bible to bless her child.
Years rolled on, but the last one sped –
My idol was shattered – my earth star fled:
I learnt how much the heart can bear,
When I saw her die in that old arm chair.

'Tis past! 'tis past! but I gaze on it now
With quivering breath and throbbing brow:
'Twas there she nursed me – 'twas there she died,
And memory flows with lava tide –
Say it is folly, and deem me weak,
While the scalding tears run down my cheek.
But I love it – I love it, and cannot tear
My soul from my mother's old arm chair. LB

3 APRIL

Modesty

Ben Azai was a rabbi who lived in Israel in the second century. He was so dedicated to the study of the word of God, that he even abandoned his wife. Not a good role model since Judaism puts a lot of emphasis on family life and the raising of children.

He liked to add a moral message to his teaching – so much so that some of his colleagues got a bit worried about how far he should insist on this. 'Do you wait till the person you are talking to wants to fight or to curse?' 'Just till they start to scold!' he reassured them.

One of his sayings sits somewhere between modesty and common sense: 'When you choose a place to sit, pick one a few steps lower than the one you think you deserve. It is better that people tell you to go up rather than to come down.' (*Avot D'Rabbi Nathan 25*) JM

4 APRIL

Unlike pubs

Unlike pubs and cinemas and places of worship, 'the gates of repentance are always open.' (*Pesikta D'Rav Kahana*) LB

Reputation

> A person is known by three things: by his cup, by his pocket and by his anger. Some say: by his laughter. (*Eruvin 65b*)

[This epigram by Rabbi Ilai, who lived in Tiberias in the third century, loses something in the translation. It is actually a pun on three Hebrew words 'kos' (cup), 'kis' (purse or pocket) and 'ka'as' (anger) – it still works, even in English.] JM

The narrow gate

Charlotte Klein was an orthodox Berlin Jewess, who became a Catholic convert and a nun. *En route*, she was married, a refugee from the Nazis, and worked for British intelligence. She could be (and often was) exasperating, but at her death five rabbis attended her requiem mass to say prayers – no mean achievement. Life had not been easy for her and she was not easy on herself. Sister Louis Gabriel (that was her other name) became a personal sister to me. Her friend and colleague, Sister Mary Kelly, wrote this to me about her.

> 'Enter by the narrow gate; for the gate is wide and the way is easy, that leads to destruction, and those who enter by it are many. For the gate is narrow and the way is hard, that leads to life, and those who find it are few.' (*Matthew 7:13–14*)

Charlotte said this was the text that impressed her when she first read the New Testament. It was at a time of great trouble in her life when she had long since abandoned Jewish observance. She never explained the significance of this text but I suspect that she was longing for that 'way that led to life', and in keeping with the 'absoluteness' of her personality, was ready to go forward to get it, cost what it may. LB

7 APRIL

The mysteries of life

The Rabbis taught that seven things are hidden from us, and these are they:

The day of death.
The day of consolation.
The extent of the judgment.
Nobody knows what is in the heart of their neighbour.
Nobody knows how they are to earn their living,
nor when the Kingdom of David will be restored (the messianic time),
nor when the reign of evil will cease. (*Pesachim 54b*) JM

8 APRIL

Motive

At my prep school we all had to line up for cocoa before bedtime. The wife of the headmaster would dole this out of a huge bowl with a ladle, Oliver Twist style. One evening when it was my turn she asked me what I wanted to be when I grew up. My ten-year-old mind was already made up so I said 'I'm going to be a priest.' She shrieked with laughter as did everyone else. From that moment my resolution stiffened and twenty years later when I preached at the School Founder's Day I much enjoyed reminding her of the incident. She was mortified! (*The Rev Malcolm Johnson,* Master of the Royal Foundation of St Katharine)

My mother also said I was becoming a rabbi 'to spite her'. It's only when you're honest about your wrong motives you know you've done right. Thank God, God purifies our motives. LB

9 APRIL

Gisela

I first met Gisela Hommel through a German pastor who wanted me to get to know her. She was a housewife who was a writer, radio broadcaster and theologian – not in any official capacity, but as someone with a passionate concern for truth and great misgivings about the German church to which she belonged.

She was heavily built and her movements were deliberate. I do not remember seeing her dressed in anything other than a dark smock which was almost her uniform. She listened more than she spoke, but you were always aware of her attentive presence. She would occasionally sigh loudly. It seemed to convey her approval or disapproval of what was being said, but it was probably only a feature of her physical condition.

Her Jewish father had died 'just in time', as the family put it, after the Nazis came to power, and the family sent her to live with a Catholic family somewhere else in Germany which enabled her to survive. When I met her she was studying Judaism. She wanted to call her first book on the subject *Judaism for Beginners*, but her publishers thought the title too flippant and saddled it with something more solemn.

She was not a conventional feminist – and was particularly critical about trends in German feminist theological writing that simply recycled old Christian anti-Jewish ideas. (Jesus was a true feminist; but all his contemporary rabbis were male chauvinist pigs.) She was her own person, with an impish sense of humour trapped in a rather solemn German frame.

I talked to her on the phone during her final illness. She knew she was dying but was her usual straightforward self, grateful for the support she had received from neighbours. Two weeks after that conversation she died.

She had thought much about her father's background and the possibility of converting to Judaism one day, though she felt she had work to do in the church. She once spoke of herself as a mother who makes the sandwiches for the outing and packs everyone on to the bus while she stays behind to clean up the kitchen. One day, she said, she would run after the bus herself and catch it. JM

10 APRIL

So much!

When Rabbi Yochanan ben Zakkai was dying he said to his disciples. 'Fear God as much as you fear your fellow human beings!' 'So little!' they exclaimed, astonished. 'So much!' he replied. (*Berachot 28b*)
LB

11 APRIL

Practical wisdom

The Rabbis had any number of good bits of advice for daily living, including the following:

> If you spit in the air it will land on your face. (*Ecclesiastes Rabbah 7:21*) JM

12 APRIL

Death

Sister Mary Kelly, of the Sisters of Sion, wrote this to me about her fellow Sister, Dr Charlotte Klein (Sister Louis Gabriel).

> The beauty of *Ecclesiastes 12:1–7* (see 'The dying city', 3 November) moved Charlotte and its acceptance of the inescapability of death. Charlotte quoted it in a broadcast she made on Good Friday 1983 (two years before she died). However she coupled it with a quotation from the Epistle to the Corinthians: 'The perishable nature must put on the imperishable, and this mortal nature must put on immortality . . . then shall come to pass the saying: "Death is swallowed up in Victory . . . O death where is thy victory? O death where is thy sting? (*Isaiah 25:8*)" (*1 Corinthians* 15:53–55) and the couplet:
>
> 'One short sleep past, we wake eternally,
> And death shall be no more:
> Death, thou shalt die.' (*John Donne* 1572–1631) LB

13 APRIL

Goodbyes

I don't know where I first heard this, but I can attest to its truth.

> Texans leave and don't say goodbye.
> Jews say goodbye and don't leave.

(I do not know how this potential conflict is resolved by Jews from Texas.)

The Rabbis of Pumbeditha, a town in Babylon which was a centre of Jewish learning in the third century, had a nice way of parting. They would say: 'May the One who gives life give you a life that is long, good and secure.' JM

14 APRIL

Lullaby

Jewish lullabies are sweet but very sad. Luckily I was too young to understand them or they might have turned my hair white. This one contrasts Jewish nobility – the Temple – and Yiddish reality, the life of a peddlar. The music is even sweeter and sadder than the words. Perhaps such early songs account for my later melancholy.

In the corner of a Temple room
The widow of Zion sits alone
Rocking a little Jewish child, her only one,
And singing him to sleep with this tender song.
'By the Jewish baby's cradle
Stands a pure white kid.
That kid has had to become a pedlar
And that's how you will make your living.
Raisins and almonds.
Sleep little Jewish baby sleep!'
(*Abraham Goldfaden* 1840–1908)

The kid is of course the chosen people. LB

15 APRIL

Passover

The story of the Exodus from Egypt has had reverberations throughout history. It is the central event of the Festival of Passover, but also almost every Jewish service is to be 'a reminder of the departure from Egypt', of God's providence. The Exodus has inspired revolutionary movements within and without Judaism and Christianity, from the struggle against slavery to 'liberation theology'. Figures like Shiphrah and Puah, the two midwives who refused to kill the firstborn Israelite boys, have become symbols of peaceful resistance to tyranny. The story of Moses' journey, from Egyptian prince to defender of the weak to triumphant leader has been a model for many. And the hope of a promised land, somewhere over there, where a new kind of society could be created, has been the basis of utopias and actual experiments in ways of living together.

But why were the children of Israel enslaved in the first place? The Rabbis suggested one reason – with their usual willingness to be self-critical and reflect on their own faults. Jacob had twelve sons, some by his wives, Rachel and Leah, some by the handmaids of his wives – Bilhah and Zilpah. But the sons of the wives used to tease the sons of the handmaids – 'You are only the children of slaves!' That is why the entire people had to endure the experience of slavery, to learn that under God all human beings are equal. JM

16 APRIL

The hand

One of the loveliest friendships in early English history is that between King Oswald and Aidan. This is an incident of that friendship recorded by Bede.

> It is reported that when he was once sitting at dinner on the holy day of Easter with Bishop Aidan and a silver dish of dainties before him, and they were just ready to bless the bread, the servant, whom he had appointed to relieve the poor, came in on a sudden, and told the king, that a great multitude of needy persons from all parts were sitting in the streets begging some alms of the king; he immediately ordered the meat set before him to be carried to the poor, and the dish to be cut in pieces and divided among them. At which sight, the bishop who sat by him, much taken with such an act of piety, laid hold of his right hand, and said, 'May this hand never perish.' Which fell out according to his prayer, for his arm and hand, being cut off from his body, when he was slain in battle, remain entire and uncorrupted to this day. LB

17 APRIL

Hope

At the end of the Passover service and the end of the Day of Atonement we say: 'Next year in Jerusalem!', in hopeful anticipation of the coming of the Messiah. With the creation of the State of Israel there has been a slight adjustment to the statement for some, referring to 'Jerusalem rebuilt', with the Temple restored. But the following anecdote by the Anglo-Jewish scholar Israel Abrahams dates back to 1906, long before the State became a reality.

> 'Next year in Jerusalem.' So have we all said since childhood. I heard a greybeard repeating it in Jerusalem itself. 'What,' I said, 'you are here and I am here. Let us say: Next year also in Jerusalem.' 'No,' replied the cheery nonagenarian, 'next year in Jerusalem the Rebuilt (*Ha-benuya*).' The old man firmly hoped that by the following spring the Temple would be restored, and he would go up with a joyous throng to the Mount of the House. Two Passovers have gone since then. The old man still lives, still hopes. He wrote to me last week: 'I am in no mood to hurry God; I am only 92.' JM

18 APRIL

Pilgrim

I was the only Jewish child at school, and my parents weren't sure if I should stay in school assembly. I was curious and decided to stay and they acquiesced. The homilies didn't touch me but this hymn, magnificently. Ever since it has been my lodestar through life. I used to sing it when I was hitchhiking and I still sing it on the underground going to work. I agree with Bunyan (1628–1688) that life is a journey and the goal is not a holiday home or villa in Spain but the Celestial City.

Who would true valour see
Let him come hither;
One here will constant be,
Come Wind, come Weather.
There's no Discouragement
Shall make him once relent
His first avow'd intent
To be a Pilgrim.

Who so beset him round
With dismal Stories
Do but themselves confound
His Strength the more is;

No Lion can him fright,
He'll with a Giant fight,
But he will have a right
To be a Pilgrim.

Hobgoblin nor foul Fiend
Can daunt his spirit;
He knows he at the end
Shall Life inherit.
Then Fancies fly away,
He'll fear not what men say.
He'll labour night and day
To be a Pilgrim. LB

19 APRIL

Down and out

There's a blues that runs:

> Nobody knows you when you're down and out.
> In your pocket, not one penny,
> And as for friends, you haven't any . . .

The same sentiments were expressed 900 years ago by the Hebrew poet Judah Halevi (see 'The Loves of Judah Halevi' 31 August):

> The day that my gold went, my friendly guest fled,
> And, despising me, he said, 'I turn away from thy countenance.'
> And I said, 'What, my son, what is my crime
> That thou art angry with me?'
> His reply was, 'Thy poverty is thy crime.'

(Again this poem loses something in the translation since there is a word play in the Hebrew between the word 'countenance' and 'poverty'.) JM

20 APRIL

Nature

These lines of Wordsworth were important for my friend Sister Charlotte, and I brood over them to understand her and her unlikely journey through life. They have become important to me, too. What do they say to you?

For I have learned
To look on nature, not as in the hour
Of thoughtless youth; but hearing oftentimes
The still, sad music of humanity,
Nor harsh nor grating, though of ample power
To chasten and subdue. And I have felt
A presence that disturbs me with the joy
Of elevated thoughts; a sense of sublime
Of something far more deeply interfused,
Whose dwelling is the light of setting suns,
And the round ocean and the living air,
And the blue sky, and in the mind of man:
A motion and a spirit, that impels
All thinking things, all objects of all thought,
And rolls through all things.
(*Tintern Abbey*) LB

21 APRIL

Spring blessing

Suddenly it is spring – whether early or delayed. And to greet it a blessing to be recited on seeing trees in blossom for the first time in the year.

Blessed are you, our Living God, Sovereign of the universe, You have not made Your universe lack for anything, and have created in it fine creatures and trees to give people pleasure. JM

Unhappy gay

Thomas Beddoes was a gay who lived at the wrong time in the early years of Victoria, poor chap. But I agree with him – the people we love don't die. They continue on many levels. For me they are more than ghosts.

If there were dreams to sell,
  What would you buy?
Some cost a passing bell;
  Some a light sigh,
That shakes from Life's fresh crown
Only a roseleaf down.
If there were dreams to sell,
Merry and sad to tell,
And the crier rung the bell,
  What would you buy?

A cottage lone and still,
  With bowers nigh,
Shadowy, my woes to still,
  Until I die.
Such pearl from Life's fresh crown
Fain would I shake me down.
Were dreams to have at will,
This would best heal my ill,
  This would I buy.

But there were dreams to sell,
  Ill didst thou buy;
Life is a dream, they tell,
  Waking, to die.
Dreaming a dream to prize,
Is wishing ghosts to rise;
  And, if I had the spell
  To call the buried, well,
    Which one would I?

If there are ghosts to raise,
  What shall I call,
Out of hell's murky haze,
  Heaven's blue hall?

Raise my loved long-lost boy
To lead me to his joy.
  There are no ghosts to raise;
  Out of death lead no ways;
    Vain is the call.

Know'st thou not ghosts to sue?
  No love thou hast.
Else lie, as I will do,
  And breathe thy last.
So out of Life's fresh crown
Fall like a rose-leaf down.
  Thus are the ghosts to woo;
  Thus are all dreams made true,
    Ever to last! LB

23 APRIL

Heavenly fire

The first great Hebrew poet to appear after the biblical period is named Yannai. Almost nothing is known about his life, except that he probably lived in the 5th century in Palestine. Yet he was the great innovator of liturgical poems that helped create a special mood for each of the different Sabbath days of the year. He based his poems on biblical themes – as here when he meditates on the bush that Moses saw, the bush that burned with fire but was not consumed. Here is the fire of heaven eternally present on earth:

Fire that consumes fire
fire that burns dry and moist alike
fire glowing in snow and ice
fire like a crouching lion
fire that appears in changing forms
fire that is and never ends
fire that shines and spreads
fire that shimmers and blazes
fire flying in a stormwind
fire burning without wood
fire that renews itself each day
fire not fanned by fire

fire that rises like palm branches
fire whose sparks are lightning
fire dark like a raven
fire curling like the colours of the rainbow.
JM

24 APRIL

The sunshine (zunsheen)

When I'm low, this poem by the 19th century Dorset poet, William Barnes, speaks to my condition. I don't wander in a field, only in a park, but it's the same.

The Spring
When wintry weather's all a-done,
An' brooks do sparkle in the zun,
An' naïsy-buildèn rooks do vlee
Wi' sticks toward their elem tree;
When birds do zing, an' we can zee
  Upon the boughs the buds o'spring, –
  Then I'm as happy as a king,
  A-vield wi' health an' zunsheen.

Vor then the cowslip's hangèn flow'r
A-wetted in the zunny show'r,
Do grow wi' vi'lets, sweet o' smell,
Bezide the wood-screen'd graegle's bell;
Where drushes' aggs, wi' sky-blue shell,
  Do lie in mossy nest among
  The thorns, while they do zing their zong
    At evenèn in the zunsheen.

An' God do meäke his win' to blow
An' raïn to vall vor high an' low,
An' bid his mornèn zun to rise
Vor all alike, an' groun' an' skies
Ha' colours vor the poor man's eyes:
  An' in our trials He is near,
  To hear our mwoan an' zee our tear,
    An' turn our clouds to zunsheen.

An' many times when I do vind
Things all goo wrong, an' vo'k unkind,
To zee the happy veedèn herds,
An' hear the zingèn o' the birds,
Do soothe my sorrow mwore than words;
  For I do zee that 'tis our sin
  Do meäke woone's soul so dark 'ithin,
    When God would gi'e woone zunsheen. LB

25 APRIL

War

In the eleventh century an extraordinary man, a great Jewish scholar, poet and statesman, Shmuel Hanagid (the Prince) (known in Arab circles as Isma'il ibn Nagrela) became the commander of the Arab armies of Granada. He lived from AD 993–1056 and spent the last twenty years of his life leading a series of triumphant campaigns against Seville. He sent poems to his son throughout that period, so who better to write the following on the illusory seduction of war.

At first war seems like a beautiful woman
every man desires to play with her.
But in the end it is like a repulsive hag,
all her lovers weep and sicken. JM

26 APRIL

Ridiculous

Religion needs a sense of the ridiculous because it's so much into role-playing. After an overdose of eastern mysticism and reincarnation I came across this parody and laughed away my mock reverence. I showed it to a guru and was relieved when he laughed with me – even more, he was in stitches! Western clergy are more uptight – alas.

I think I remember this moorland,
  The tower on the tip of the tor;
I feel in the distance another existence;
  I think I have been here before.

And I think you were sitting beside me
In a fold in the face of the fell;
For Time at its work'll go round in a circle,
And what is befalling, befell.

'I have been here before!' I asserted,
In a nook on a neck of the Nile.
I once in a crisis was punished by Isis,
And you smiled, I remember your smile.

I had the same sense of persistence
On the site of the seat of the Sioux;
I heard in the tepee the sound of a sleepy
Pleistocene grunt. It was you.

The past made a promise, before it
Began to begin to begone.
This limited gamut brings you again . . . Damn it,
How long has this got to go on? (*Morris Bishop*)

LB

27 APRIL

The chains of earth

I remember a line from a Bob Dylan song, 'Is a bird free of the chains of the sky?' In the eleventh century the great Hebrew poet, Shmuel Hanagid (see 'War' 25 April), expressed a similar sentiment.

For man, earth is a prison all his days,
so I say this truth to the fool,
you rush around – but the sky is all around you,
arise and get out if you can! JM

28 APRIL

Dead queens

The tombs of dead queens worry me. There's Catherine of Aragon buried under the flags of Castille and Aragon, but in an Anglican cathedral, which she would have hated. And even worse, there's Mary Tudor buried beneath her sister Elizabeth, whose legitimacy she couldn't recognize and whose triumph would have mocked her own failure, if she had known it. Fortunately she never lived to see it. In Westminster Abbey I felt sorry for her.

Mortality, behold and fear
What a change of flesh is here!
Think how many royal bones
Sleep within these heaps of stones;
Here they lie, had realms and lands,
Who now want strength to stir their hands,
Where from their pulpits seal'd with dust
They preach, 'In greatness is no trust.'
Here's an acre sown indeed
With the richest royallest seed
That the earth did e'er suck in
Since the first man died for sin:
Here the bones of birth have cried
'Though gods they were, as men they died!'
Here are sands, ignoble things,
Dropt from the ruin'd sides of kings;
Here's a world of pomp and state
Buried in dust, once dead by fate.
(*Francis Beaumont* c.1584–1616) LB

29 APRIL

A hymn to failure

This little hymn to failure was penned by Abraham Ibn Ezra (see the other passage in his name, 9 January). For once his sarcasm (or his irony) is turned upon himself.

I struggle to succeed but cannot
for my heavenly stars have destroyed me.
If ever I took up selling shrouds
for the rest of my life no one would die! JM

Time with a gift of tears

I first came across these words in a novel by Clifford Bax and they lingered in my mind. Later on I looked up the poem they came from. I was a prude and wanted to dismiss Swinburne, who was 'not quite', sexually or socially. But I agreed with his recipe for the creation of man (and woman).

Before the beginning of years
  There came to the making of man
Time, with a gift of tears;
  Grief, with a glass that ran;
Pleasure with pain for leaven;
  Summer, with flowers that fell;
Remembrance fallen from heaven,
  And madness risen from hell:
Strength without hands to smite;
  Love that endures for a breath:
Night, the shadow of light,
  And life, the shadow of death.

And the high gods took in hand
  Fire, and the falling of tears,
And a measure of sliding sand
  From under the feet of the years;
And froth and drift of the sea;
  And dust of the labouring earth;
And bodies of things to be
  In the house of death and of birth;
And wrought with weeping and laughter,
  And fashioned with loathing and love,
With life before and after
  And death beneath and above,
For a day and a night and a morrow,
  That his strength might endure for a span
With travail and heavy sorrow,
  The holy spirit of man . . . LB

MAY

1 MAY

Codeword

It was during the final years of the communist regime in the Soviet Union. For many years Soviet Jews who had applied to leave the country had been stripped of their jobs and left to languish in a state of limbo, always subject to arrest as 'parasites' – because they were unemployed! Jews from different parts of the world would visit these 'refuseniks', to show them solidarity and to provide them with clothing, goods to barter with and Hebrew literature.

A major conference was planned to send over a dozen academics in Jewish studies to help them improve their Jewish knowledge. In the end the authorities would not permit it, but in the weeks before it was meant to take place we began feverish preparations. At the last meeting, one of the professors expressed his anxieties about visiting the Soviet Union. What if the KGB harassed us or even arrested us? Building on his paranoia (which was only partly paranoia!) he came out with the suggestion that we should have a codeword which we could telephone to someone in London. If we mentioned that word, they would know we were in trouble and immediately contact the British government for help. We tried to take him seriously – though those of us who had visited before thought it a bit absurd.

There are not many occasions when we can get to play the hero, even if it is a bit make-believe. But sometimes we have to take that kind of risk for a cause dear to our hearts.

After much debate about this 'codeword', the question arose – what word should we use? It was our colleague Albert Friedlander (see 9 November) who came up with the ideal solution – something totally appropriate that sent us off into hysterics. He said: 'How about "Mayday!"?' JM

2 MAY

Home

I have never felt at home in this world, and eternal my earthly homes are not! I've known this ever since I considered the hole which once was my home after a bombing during the blitz. I sang this hymn of Isaac Watts (1674–1748) when I was sent to the country soon after and it made sense.

O God, our help in ages past,
  Our hope for years to come,
A shelter from the stormy blast,
  And our eternal home;

Beneath the shadow of thy throne
  Thy saints have dwelt secure;
Sufficient is thine arm alone,
  And our defence is sure.

Before the hills in order stood,
  And earth received her frame,
From everlasting thou art God,
  For endless years the same.

A thousand ages in thy sight
  Are like an evening gone;
Short as the watch that ends the night
  Before the rising sun.

Time, like an ever-rolling stream,
  Bears all its sons away;
They fly forgotten, as a dream
  Dies at the opening day.

O God, our help in ages past,
  Our hope for years to come,
Be thou our guard while troubles last,
  And our eternal home. LB

---

3 MAY

The miser

I must apologize for the slight crudeness of the following poem. It is the creation of yet another of the astonishing array of gifted poets who flourished in the 'Golden Age of Spain'. Judah Al-Harizi (about 1170 until after 1235) grew up in Christian Toledo and travelled extensively in the Near East. He was a translator of Arabic poetry as well as an original writer himself. The following piece seems to reflect a degree of disenchantment with a certain Solomon.

They asked me about the generosity of Solomon.
I replied: He and it are as distant as fire and rain-water.
The tongue of his cup sticks to its palate with thirst,
the lips of his table faint with hunger.
He is afraid to pass water in case he thirsts,
and is scared to open his bowels in case he hungers. JM

4 MAY

Bones

Unidentified bones were discovered in a field in Norfolk, engendering the magnificent prose of Sir Thomas Browne (1605–1682). So they had their continuance, albeit unexpectedly. *Urn Burial* is the best text-book on mortality and a proper companion to every graveyard. Sir Thomas was well acquainted with death being a physician. Unfortunately, like his contemporary Bunyan, he believed poor old women could be witches, which saddens me because I admire them both.

What Song the *Syrens* sang, or what name *Achilles* assumed when he hid himself among women, though puzzling questions are not beyond all conjecture. What time the persons of these Ossuaries entred the famous Nations of the dead, and slept with Princes and Counsellors, might admit a wide solution. But who were the proprietaries of these bones, or what bodies these ashes made up, were a question above Antiquarism. Not to be resolved by man, nor easily perhaps by spirits, except we consult the Provincial Guardians, or tutelary Observators. Had they made as good provision for their names, as they have done for their Reliques, they had not so grosly erred in the art of perpetuation. But to subsist in bones, and be but Pyramidally extant, is a fallacy in duration. Vain ashes, which in the oblivion of names, persons, times, and sexes, have found unto themselves a fruitlesse continuation, and only arise unto late posterity, as Emblemes of mortal vanities; Antidotes against pride, vainglory, and madding vices. Pagan vain-glories which thought the world might last for ever, had encouragement for ambition, and finding no *Atropos* unto the immortality of their Names, were never dampt with the necessity of oblivion. Even old ambitions had the advantage of ours, in the attempts of their vain-glories, who acting early, and before the probable Meridian of time, have by this time found great accomplishment of their designes, whereby the ancient

Heroes have already out-lasted their Monuments, and Mechanical preservations. But in this latter Scene of time we cannot expect such Mummies unto our memories, when ambition may fear the Prophecy of *Elias*, and *Charles* the fifth can never hope to live within two *Methusela*'s of *Hector*. LB

5 MAY

The poetry of war

War creates 'might-have-been's'. The tragic, senseless loss of life is often most keenly felt in the writings of the gifted poets who died too soon. World War I produced its harvest of such tragedies, among them the poet and artist Isaac Rosenberg (1890–1918). He left behind a handful of 'trench poems' including this one, 'Break of Day in the Trenches'.

The darkness crumbles away –
It is the same old Druid Time as ever.
Only a live thing leaps my hand –
A queer sardonic rat –
As I pull the parapet's poppy
To stick behind my ear.
Droll rat, they would shoot you if they knew
Your cosmopolitan sympathies.
Now you have touched this English hand
You will do the same to a German –
Soon, no doubt, if it be your pleasure
To cross the sleeping green between.
It seems you inwardly grin as you pass
Strong eyes, fine limbs, haughty athletes
Less chanced than you for life,
Bonds to the whims of murder.
Sprawled in the bowels of the earth,
The torn fields of France.
What do you see in our eyes
At the shrieking iron and flame
Hurled through still heavens?
What quaver – what heart aghast?
Poppies whose roots are in man's veins
Drop, and are ever dropping:
But mine in my ear is safe,
Just a little white with the dust. JM

6 MAY

Shaken

The opening of the Koran shakes me. Even in the English it communicates the urgency, the incisiveness and clarity of the message. There is no fooling around with religion here. What must it be like in the Arabic?

> In the name of Allah, the Beneficent, the Merciful.
> Praise be to Allah, Lord of the Worlds,
> The Beneficent, the Merciful.
> Owner of the Day of Judgment,
> Thee alone we worship; Thee (alone) we ask for help.
> Show us the straight path,
> The path of those whom Thou hast favoured;
> Not the path of those who earn Thine anger nor of those who go astray. LB

7 MAY

Bookplate

I don't know what causes me more anxiety – to borrow a book or to lend one. To borrow a book means a great responsibility – to read it in time and return it undamaged. But lending books creates a whole lot of other problems – including how to ensure that you remember who now has it. A friend puts a bit of cardboard in the gap with the name of the borrower on it. But the problem is that casual moment when someone asks and you agree – and forget to make the note.

That's how bookplates get born – whether a simple name stuck on the inside of the cover or an elaborate artistic representation of the owners' particular interests or fantasies about themselves.

Someone once found in a second-hand bookshop an *Introduction to Hebrew Grammar* that I had owned as a child. There I had carefully inscribed Jonathan Magonet, 69 Bedford Road, Clapham, London, England, Europe, The World, The Universe. Good to know that I was a convinced European even in those days.

In the Jewish schools of the Ukraine before the war, a slightly different kind of 'personalization' in simple Hebrew was popular.

To whom does this book belong?
To whomever it belongs – it belongs.
Even so, to whom does it belong?
It belongs to the owner of the book.
So who is the owner of the book?
The one who bought it.
So who is the one who bought it?
Whoever had the money – that's the one who bought it.
So who had the money?
The one who bought the book.
And who bought the book?
The Owner of the book bought it.
And who is the owner of the book?
The one to whom the book belongs.
So to whom does the book belong?

After which frustrating exchange the 'owner' proudly attached his name. JM

8 MAY

The sparrow

When I went to Oxford, they gave me Bede's *Ecclesiastical History of the English People* to study, which was a turn-off as I was a Marxist, eager to learn about revolution. My Latin wasn't that hot either. Then I came across this story of the sparrow. I don't know who that 'thane' was, but he asked my question.

> Another of the thanes of the king giving assent to his persuasion and prudent words, forthwith added, saying, 'The present life of man on the earth appears to me, O king, in comparison of that time which is unknown to us, such as if – when you are sitting at supper with your leaders and ministers, in the wintertime, a fire indeed having been lighted and made to glow in the middle of the supper-room, but storms of wintry rain and snow raging everywhere without – a sparrow should come and fly very quickly through the house, entering by one door and going out afterwards by another. During the very time, indeed, in which he is within, he is untouched by the wintry storm, but yet after that very small space of serenity is in a moment passed through, presently returning into the stormy winter

that he quitted, he glides from your eyes. So this life of men appears for a short time, but of what follows or of what preceded we are altogether ignorant. Wherefore, if this new doctrine has brought anything more certain, it seems that it ought deservedly to be followed.' LB

9 MAY

Job's comforters

Job's friends, who tried to comfort him after the loss of his family and wealth are familiar figures. Instead of comforting him they actually managed to insult him, suggesting that his loss was really his own fault because he had sinned, though Job was convinced of his innocence. In the end God had to intervene and justify Job's view. The following story is both moving and slyly amusing, as the pupils of the great Rabbi Yochanan ben Zakkai tried to comfort him after the death of his son.

Rabbi Eliezer entered, sat down before him and said to him: 'O master, is it your will that I should say something to you?' He replied: 'Speak.' Rabbi Eliezer then said: 'Adam had a son who died, and yet he accepted consolation for him. How do we know that he accepted consolation? Because it is written: "And Adam knew his wife again" (*Genesis 4:25*). Accept consolation for yourself.' Rabbi Yochanan said to him: 'Is it not enough that I am grieved that you have to remind me of Adam's grief?'

Then Rabbi Joshua entered and said: 'O master, is it your will that I should say something to you?' He replied: 'Speak.' Then Rabbi Joshua said to him: 'Job had sons and daughters all of whom died in one day, and yet he accepted consolation for them. Accept consolation for yourself. How do we know that Job accepted consolation? Because it is written that Job said: "The Eternal gave, the Eternal has taken away, blessed be the name of the Eternal." (*Job 1:21*) At which Rabbi Yochanan said to him: 'Is it not enough that I am grieved that you have to remind me of Job's grief?'

Then Rabbi Jose entered, sat down before him and said: 'O master, is it your will that I should say something to you?' He replied: 'Speak.' Then Rabbi Jose said to him: 'Aaron had two grown-up sons both of whom died on the same day, and yet he accepted consolation, as it is written: "And Aaron held his peace." (*Leviticus 10:3*) Now silence implies consolation. So accept consolation for yourself.' Rabbi Yochanan said to him: 'Is it not enough that I am grieved that you have to remind me of Aaron's grief?'

The Rabbi Simon entered and said: 'O master, is it your will that I should say something to you?' He replied: 'Speak.' Rabbi Simon said to him: 'King David had a son who died, and yet he accepted consolation. So accept consolation for yourself. How do we know that David accepted consolation? Because it is written: "And David comforted Bathsheba his wife, and went in to her and lay with her and she bore a son and he called his name Solomon." ' (*2 Samuel 12:24*) At which Rabbi Yochanan said: 'Is it not enough that I am grieved that you have to remind me of David's grief?'

Rabbi Eleazar ben Arak entered. As soon as Rabbi Yochanan saw him he said to his servant: 'Take his garments and walk after him to the bathhouse (i.e. pay him respect) for he is a great man and I cannot withstand him!' Rabbi Eleazar entered, sat down before him and said to him: 'I shall give you a parable to which this matter is like: it is like a man to whom the king gave something in trust. Every day the man would weep and cry, saying: "When shall I be freed of this trust in peace?" That is your situation, O master. You had a son who studied the whole of our religious tradition and departed from this world without sin. You should accept consolation for him since you have restored your trust unimpaired.' Then Rabbi Yochanan said: 'Eleazar my son, you have comforted me in the way people should comfort.' (*Avot D'Rabbi Nathan 14*) JM

10 MAY

The cage

'A cage went to look for a bird' – (*Kafka*)

Life closes in on you, doesn't it? Try not to be trapped – at least in the spirit. LB

11 MAY

The way of all flesh

Bachya Ibn Pakuda probably lived in the second half of the eleventh century in Muslim Spain, another product of that extraordinary 'Golden Age' of creativity. He wrote a book on ethics called *Hovot ha-Levavot, The Duties of the Heart*, with sections on topics like humility, repentance, spiritual accounting, abstinence and the love of God. The following short extract comes from one of the closing chapters of the book, an admonition to the soul to prepare itself for its final end and reckoning. But he starts with a short poem of marvellous energy:

> O my soul, stride forward bravely and bless the One who is your rock. Put your request for grace before Him in an orderly fashion; and pour out your supplication before Him. Arouse yourself from your sleep and consider your situation, where you have come from and where you are going . . .
>
> O my soul, set your mind on the highway, the way on which you have walked. For all came from the dust, and indeed shall return to the dust. Every thing that was created and fashioned has an end and a goal, to return to the earth from which it was taken. Life and death are brothers, they dwell together; they are joined to one another; they cling together, so that they cannot be separated. They are joined together by the two ends of a frail bridge over which all created beings travel. Life is the entrance and death the exit. Life builds, and death demolishes; life sows and death reaps; life plants and death uproots; life joins together and death separates; life links together and death scatters. So please understand and see that the cup will also pass to you, and you shall soon go from the lodging place which is on the way, when time and chance happen to you, and you return to your eternal home. On that day you shall delight in your work and take your reward for the work in which you laboured in this world, whether it be good or bad. JM

12 MAY

The department store window

I remembered these words of the 'Old Boy' (Lao-Tse) as I looked at poor whites and blacks looking at the riches in a New York department store window – which they would never get despite the Great American Dream. I watched their awe turn into envy and then into the beginnings of hate. The Old Boy proposed a very different solution for society.

> If you don't give honours, people won't compete.
> If you don't prize things, people won't steal.

If you don't advertise, people won't covet.
Therefore rule wisely by damping down desires, filling people's tummies and keeping them content and healthy. LB

13 MAY

The golden mean

We can meet elsewhere in this book Judah Halevi the poet, but here he is in his other garb, as the author of a major philosophical work in Arabic, which is known from its Hebrew translation as *The Kuzari*. The king of the Khazars converts to Judaism and then invites representatives of the teaching of Aristotelianism, Judaism, Christianity and Islam to discuss their beliefs with him. Naturally, this allows Halevi to show the superiority of Judaism. Here the 'Rabbi' discusses the middle path that Judaism recommends.

The divine law does not impose asceticism upon us. Rather it prefers that we keep to the golden mean and give to every mental and physical faculty its appropriate share, without giving too much to one faculty and too little to another. Thus, someone who is inclined to lust decreases his thinking faculty; and on the other hand, someone who is inclined to abstinence decreases some other faculty. Fasting for a long period is no act of piety for someone whose appetites are weak, whose faculties are feeble and whose body is thin; instead he should pamper his body. Nor is decreasing your wealth an act of piety, if you happen to have earned it in a lawful way without trouble, and owning it does not keep you from studying and performing good deeds, especially if you have dependants and children and your desire is to spend money for the sake of God – better that such a person should amass wealth.

As a general rule, our Torah, the teaching of God, is divided into fear, love and joy, by each of which you may draw near to God. JM

14 MAY

Old boy

Tradition says Lao-Tse (Old Boy) was the prime minister of a Chinese king about the time of the prophet Isaiah. When he was very old, he quit his post to become a hermit in the wilderness. But the border guard would not let such an eminent person pass through till he had written down his wisdom.

Lao Tse finally gave in and scribbled some words on a scroll. 'I do not think it will be of use to you' he said. 'If you do not already understand these thoughts, this scroll will not help you. And if you do it is superfluous.'

That scroll became the scripture of Taoism. And as for the Old Boy, he went on into the wilderness and was never heard of again.

Some of his thoughts are strikingly similar to sayings of the early Rabbis, both in content and expression. It is a coincidence, of course, which just goes to show that spiritual teachers teach alike. Only spiritual pygmies are obsessed by differences.

> Who is wise? Whoever learns from everyone.
> Who is mighty? Whoever controls their passions.
> Who is rich? Whoever is happy with what they have.
> Who is honourable? Whoever honours other people.
> (*Sayings of the Fathers 4:1*)

The Old Boy put it like this:

> One who learns from others is wise.
> One who learns from himself is wiser.
> One who subdues others is strong.
> One who subdues himself is stronger.
> One who is content is rich. LB

15 MAY

Humility

The following Rabbinic teaching needs no introduction:

> Do not be like a big door which lets in the wind; or a small door which makes the worthy bend down; but be like the threshold on which all may tread, or a low peg on which all can hang their things.
> (*Derech Eretz Zuta 1:3*) JM

16 MAY

The hardest task

'The hardest task in life is letting go' (Japanese saying.): memories, hurts, loved ones, certainties, youth . . . . LB

17 MAY

Self-improvement

Suddenly bookshops are full of volumes on self-improvement. In the old days the selection was relatively small – 'How to Make Friends and Influence People', 'It Pays to Increase Your Word Power' – but now there is hardly a bit of our personality, anatomy or soul that cannot be improved, extended, healed or 'made whole' through books, tapes or videos.

The practice is not new, simply the number of things that are apparently disastrously wrong with us and the range of heavenly states we can reach. In the Middle Ages Jewish fathers produced 'ethical wills' for the edification of their sons (less often their daughters!). Moses ben Nachman, also known as Nachmanides, was an extraordinary figure – Rabbinic scholar, physician, mystic and Bible commentator. Born in Gerona about 1195 he died in Palestine about 1270. His 'ethical will' contains the following ideas on how to obtain humility.

> Now, my son, I will set out for you how to conduct yourself according to the quality of humility, to follow it constantly. Let all your words be spoken with gentleness, with respect, good manners and love; with a friendly expression and a bowed head. Your eyes should be cast downward but your heart directed upwards. Do not stare at people when you speak to them. Let every person seem to you greater than yourself. If they be rich, honour them as did our saintly teacher; if they be poor and you are rich, you should have mercy and compassion on them and honour God with your wealth. If you are wiser remember that you are guilty and they innocent, for they sin unwittingly but you knowingly – as our Rabbis of blessed memory taught: 'The errors of the sages are considered as wilful sins' (*Baba Metzia 33b*). In all your thoughts, words and deeds, and at all times and seasons, consider yourself as standing before the supreme King of Kings, the Holy One, blessed be He.

Why not produce your own ethical will? JM

18 MAY

What

‘What is God?’ asked the young Thomas Aquinas.

Not ‘Who?’ – an anthropomorphic question, inviting a sentimental answer. Very perceptive for a boy! I was never as bright as that. LB

19 MAY

Three sins

The following saying of the Rabbis seems a bit shocking at first. But any tabloid newspaper will confirm the first two and the existence of tabloid newspapers confirms the third.

> Most are prone to robbery, few to incest, all to gossip (or slander)! (*Baba Batra 165a*) JM

20 MAY

Confined to bed

‘You don’t need to go out of the door to see the world. You don’t need to look out of the window to see heaven.’ (Adapted from the *Tao-teh-king*) LB

21 MAY

Knowall

I don’t remember much of the chemistry he taught me at my prep school, but I do recall that at the end of term he would sometimes sit us in a lecture room and read Thurber’s ‘The Night the Bed Fell on Father’. We laughed till we ached – though it has never seemed so funny since.

There must have been some game he played with us about knowing so much about everything. Perhaps it was during one of those Thurber sessions that he explained: ‘Someone asked me if I was omniscient. But I said, ‘No’, I once thought I was wrong!’ JM

22 MAY

The mother-in-law

The most sublime words of love in the Hebrew scriptures are said by a young woman to her mother-in-law, the butt of so many music hall jokes.

> 'Entreat me not to leave thee, and to return from following after thee; for whither thou goest, I will go; and where thou lodgest, I will lodge; thy people shall be my people, and thy God my God'; where thou diest, will I die, and there will I be buried; the Lord do so to me, and more also, if aught but death part thee and me.' (*Ruth 1:16–17*) LB

23 MAY

Politician

The trouble with the following definition is that the person who gave it, a politician, meant it as a positive quality.

> I believe in leadership. I believe in leading the community from the front in the direction in which they wish to go. JM

24 MAY

Earning

'Each day you earn salvation as you earn your living': (*Genesis Rabbah*) LB

25 MAY

Tucholsky

Born in Berlin, Kurt Tucholsky (1890–1935) became a pacifist and socialist after his experiences as a conscript in the First World War. As a journalist and satirist he had an amazing output of essays, stories, poems and cabaret songs, often writing under comical pseudonyms. He hated the excesses of Communism but despaired at the success of Nazism, eventually taking his life in Sweden.

I saw this piece of his written on the wall by the telephone kiosk in Koblenz Station. It is good to know that there are such literate graffiti writers in Germany, but I wonder how Tucholsky would have reacted.

Nichts ist schwerer und nichts erfordert mehr Charakter als sich in offenen Gegensatz zu seiner Zeit zu befinden und laut zu sagen Nein.

Nothing is harder and nothing builds more character than to find oneself in open opposition to one's time and to say aloud: 'No!' JM

26 MAY

Sweat

Everybody in life experiences a beautiful day when the world seems like Eden and love is trouble free. But when the day's over, you earn love, as you earn your living, by the sweat of your brow. (*Ludwig Boerne* 1786–1837)

Beware of being 'in love'. It can be so misleading and so self-centred. LB

27 MAY

Lost love

The Rabbis expressed it in this way. 'When love was strong we could have made our bed on a sword's blade. Now, when it has become weak, a bed of sixty cubits is not large enough for us.' (*Sanhedrin 7a*)

Israel Zangwill (1864–1926) put it this way:

Once between us the Atlantic,
Yet I felt your hand in mine;
Now I feel your hand in mine,
Yet between us the Atlantic. JM

28 MAY

Sad truth

One parent supports a dozen children, but a dozen children can't support one parent. (*Jewish Proverb*) LB

Lorelei

I was disappointed when I first passed the Lorelei on a Rhine ferry boat. To tell the truth I was not sure where they were pointing or what I was supposed to see. High cliffs, dangerous rocks, and the legend of the beautiful girl who combs her hair and lures sailors to destruction. Perhaps some of my disappointment was reflected in a little poem I wrote:

I met the Lorelei
in a Dusseldorf discotheque
combing her dandruff
into a coke.

Despite a sore throat
she gave a fair imitation
of Joan Baez.

Heinrich Heine wrote the definitive poem about her which became a popular folk song. In fact so popular that the Nazis could not eliminate this significant item of German culture despite it being written by a Jew! Their solution was to make sure that whenever it was published it carried the tag 'Anonymous'. To spite them, here it is; in the translation by Emma Lazarus, an American Jewish woman poet, who worked on behalf of the immigrants coming to America. Her own sonnet about the European 'huddled masses yearning to breathe free' was affixed to the Statue of Liberty, another alluring lady.

I know not what spell is o'er me,
That I am so sad today;
An old myth floats before me –
I cannot chase it away.

The cool air darkens, and listen,
How softly flows the Rhine!
The mountain peaks still glisten
When the evening sunbeams shine.

The fairest maid sits dreaming
In radiant beauty there.
Her gold and her jewels are gleaming.
She combeth her golden hair.

With a golden comb she is combing;
A wonderous song sings she.
The music quaint in the gloaming,
Hath a powerful melody.

It thrills with a passionate yearning
The boatman below in the night.
He heeds not the rocky reef's warning.
He gazes alone on the height.

I think that the waters swallowed
The boat and the boatman anon,
And this, with her singing unhallowed
The Lorelei hath done. JM

30 MAY

Mugging

If God came down to earth, people would smash bricks through His windows. (*Jewish Proverb*) LB

31 MAY

I only hope I remember all this next time

Friends often tell me that my life seems to lurch from one disaster to another. I devise a plan for my life, such as becoming a nun, and then get violently deflected from it and have to flail around desperately to get started again. In 1974, for example, I was devastated when my doctoral thesis was turned down by Oxford University: this completely put paid to my ambition to become an academic. I could not even fail quietly, since the decision caused a minor scandal and for about five months members of the faculty rancorously and publicly debated my fate. I had just got over that and settled into a teaching career, when I was told that I would have to leave my school because of my epilepsy. Both times I was frightened, angry and extremely unhappy. I could see no light, no hope and my life seemed in ruins. Now I am extremely glad of both these setbacks, since if they had not happened I would have missed so much in the way of friendship, interests and opportunities to learn. I realize today that I was quite unsuited to academic life and that I would have found it far too constricting. If I had not got the sack, I would never have had the nerve to become a freelance writer. In some ways, therefore, I feel I have had a charmed life, if not always a peaceful one.

I am no Pollyanna and certainly don't think that there is always a silver lining. The human tragedies that we have seen in our century alone forbid us to take that facile line. Nor do I believe that God was arranging things, to guide me onto a better path. I find the idea of such a celestial Big Brother, however benign, rather repellant. But I think I have learned that some minor disasters can remind us that our hold on joy is fragile. They can also make us reach deeply into ourselves to find an alternative and this (like a difficult examination paper) can help us to discover things within ourselves that we did not know we had. I only hope I remember all this next time . . ..

(*Karen Armstrong* – writer, friend and former nun) LB

JUNE

1 JUNE

Relaxed

My heart isn't proud
And my eyes aren't ambitious.
I'm not meddling with things
Too big or wonderful for me.
Instead, I've relaxed
Quietly and peacefully
Like a child at its mother's breast.
I feel like a weaned child. (*Psalm 131*)

Try to put the Psalms into your own words. That way they'll work for you. I say this before going to sleep. LB

2 JUNE

Her Majesty's Consul-General

In April 1967, having completed my medical 'house jobs', I travelled to Jerusalem to learn Hebrew prior to starting Rabbinic studies in the autumn. My parents were worried about my going there as hints of war were already in the air. Ironically our plane made a stopover in Greece and we had to camp out in the airport for twenty-four hours because of the revolution.

In the weeks leading up to the Six Day War I thought a lot about whether to return home or stay on. Whether out of an atavistic Jewish loyalty, or sheer inertia, I decided to stay and offered my services to the Hadassah Hospital. But there was one moment when I hesitated – the arrival of a stencilled letter from the British Consulate-General. I suspect that some version of this must be on file in British Embassies around the globe. It certainly put the frighteners on me – as much because of its stilted language as the curious undertone of concern mixed with a delicate washing of the hands.

British Consulate-General,
Jerusalem
Sir/Madam,

In view of the present situation I would suggest you should urgently consider the desirability of leaving Jerusalem without delay. This may only be possible while public transport services exist, and I must make it clear that Her Majesty's Representatives have no special means for providing transport for you and your family should you fail to act upon this warning and public services cease to operate.

Whatever action you may decide upon as the result of this warning must be taken on your own responsibility, but in reaching a decision you should remember that the longer you delay the more difficult your subsequent departure may become.

I should be grateful if you would inform me of your decision at the earliest possible moment.

I am,
Sir/Madam,
Your Obedient Servant
Her Majesty's Consul-General
JM

3 JUNE

Bump

'From ghoulies and ghosties and long leggity beasties and things that go bump in the night, good Lord deliver us.'

I was taught this in the West Country during the wartime air raids. Some say it before they look under the bed. LB

4 JUNE

On choosing leaders

We have a strange attitude to leaders. We either put them on a pedestal as if they can do no wrong or spend our time trying to find faults with which to attack them. I wonder what the statistics would look like if we tried to find out what proportion of politicians were genuinely altruistic and working for the common good; how many were in it for fame or power, but nevertheless realized they had to do as good a job as possible just to stay in business; and how many are downright corrupt. Probably most of them are a mixture of all of these things. We get very shocked when some kind of corruption is discovered – though different societies get hot under the collar about different things.

The Rabbis had one odd idea about the right way to pick a community leader:

You do not set up a leader over the community unless he has a basket of reptiles hanging over his back! For if he becomes arrogant, you can say to him: 'Look what's hanging behind you!' (*Yoma 22b*) (The Rabbinic commentaries assume that the 'bag of reptiles' refers to scandals in the family tree, but any past blemish would probably do.) JM

5 JUNE

The fat lady

'The party's not over till the fat lady sings'.

I don't know where it comes from or what it means but in a depression, it popped into my mind and gave me a lift. I passed it on and it has the same effect on others – especially in hospital. We shouldn't be spiritual snobs. LB

6 JUNE

Healthy

My father was a doctor who pioneered the use of hypnosis for medical conditions, particularly psychosomatic disorders. He used to say that his office was a place of last resort for people who had been everywhere else. Yet he was very successful, because he knew how to listen to people's problems and used a lot of common sense in treating them. He had a little rhyme to help encourage his patients to check out the health of key areas of their life. I heard it so often it used to annoy me, but now I realise how much sense it made.

Happy at work.
Content at play.
Someone to love.
And faith to pray.

It's worth trying it out from time to time. JM

7 JUNE

Too heavy

'Don't take it too heavy, dearie, don't take it too heavy!'

A young man was pouring his heart out. 'My parents never understood me,' he wailed. 'We never related . . .'

My friend who was built like an amiable blonde gorilla listened to him kindly, while continuing to play patience, and comforted him with the advice above.

I'm not sure if my parents never understood me, or understood me only too well. But I often repeat my friend's advice when I'm tied up in an emotional knot. Try it! LB

8 JUNE

Knowing our place

> 'God is called the place of the world, but the world is not called His place.'

Much of our time is spent trying to make career decisions. Many of us are subject to perennial doubts about our role, our 'place' in the world. Some of us spend hours imagining that the grass would be greener in some other job, some other country, some other community, some other relationship . . .. If God is the only *real* place . . . does it actually matter where we are or what we do so long as we know how to stand still and consider what it is He might be showing us on our own doorstep in the here and now?

(*Norman Davies* – Musician and Mystic) JM

9 JUNE

The light

In the bad old days you could never admit that another religion could equal or do something as good as your own. (Over-compensation through insecurity? Jargon perhaps but still true.) Well, the opening of St John's Gospel is the creation account which makes me thrill with awe, though I know it's a rather anti-Jewish gospel and an exclusive one, which I disapprove of.)

> In the beginning was the Word, and the Word was with God, and the Word was God. The same was in the beginning with God. All things

were made by him; and without him was not any thing made that was made. In him was life; and the life was the light of men. And the light shineth in darkness; and the darkness comprehended it not. LB

10 JUNE

On the vanity of earthly greatness

The thought has been expressed in more grandiose terms – see Ozymandias (2 September). But this little poem by Arthur Guiterman (1871–1943), an American writer of light verse is very clear on the transience of earthly greatness:

The tusks that clashed in mighty brawls
Of mastodons are billiard balls.

The sword of Charlemagne the Just
Is ferric oxide, known as rust.

The grizzly bear whose potent hug
Was feared by all is now a rug.

Great Caesar's bust is on the shelf,
And I don't feel so well myself! JM

11 JUNE

So ordinary

And, behold, two of them went that same day to a village called Emmaus, which was from Jerusalem about threescore furlongs. And they talked together of all these things which had happened. And it came to pass, that, while they communed together and reasoned, Jesus himself drew near, and went with them, but their eyes were holden that they should not know him . . .

And they drew nigh unto the village, whither they went; and he made as though he would have gone further. But they constrained him, saying, Abide with us: for it is toward evening and the day is far spent. And he went in to tarry with them. And it came to pass, as he sat at meat with them, he took bread and blessed it, and brake, and gave to them. And their eyes were opened, and they knew him; and he vanished out of their sight. (*Luke 24:13–16, 28–31*)

We bump into the divine but don't register it, because it seems so ordinary. LB

12 JUNE

The best religion

Heinrich Heine has appeared elsewhere in this collection. This little gem needs a bit of explanation. *'Shobbos'* is the East European way of pronouncing 'Shabbat', the Jewish Sabbath. The Jewish community of Frankfurt was renowned for its piety and the butt of a number of in-jokes as a result. Heine puts it into a certain kind of perspective.

> To Frankfort I on *shobbos* came,
> Where dumplings were my food.
> They have the best religion there;
> Goose-giblets, too, are good. JM

13 JUNE

Dolce vita

> I made me great works; I builded me houses; I planted me vineyards; I made me gardens and parks, and I planted trees in them of all kinds of fruit; I made me pools of water, to water therefrom the wood springing up with trees; I acquired men-servants and maid-servants, and had servants born in my house; also I had great possessions of herds and flocks, above all that were before me in Jerusalem. I gathered me also silver and gold, and treasure such as kings and the provinces have as their own; I got me men-singers and women-singers, and the delights of the sons of men, women very many. So I was great, and increased more than all that were before me in Jerusalem; also my wisdom stood me in stead. And whatsoever mine eyes desired I kept not from them; I withheld not my heart from any joy, for my heart had joy of all my labour; and this was my portion from all my labour. Then I looked on all the works that my hands had wrought and on the labour that I had laboured to do; and, behold, all was vanity and a striving after wind, and there was no profit under the sun. (*Ecclesiastes 2:4–11*)

Whether it's Jerusalem over two thousand years ago, Rome ancient or modern, Manhattan or the Riviera – it's still the same. LB

14 JUNE

The cure

I was a medical student a long time ago and I am sure that many of the attitudes that went with the profession in those days have changed, particularly in this age of consumer information. Even then there was the beginning of a realization that the patient was entitled to know much more about their condition, but there was still a kind of conspiracy to keep them in partial ignorance and maintain the medical mystique.

So we learnt a special vocabulary, partly, it must be admitted, to protect the sensibilities of the patient and their family. Thus 'syphilis' was 'specific disease'. 'Cancer', with a bit more justification, had a number of euphemistic alternatives. (I remember the cautionary tale about the new houseman who decided that integrity demanded that he tell everyone on the cancer ward precisely what their condition was; as a result, two jumped out of the window and others did equally drastic things. Thank heavens for the hospice movement and a proper approach to this difficult and painful subject.)

But my favourite word, that still seems to crop up, is 'iatrogenic'. It sounds very impressive, as, presumably it was intended to be. What it means is that the current state of ill-health of the patient is the result of the medication he or she has been given.

The problem is not new. In the middle ages, Moses Maimonides, who as well as being a philosopher and legal authority, was also a physician to the court of Saladin, produced a number of treatises on medicine. Clearly his cures were somewhat limited to dietary approaches, physical treatment and certain herbs and medicines, but he put the issue very clearly in one of his warnings to fellow physicians:

'Don't make the cure worse than the disease from which the patient is suffering!' JM

15 JUNE

Question and answer

Q. How shall I come into the presence of the Lord, and bend low before God on high?

A. O man, He has told you what is good and what the Lord asks of you! Is it not to do justice, to love mercy, and to walk humbly with your God! (*Micah 6:6–8*) LB

The dog that did not bark

The singular matter of the dog that did not bark is a classical Sherlock Holmes paradox. It is the silence of the dog, the fact that it did not bark when it might have been expected to, that sets the great detective off in his pursuit of truth.

The religious equivalent must be all the disasters that do not happen to us in this dangerous world through which we journey, deflected by Divine providence. One of the Jewish prayers talks about 'Your miracles that are daily with us'. If all of life is a miracle then each ordinary moment is potentially extraordinary, everything secular is potentially holy and it is up to us to see it or to make it that way.

There is one special day in the Jewish calendar, it is even called *yom hameyuchas*, 'the special day', and it is called that because absolutely nothing special happens on it! It comes between two festival days that precede it, the new moon of the month of *Sivan* and the three special days that follow it, leading up to the revelation on Mount Sinai celebrated at the festival of *Shavuot*, Pentecost. So what is special about this day that is actually 'normal'?

There is a parable told about a king who asked four artists to each decorate a wall of a room. Three of them set about with their paints designing and decorating their own particular wall to the very best of their ability. Meanwhile the fourth artist spent his time with a slide rule and sheets of paper making calculations. When the others had finally finished he brought in polished mirrors which he fixed to the fourth wall in such a way that they reflected and enhanced the designs on the other three walls, thus completing the exquisite beauty of the whole composition.

The 'normal' day between the festival ones helps to show off their special nature. We cannot always live on the peaks of life but appreciate them more for the normal times between, and so we should appreciate the normal days because they give us the basic structures and security of our lives that enables us to experience and survive the peaks. JM

17 JUNE

The question

When I told my mother proudly I was going to become a rabbi, she said curiously, 'Lionel, does religion make people nicer? Will it make you nicer?'

Does it? Did it? Does it make people in Ulster or Bosnia or the Holy Land nicer? LB

18 JUNE

Books

It was Islam that defined Jews (and Christians too) as the 'People of the Book' – by which was meant that they too had received the same divine revelation through their 'prophets', as recorded in *the* Book, the Bible. But the term fits Jews for another reason, since books have so long been an essential part of our culture, self-image and obsession. No wonder that the following thoughts by Judah Ibn Tibbon, the twelfth-century Spanish translator of classical Jewish philosophical works from Arabic into Hebrew, have come to adorn bookmarks and book token cards:

> Let your bookcases and your shelves be your gardens and your pleasure grounds. Pluck the fruit that grows therein, gather the roses, the spices and the myrrh. If your soul be satisfied and weary, change from garden to garden, from furrow to furrow, from prospect to prospect. Then your desire will be renewed and your soul be filled with delight. JM

19 JUNE

Now you know

> If A asks B, 'Lend me your sickle' and B says 'I won't' and then the very next day asks A 'Lend me your hammer' and A says 'You wouldn't lend me your sickle, so I'm not going to lend you my hammer' – that's revenge.
>
> But if A says 'Take the hammer. I'm not going to behave to you like you behaved to me' – that's bearing a grudge! (*Sifra on Leviticus 19:18*) LB

20 JUNE

Life studies

Your successes make you clever, but your failures make you wise. LB

21 JUNE

Don't bottle it up

> If someone hurts you, don't bottle it up and say nothing. Have it out with him (or her) and ask 'Why did you do that to me?' (*Maimonides* 1135–1204)

Bottled-up anger gives you a depression. LB

22 JUNE

Friendliness

Walter Benjamin deserves more than a casual mention. A philosopher and literary critic he was one of the key thinkers of the interwar years in Germany. With the rise of the Nazis he settled in Paris, but, ironically, was interned there as a German citizen when war broke out. Released he fled to the South of France and was about to cross the border into Spain with other refugees when the police chief of the border town threatened to send them back to France. Benjamin took his own life.

So this remark of his is doubly poignant.

> Friendliness is not the abolishing of distance but the bringing of distance to life. JM

23 JUNE

Freebies

> Come all who are thirsty come to the water.
> You without money, come and buy and eat!
> Come and buy without money or price
> Wine and milk. (*Isaiah 55:1*)

Lots of things cost you nothing – a bit of encouragement, spirituality, the vision of God, keeping your temper, a prayer, a joke . . . LB

Heroes

24 JUNE

I was first introduced to the writings of Bertolt Brecht by my German teacher at school. It was very imaginative on his part to take us out of elementary shopping instructions into drama, and Brecht's direct and straightforward prose style meant we could understand a lot from the beginning. Feeling comfortable with the language helped pave the way for my own first visit to Germany and the confrontation with the problems of Jews and Germans.

We read a play called 'Leben des Galilei', the life of Galileo, and one phrase stuck in my mind. I suppose that at first I enjoyed quoting it as a way of showing off – look how much German I can speak!

But it remains a very powerful challenge to over-simple ideas about leadership and heroism. I find it helpful whenever I start wishing for an instant solution to a problem – if only the perfect person would come along and make everything right. It is the sort of feeling on which messianic expectations and hopes are built – and on which false messiahs attain power, usually at the cost of everyone else.

Galileo the scientist has concluded that the sun, and not the earth is the centre of the universe. But faced by the church's powerful opposition to this heretical idea he is forced to recant or risk death. The following dialogue, his servant's comment and Galileo's reply, depends in the German on the change of just one word:

> Servant: Unfortunate the land that has no heroes.
> Galileo: Unfortunate the land that needs heroes.

JM

The buck

25 JUNE

Why was the Temple destroyed? These answers come from different tractates of the Talmud.

> Because someone was put to shame publicly and nobody could be bothered to stop it. (*Gittin*)
>
> Because although lots of good deeds were done in the Temple, people hated each other without any real reason. (*Yoma*)
>
> Because judges kept to the strict letter of the law and didn't get to the truth behind it. (*Baba Metzia*)

Because people didn't correct each other. (*Arachin*)

The Rabbis didn't blame the Romans, though they disliked them, just themselves. Unlike self-righteous, defeated nations today, they didn't pass the buck. LB

26 JUNE

Jotham's fable

Part way through the biblical Book of Judges comes this little parable (*Judges 9:8–15*). It is told by Jotham, the only survivor of his family wiped out by the ambitious Abimelech. Jotham stands on a hill and shouts out these words to the men of Shechem who had conspired in the murderous act.

> The trees once went out to anoint a king over them. They said to the olive tree: 'Reign over us.' But the olive tree said to them: 'Shall I leave my oil, by which gods and men are honoured, and go to hold sway over the trees?'
>
> So the trees said to the fig tree: 'Come along and reign over us.' But the fig tree said to them: 'Shall I leave my sweetness and my good fruit and go to hold sway over the trees?'
>
> So the trees said to the vine: 'Come along and reign over us.' But the vine said to them: 'Shall I leave my wine which makes gods and men rejoice and go to hold sway over the trees?'
>
> Then all the trees said to the thornbush: 'Come along and reign over us.' And the thornbush said to the trees: 'If you really intend to anoint me to rule over you then come and take refuge in my shade; but if not, let fire come out from the thornbush and burn up the cedars of Lebanon.'

In the biblical tale the threat of the 'thornbush'/Abimelech comes true and it all ends in disaster and mayhem. But what does the parable mean? Most people who answer point out that it simply proves that those who actually are ambitious to lead society are the least productive, most unworthy, and perhaps the most dangerous!

But the great philosopher and Bible commentator Martin Buber (1878–1965) had a different reading. He pointed out that it is precisely when the 'productive' people duck their leadership responsibilities, thinking that their oil, figs or wine are all that matters, that the thorn-bushes get to power. JM

27 JUNE

The tingle factor

Let us bless and let us extol, let us tell aloud and let us raise aloft, let us set on high and let us honour, let us exalt and let us praise the Holy One, blessed be He, though He is far beyond any blessing or song, any honour or any consolation that can be spoken of in this world.

An Aramaic, pharisaic prayer (the Kaddish) current at the time of Jesus, and perhaps the basis for phrases in the Lord's Prayer. It has the 'tingle factor'. LB

28 JUNE

You're never alone with a book

The title of this piece comes from a famous cigarette commercial. Under a lamppost stood the hero in a trenchcoat smoking a cigarette, while a voice intoned: 'You're never alone with a Strand.' It won prizes for its artistry – and sales are said to have slumped because no one wanted to buy a cigarette that suggested you would end up being so lonely!

Since you can't do much with a cigarette except smoke it, a good book is probably a better bet as a companion in solitude. That is the view of Moses Ibn Ezra, another of these astonishing twelfth-century Hebrew philosopher/poets writing in Muslim Spain.

A book is the most delightful companion .... An inanimate thing, yet it talks .... There is in the world no friend more faithful and attentive, no teacher more proficient .... It will join you in solitude, accompany you in exile, serve as a candle in the dark, and entertain you in your loneliness. It will do you good, and ask no favour in return. It gives, and does not take. JM

29 JUNE

Relationships

Relationships need definition, whether human or divine. Abelard and Heloïse defined their relationship in their letters. In a similar way Jews defined their relationship to God in their liturgy.

We are Your people and You are our God.
We are Your children and You are our Parent.
We are Your servants and You are our Master.
We are Your community and You are our Purpose.
We are Your inheritance and You are our Destiny.
We are Your flock and You are our Shepherd.
We are Your vineyard and You are the Planter.

Try to define your relationship with someone you love, human or divine! LB

30 JUNE

It must be true . . .

That was the title of a book: *It Must Be True It Was In the Papers.* The same scepticism was expressed by the great medieval philosopher Moses Maimonides in a letter he wrote to the Jewish community in Yemen:

> Do not consider that something is true simply because it is written in books, for a liar who will deceive with his tongue will not hesitate to do the same with his pen. JM

JULY

Retirement

> Tho' much is taken, much abides; and tho'
> We are not now that strength which in old days
> Moved earth and heaven; that which we are, we are;
> One equal temper of heroic hearts,
> Made weak by time and fate, but strong in will
> To strive, to seek, to find and not to yield. (*Tennyson*)

There are certain advantages in becoming an OAP. You no longer have to carry as much expectation. What you've done, you've done, and the rest is gravy. You also begin to live in the present, not the past or the future. And of course you get your state pension! It's fine provided you don't yield to your crumbling body. LB

The master

Gurus and spiritual masters seem to be popping up nowadays all over the place, in traditional religions and in the newer 'cults'. Sometimes it is hard to tell the authentic from the phoney: those who just manipulate emotions for their own purpose and those who are so 'transparent' that all may find themselves and their own spiritual nature and journey through this teacher. But the phenomenon is not new – nor is a bit of gentle mickey-taking at their expense.

At the end of the Sabbath the master used to give his students a special 'teaching', for them to meditate on in the coming week. 'Life' he said solemnly on one occasion, 'is like a waterfall', and he sighed deeply. His students nodded enthusiastically, truly a marvellous teaching to contemplate. For the following week they sat and discussed at every possible moment this word of their master. They argued this way and that, consulted the great volumes of the tradition and sought out the opinions of their teachers. When the Sabbath came round again they could hardly contain their impatience to learn from the master the true meaning of this mysterious saying. Finally when the time came to talk, one of them plucked up the courage to say: 'Rebbe, we have thought about and discussed the entire week your teaching of last week: 'Life is like a waterfall'. But however much we consider it and argue, we cannot fathom its depths or understand its hidden meaning. Please tell us, in what way is life like a waterfall?'

The master smiled at them and his eyes glazed over as he went into himself and entered the innermost part of his soul, rising through the seven heavens to the very throne of glory in search of the answer to this deepest of mysteries. There was silence in the room for five minutes, then half an hour, eventually it was two full hours before the teacher returned from this exploration to give his answer. He looked around the room at his expectant disciples, smiled, shrugged his shoulders and said: 'Nu! so life isn't like a waterfall!' JM

3 JULY

Bitter fruit

A young rabbi, the son of two refugees, tastes the bitter fruit of the thirties and forties. It is a medicine our generation cannot avoid.

I made my first visit to Germany when I was nineteen years old, as one of a party of Jewish students. I spent three tense weeks in Germany thinking bitter, angry thoughts. (How many Jews had once lived in this place? What was that old man doing during the war?) I relaxed when we visited Kiel University. The German students we met were all born after the war. They also had long hair and jeans. They invited us to the local beer cellar, and the conversation and drink flowed easily.

At midnight I stood up in order to leave.

'Please' said one of the German student leaders, 'will you stay and talk to me?'

'Yes, of course' I said, and sat down.

The student asked me in which concentration camps had members of my family been. I mentioned names and places, including the fact that one of my grandparents had died in Auschwitz in 1942.

'In 1942,' he said, 'my father was an S.S. guard in Auschwitz.'

Suddenly I was sober. I did not know what to say. Thoughts came rushing into my mind. I did not want this meeting. I wanted to be anywhere else in the world, but not in this place with this boy. We had met before, he and I, through our families. What sort of meeting had that been, and in what conditions! I stared and said nothing. I did not know his position. Did he in any way sympathize with his father's actions?

He answered my unspoken thoughts: 'I found this out three years ago. I left home, and have not spoken to my father since that day.'

I sat back and tried to imagine myself in his position. What would it be like to find out that my father, the man who brought me up, the man that I loved, had done such things? What would it be like to be bone of such bone and flesh of such flesh!

Then he said, 'I have been waiting for you to come. I want to know what I should do.'

We had a long and difficult conversation. In effect he was asking my permission to see his father again. I hope I helped him. I now realize that he helped me. It took a trip to Germany to make me realize that a German can really be a human being. It took a journey into myself, with the help of some years of analysis, to make me realize how human and angry a Jew can be. All humanity has eaten of the fruit; possibilities for good and evil couch in us all. (*Rabbi Daniel Smith*) LB

4 JULY

Dissidents

It seems that societies can only take so much truth about themselves. When something becomes too dangerous to hear there are two options for dealing with those brave or foolhardy enough to speak out. Authoritarian regimes suppress the dissidents and ban their words. Democracies turn them into pop heroes, market their message, sell the T-shirt and neutralize their word through over-saturation.

But there is nothing new in any of this. In the Bible they did the same thing with their own dissidents, the prophets. Amos was deported, Jeremiah imprisoned and Uriah ben Shemaiah was executed for treason. Ezekiel complained that he got the other kind of treatment:

> You are to them like one who sings love songs with a beautiful voice and plays well on an instrument, for they hear what you say, but they will not do it! (*Ezekiel 33:32*) JM

5 JULY

A visionary meal

There is the spiritual meal described by George Herbert (see The Meal 1 February). Here is a visionary one. It is a truth told in many versions. This is from Rabbi Daniel Smith.

> At night God appeared to a rabbi in a dream saying, 'You have been a good man. I will grant any wish you want.' The rabbi said, 'There is one thing. I would like to see heaven and hell before I die.'
>
> Invisible hands led the rabbi to a coach, and they drove until they came to a huge castle. The castle doors opened to reveal a huge hall, so big you could not see the other end of it. Down the centre of the hall was a long table with lots of good food and good drink. On either side of the table on long benches there sat next to each other rows of people, but they could not eat. Their arms had been bound with wooden splints, so that they could not bend their arms to feed themselves. They were miserable and crying, and the rabbi cried for their sake as he was led away back to the coach.
>
> Again the coach drove, until they came to another castle and the rabbi heard sounds of singing and laughter. This also had a hall so big you could not see the end of it. Here also was a long table with lots of good food and good drink. On either side of this table too there sat next to each other rows of people whose arms had been placed in wooden splints so that they could not bend the arm to feed themselves. But this was heaven; this was different. In heaven everyone simply fed the person next to them.
>
> It was the same conditions but the people of heaven thought of others, and not only of themselves. It is up to us whether we create a heaven or a hell on earth. LB

6 JULY

Au clair de la lune

I learnt it as a child, and can remember at least the first verse. But like so many folk-songs or nursery rhymes, the more you try to fathom them the more mysterious they become.

> Au clair de la lune
> Mon ami Pierrot

Prête-moi ta plume
Pour écrire un mot.
Ma chandelle est morte
Je n'ai plus de feu
Ouvrez-moi ta porte
Pour l'amour de Dieu.

In the light of the moon
my friend Pierrot
lend me your pen
to write a word.
My candle is out,
I have no more fire.
Open the door for me
for the love of God.

In the second verse Pierrot rather ungraciously sends his friend off to the neighbour since he has no fire and anyway he's in bed. But what is this 'word' that he is so desperate to write? A love letter he must compose at once to his beloved? A poem bursting out of him demanding to be put on paper? An income tax return that is overdue? And is the 'love of God' simply an idiom or a statement of profound faith?

I know that behind this somewhere is the Commedia del Arte and the figures of Pierrot and Columbine. There is probably a good scholarly explanation of the origins, meaning, 'sitz in leben' and provenance of the poem together with textual variants and reconstructions of the presumed original, uncorrupted version. For the time being I prefer to leave it as part of childhood French and an evocative mystery. JM

7 JULY

A touch

I no longer say much to terminal patients in hospital. I just hold their hand. The body is more direct (and more honest) than the mind.

In 1978 I had a serious operation and had an extraordinary amount of pain after it. If the church needed martyrs today it would have to look elsewhere, but I did try to suffer in silence. In the middle of the night I got out of bed and put my head on the sheet and wept.

Suddenly I felt the charge nurse's arms around me in a huge hug and I immediately felt reassured. Some stronger sleeping pills were fetched but the nurse's 'tender loving care' meant almost as much. Why do we touch each other so little? (*The Rev Malcolm Johnson,* Master of the Royal Foundation of St Katharine) LB

8 JULY

Speechwriters

A friend of mine is a personal assistant to the head of a private company. This means that amongst his tasks is to write important speeches for his boss. I suppose we are used to this from politicians; after all why have researchers and civil servants if not to provide an official line and text, and how can any single person be expected to be up on all the different subjects and nuances? Nevertheless it becomes a bit strange when the speeches appear in a book of 'original thoughts'.

On one occasion when his boss received a foreign award, my friend had to write the speech of modest acceptance. He also had to write the speech of the official who presented the award – who would otherwise know nothing about the boss and the reason why he deserved the award in the first place. Then he had to write the speech for the person who chaired the proceedings who would otherwise have no idea what the evening was about. Then he wrote the words of welcome by the owner of the community centre in which the event took place to the guests who had gathered for this significant event. Naturally he also wrote the press release that went out beforehand and the report of this marvellous occasion that went to the newspapers.

Each speech had to be personalized in the presumed style of the one giving it. My friend is currently looking for other work. JM

9 JULY

It's not cricket

I have been much influenced by the Gita, its doctrine of our deep interconnectedness, and how goodness and the Godhead reincarnate and return to every generation.

I tried to see my western life in this eastern way – not always with success though with great profit. Andrew Lang (1844–1912), I was relieved to find, had similar problems applying this mystical wisdom to English cricket.

If the wild bowler thinks he bowls,
Or if the batsman thinks he's bowled,
They know not, poor misguided souls,
They too shall perish unconsoled.
I am the batsman and the bat,
I am the bowler and the ball,
The umpire, the pavilion cat,
roller, pitch, and stumps, and all. LB

10 JULY

Memories are made of this

The worst part of school, and for that matter much of my later education, was the task of memorizing information. In medical school I was given a marvellous mnemonic for learning the cranial nerves – alas far too vulgar to reproduce here in its entirety. The mnemonic was easy enough to remember (it began: 'Oh! Oh! Oh! to touch and finger . . .) but I still could not remember which 'Oh!' or which 'T' referred to which nerve. Not being at the time a Jewish scholar I had never heard of the *Sefer Raziel*, a seventeenth century collection of mystical and magical works which might have solved my problem. It contains the following recipe for instant and everlasting memory.

> The following has been tried and found reliable, and Rabbi Saadia ben Joseph made use of it. He discovered it in the cave of Rabbi Eleazar Kalir, and all the wise men of Israel together with their pupils applied this remedy with excellent effect: At the beginning of the month of Sivan take some wheatmeal and knead it, and be sure to remain *standing*. Make cakes and bake them, write upon them the verse, 'He has made memory among His wondrous acts; gracious and merciful is the Eternal.' Take an egg and boil it hard, peel it, and write on it the names of five angels; eat such a cake every day, for thirty days, with an egg, and you will learn all that you see and never forget. JM

11 JULY

Preaching

How long should a sermon be? Some people can make an hour seem like ten minutes and others can do the opposite. The problem is not new and it was addressed in classical Victorian style by the Rev Simeon Singer. He was an English Orthodox rabbi (1848–1906) who edited and translated the Jewish prayerbook so successfully that the 'Singer's Prayer Book' became the standard one adopted in Orthodox synagogues throughout Britain and the Empire. He belonged to a time when British Orthodox rabbis were often quite progressive in their views, and his enormous output of lectures, and indeed sermons, on Jewish historical themes are always fascinating, enlightening and entertaining.

His views on preaching are included in a challenging lecture called 'Where Clergy Fail'. Here he is on the length of the sermon:

> Of all the preacher's sins, the one for which pardon is hardest to obtain is preaching at inordinate length. Not many of us, I fear, have a perfectly clean record in that respect. What is long or short in a sermon depends, of course, to a great extent, upon the appetite of your congregation. There are people, our own people, too – need I say they are not English Jews? – who do not object to sit for two or three hours at a homiletic meal. But very few of us are likely to have to cater for such a congregation. And very few of us, to speak candidly, have the right to speak at great length. It is all very well to plead, 'But I must do justice to my subject.' In doing justice to our subject are we excused showing mercy to our hearers? Besides, what is the use of talking of justice to our subject when the jury will not listen, and become impatient, irritable and irate? Is not that the very way to prevent justice being done to our subject? A barrister who acted in that manner would soon be left without clients. JM

12 JULY

The journey of Moses

In 'The Trial' Franz Kafka included the parable of the man from the country who stood before the law. He was refused admission by the guard who warned him that if he got past he would only discover a second gate with an even more fearsome guard and so on through ever more frightening hurdles. So the man sat down outside the gate and waited till eventually he died. Kafka's modern hero stops at the first hurdle. In the Rabbinic tale that probably inspired him, when Moses went up Mt Sinai to get the 'Torah', God's teaching, he encountered a similar problem, but with a different result.

When Moses went up to Mount Sinai to receive the Torah a cloud appeared at his feet. Its mouth opened and he entered it, walking as if on solid ground. Then he met Kemuel, the porter, the angel who is in charge of the guardians of the entrance to heaven. He spoke harshly to Moses: 'What are you doing here, son of Amram, in this place that belongs to angels of fire?' Moses answered: 'I come with the permission of the Holy One, blessed be He, to receive the Torah and take it down to Israel.' But Kemuel would not let him pass, so Moses pushed him aside and went on.

Then there appeared the angel Hadarniel, who is sixty myriads of parasangs taller than the other angels, and as he speaks, lightning blazes out. He roared at Moses: 'What are you doing here, son of Amram?' Moses was terrified and would have fallen from the cloud, had not God taken pity on him and spoken to Hadarniel. At once this angel became like a servant of Moses, leading him on to the next angel Sandalfon before whom even he was afraid. But again God intervened and Moses was led stage by stage through all the angels that guard it until he reached the Torah. JM

13 JULY

The lady

St Francis fell in love with a lady, like any knight of chivalry, 'richer and fairer than any other'. She was his dream, and he devoted his life to her service.

In our eyes she appears very different – loathsome even, because we do not look upon her with love. She is My Lady Poverty – a pock-marked hag to us, a great and beautiful lady to him.

Who sees her truly? LB

The daily sins

14 JULY

The prayerbook allows for a daily acknowledgement of our sins, but a lot of Jews tend to save them up for a once a year binge on the Day of Atonement. The Rabbis saw an advantage in having an entire season devoted to the exercise of confession, repentance and atonement. They pointed out that if you sell goods in the market out of season, people will inspect them more carefully. In season, no one pays so much attention. It is the same with sins – the odds are that you can smuggle your worst ones through with those of the rest of the community.

Why do we need to confess daily? Because, the Rabbis observed, there are at least three sins that no one can escape on any given day: sinful thoughts; the presumption that God must answer our prayers, and the 'dust of slander' (*Baba Batra 164b*). JM

The hard stuff

15 JULY

'Don't let the bastards get you down!'

> In 1988 various church leaders forced me to evict the members of the Lesbian and Gay Christian Movement from their office in the tower of my church, St Botolph, Aldgate. They had been there for twelve years and I felt it was strongly symbolic that they were welcome in a church building. Here of all places people could put their faith and sexuality together. Alas, a costly court case defeated me and at the height of it all when the tabloids joined in the persecution I received from a friend a telegram containing these words. (*The Rev Malcolm Johnson*, Master of the Royal Foundation of St Katharine)

I imagine all the biblical prophets said the same thing under their saintly breath. LB

Lost and found

Junk shops, bric-a-brac stalls and auctions have a certain gloomy attraction. There is always the chance of a bargain, but it is also strange to see the remnants of other people's lives exposed, the precious and trivial things that once were important and now have to take their chances in the market place. Will they find a good home or simply be junked when space is no longer available.

I don't know if it still happens, but the Post Office in Jerusalem used to auction off unclaimed packages at regular intervals. Being Jerusalem the majority of the items were inevitably books:

Such, indeed, is the holiness of
Jerusalem
that the Post Office auctions it off
at regular intervals
in bulk.

'Holy books'
that by some oversight of divine providence
(and the aforementioned Post Office)
have strayed from their destined path
can be redeemed in anonymous packages
by those with a feeling for the sacred
– or facilities for re-marketing
at a price more suited to their worth.

Scattered among crates
of assorted underwear
of twenty identical parts to an unidentified machine
of shoes and tubes of toothpaste
of sardines, children's games and one coffee tin
of endless clothing
of an incomplete set of Shakespeare in French
of a complete set of something in Polish,
are these jewels of religious wisdom
of perceptive commentary
of refutation and polemic
of saintly dreams
of pious admonitions
– prayers of the holy people

tossed about in the familiar indignity
of yet another temporary exile.

Going for the first time,
going for the second time,
GONE!! JM

17 JULY

Water

Creator God,

Without water land cannot live;
It contracts and cracks.

Without water plants cannot grow;
Dry seeds stay dormant.

Without water we cannot live.

So, too,
We need divine water
To pour into our cracked and dry lives.

Creator God,
Soak us with Your Spirit
That we may grow as people. (*John Newbury*)

John is a Methodist who guided me and 'produced' me for the BBC 'God slots'. He took enormous unselfish care for which I'm grateful. He is a Methodist Minister now with the World Council of Churches in Geneva. LB

18 JULY

Who's in charge?

I once met a Yiddish writer in Jerusalem who told me about an experience on a bus. Some man got on who immediately started rearranging the seating for everyone – 'You move over there, then he can sit next to her, then you can put your parcels in that place, while they . . .' 'I closed my eyes', he said, 'and relaxed. It was good to know that someone else was in charge of the world for a while'.

We are all in charge of our own little corner of the universe – or at least try to sort out the things that fate or providence brings our way.

Like the man on the bus, I enjoyed the performance of this remarkable character on the corner of Broadway and 65th Street, New York.

The guy who runs Lincoln Center
from his ice-cream parlour across the road
has a banana-split belly
and knows how to spot a panhandler:
'You just have to look at their shoes.
I've seen one guy in a tuxedo and bare feet!'

As a philosopher he's against Pride.
'Look at the French,
they hate us Americans.
They can never forgive what Truman did for De Gaulle.
They treat us like dirt.
If I had my way I'd put such a tariff on their goods
they'd never get into the country!'

Between placing customers
and figuring which show people will be in today
he monologues with his waitresses,
smart in white blouses, black slacks,
on techniques of the trade
on their private pains and diseases
on the name of that actress,
well-stacked,
used to be in all those Sinatra–Dean Martin movies
what was her name? . . .

A lot of managers come in.
Sure I get offered complimentary tickets.
One guy told me: Ask at the box office.
Four tickets in the name of 'Irv'.
I was embarrassed to ask.
Is that I-R-V or E-R-V?
Sure they were there.
Twenty dollars apiece.
Some complimentary!

What's that?
He wants half a tea-bag?
That's OK
He's the customer! JM

Loving touch

I help with a retreat for people with the HIV virus. (They help me too because they're the most courageous bunch I've met.) Such retreats bring out the goodness of people. Out of the blue, a masseur wrote to us offering his services free. We accepted. At the retreat I told another helper, a nun, that I didn't like the idea of another person pummelling me. She agreed, but risked a massage (upper parts only). I couldn't seem behind, so I had one too. The relaxation that resulted was like the peace that comes with meditation. I'd forgotten how the Holy Spirit works through your muscles as well as your mind – when the massage is done with spiritual love.

The masseur Graham Tyler wrote this:

> It seems entirely natural to me that massage should be a means of expressing my spirituality, for touch is the first of the senses to develop in the unborn child, and brackets our spirit's sojourn in the physical body, remaining with us to this life's end. My understanding of the spirituality of my work is very simple: I can achieve nothing of any consequence on my own – mere technique is not enough. Anything in my work which is of real value comes not from me, but *through* me, and on a level way beyond my comprehension. All that is required of me is to perform the massage to the best of my ability, but more importantly, to give it with unconditional Love. By this I don't mean to suggest any emotional involvement, but rather that Love which is simply to treat with the greatest of care and utmost respect, every person who comes to me, whatever their background or present condition. It is only when I set my 'ego' to one side, and give myself entirely to the person I am massaging, that my work begins to have any real benefit beyond the comfort which a massage brings on a purely physical level.

Since that massage I try to touch people differently, not roughly but with respect and affection. LB

God and nature

The Hebrew Bible contains one central and highly curious idea that must have seemed to fly in the face of the experience of those who live close to the earth, and of plain common sense. That behind all the different forms of nature, the dreadful powers of storms, earthquakes, droughts and mysterious diseases, there is a single force at work; that nature itself is not the supreme reality, nor the sun or moon or stars, but God. It is such a strange idea that the struggle to establish it can be seen across the thousand years of the composition of the Bible. And the exact relationship between God and nature is always being questioned, explored and re-interpreted till today.

In the 10th century, Saadiah Gaon, who was born in Egypt and lived in Baghdad, composed this Hebrew hymn to the way nature reveals the power of God:

We know You through the universe You created;
because of the sun when it rises and when it sets;
because of the moon when it stands in the midst of the heavens;
because of the stars when they shoot their arrows on the earth,
and when they grow dark and withdraw their shining;
because of the heavens which are sometimes bright,
and sometimes gloomy, clothed with darkness;
because of the lightnings when they dart about;
because of the arrows when they fly;
because of the whirlwind when it blows;
because of the storm when it rages;
because of the clouds when they pour out water,
and the skies when they give out sound;
because of the rain when it comes pouring down;
because of the torrents that flood the earth;
because of the earth when it sends out grass;
because of the fruit tree when it yields its fruit;
because of life when it is sown, ripens and is born;
because of the strength of the young and splendour of the old;
because of the day when it gives us light;
because of the night when it grows dark about us;
because of the months when they are renewed;
because of the years when they are changed . . .

God is mentioned on the earth and it quakes;
on the lightning and it races away;
on the burning coals and they are extinguished;
on the pestilence and it rages;
on the mountains and they break apart;
on the child and it goes forth;

on the storms and they calm;
on the woman with child and she gives birth;
on the wounded and he is made whole;
on the sea and it is divided;
on the chain and it is loosened;
on the lion and he turns back;
on the waters and they stand still;
on the river and it flows backwards;
on the adversary and he is silenced;
on the world and it exists;
on the afflicted and he is healed;
on the rock and it brings out water;
on the eloquent and he is speechless;
on the thunder and it ceases;
on the unyielding and it shatters;
on the depth and it overflows.

Yet in every generation You make part of the mystery clear. JM

21 JULY

Don't run a race with yourself

From Kim Holman, the yacht designer, the winner of many races and medals:

> As a nine-year-old, recently having learned to swim but still perhaps a little apprehensive, my prep school headmaster's sister decided to teach me to dive off the high board.
>
> Her maxim was: 'always face up to a challenge. Next time one comes along it will be less difficult. If you don't face it, next time will be more difficult.'
>
> When I had worked my way up to the top diving board I heaved a sigh of relief, 'I've done it!' 'Oh no you have not', she says, 'go on diving several times each day until you are no longer afraid.'
>
> The only snag was that I then tended to face up to all sorts of challenges which I should not have done. Getting myself over-promoted and taking on tasks to which I was unsuited! LB

22 JULY

Fresh air

We are very conscious today of air pollution, a diminishing ozone layer and a thousand other environmental hazards. Sometimes we imagine that it was much better in the past before car fumes poisoned the atmosphere and other modern pollutants made life miserable. But in the twelfth century, Moses Maimonides (Rabbi and Religious Philosopher) gave the following advice:

> The quality of urban air compared to the air in the deserts and forests is like thick and turbulent water compared to pure and light water. And this is because in the cities with their tall buildings and narrow roads, the pollution that comes from their residents, their waste, their corpses, and offal from their cattle, and the stench of their adulterated food, make their entire air malodorous, turbulent, reeking and thick, and the winds become accordingly so, although no one is aware of it.
>
> And since there is no way out, because we grow up in cities and become used to them, we can at least choose a city with an open horizon . . . And if you have no choice, and you cannot move out of the city, try at least to live in a suburb created to the northeast. Let the house be tall and the court wide enough to permit the northern wind and the sun to come through, because the sun thins out the pollution of the air, and makes it light and pure. JM

23 JULY

Beatitudes for special people

Blessed are you who take time to listen to difficult speech, for you help us to know that if we persevere we can be understood.

Blessed are you who walk with us in public places, and ignore the stares of strangers, for in your friendship we feel good to be ourselves.

Blessed are you who never bid us to 'hurry up' and, more blessed, you who do not snatch our tasks from our hands to do them for us, for often we need time rather than help.

Blessed are you who stand beside us as we enter new and untried ventures, for our unsureness will be outweighed by the times when we surprise ourselves and you.

Blessed are you who ask for our help and realize our giftedness for our greatest need is to be needed.

Blessed are you who help us with the graciousness of Christ, for often we need the help we cannot ask for.

Blessed are you when, by all things, you assure us that what makes us individuals is not our particular disability or difficulty but our beautiful God-given personhood which no handicapping condition can confine.

Rejoice and be exceedingly glad for your understanding and love have opened doors for us to enjoy life to its full and you have helped us believe in ourselves as valued and gifted people. LB

24 JULY

Predators

Animal fables have long been a favourite way of describing the behaviour of human beings. This one about the wolf and the lamb comes from a medieval Hebrew collection. I can think at once of half a dozen trouble spots in the world where the technique of the wolf is being employed.

A wolf was drinking in a stream when he noticed a lamb drinking a bit further down the hill.

'How dare you muddy the water from which I am drinking!' he snarled.

'That cannot be the case,' answered the lamb, 'since the water is running from you down to me.'

'Well,' said the wolf, 'why did you call me bad names last year?!'

'That can't have been me,' said the lamb, 'since I was only born this year.'

'I don't care,' said the wolf, 'if it wasn't you it was your father!'

And he gobbled up the lamb. JM

25 JULY

An atheist's spiritual advice to ministers of religion

Richie McMullen – partner, friend, colleague who labelled himself as an atheist, reminded me of what he thought was the essential ingredient for anyone daring to be involved within the ministry of the Christian movement. For him, 'no one should even consider

being a minister or priest unless he or she were prepared to be first and foremost someone who could remain vulnerably human.' He also was very adamant, 'you cannot be a Christian minister or priest without being a political person, as well as being a radical for love.' They are, he would say, 'both sides of the same coin'.
(*Fr Bill Kirkpatrick*) LB

26 JULY

Something for nothing

It is the basis of most con tricks – from the shell game at a fairground to an elaborate scam on the stock market: the greed to acquire something for nothing. The following little parable was told by the Maggid of Dubno, Jacob ben Wolf Kranz (1741–1804).

A cunning man came to his rich neighbour and asked to borrow a silver spoon. The neighbour agreed and when the man returned it he brought with him a small silver spoon as well. 'What is this?' asked the rich man. 'Your spoon gave birth to this little one, and obviously it belongs to you.'

Some time later the same man came to borrow a large silver bowl from his rich neighbour, and when he returned it he brought with him another small silver bowl in addition. When the rich man asked what this was, he received the same answer, that the bowl had given birth.

The next time the cunning man came he asked to borrow a large gold salver of great value. Expecting a reward for his loan, the rich man gladly gave it. But as time passed and the salver was not returned he began to get anxious and went to find out what had happened. The man greeted him with a sad countenance and said, 'I'm afraid that the salver died!' 'How can a salver die?' demanded the rich man. 'If a silver spoon and bowl can give birth, then a salver can die', came the reply. JM

27 JULY

The outsider's saint

In the early sixties, when I first became aware of being drawn towards the Christian movement, I dared to mention this to a friend who listened and said nothing. However the next day he sent me a copy of *Waiting On God* by Simone Weil. I was and am impressed by her integrity and her courage to remain an outsider for outsiders. I believe she has been called 'The Outsider's Saint'. Simone wrote much that I have found I could identify with. Such as, 'I have the essential need and I think I can say vocation, to move among men of every class and complexion, mixing with them and sharing their life and outlook, so far that is to say as conscience allows, merging into the crowd and disappearing among them, so that they show themselves as they are, putting off all disguises with me. It is because I long to know them, so as to love them just as they are. For if I do not love them as they are, it will not be they whom I love, and my love will be unreal.'

Strange how years later, I find myself echoing this same statement through my own experience. 'If I can unite in myself through contemplative action with all the peoples of the world; if I can prepare in myself for the reunion of all, especially those who are the rejects of society, through seeing the mystery of God within every person hidden behind labels, which so often depersonalize, then I will be on the way to becoming a person of reconciliation: a person who accepts that we are all not only "loned" to God, but also to each other and to the community of all the "peoples of God", our ultimate lover, who does not know how to reject.'
(*Fr Bill Kirkpatrick*)

I have always relied on insiders for religion, but on outsiders for spirituality. LB

28 JULY

Fundraising

Anyone who has been involved with a voluntary organization knows the joys (or pains) of fundraising. It does not appear to matter how large or small the sum, the same amount of work seems to be involved; it is just the target audience for the appeal that differs.

When I began to raise money for my college an American colleague told me this story which is a useful icebreaker when preparing an audience for the sales pitch.

A new rabbi was appointed to a congregation and among his tasks was to raise money for special charities. He discovered that though most people gave generously there was one very rich man who had refused to donate anything, even though successive generations of rabbis had tried to persuade or convince him. So the rabbi decided to try his luck, visited the man and told him about the important charitable works that the congregation was engaged in that needed support. Would he contribute?

'Let me tell you something, rabbi,' replied the man. 'I want you to know that my wife has something of a drinking problem and she has to spend several months a year in a sanatorium. It is a marvellous place with a high level of care, but, of course, it is enormously expensive. Now my brother has been having financial troubles with his business and is on the verge of bankruptcy. He needs a very large sum of money to keep him afloat and prevent him being utterly ruined. My daughter has unfortunately managed to get herself pregnant, insists on having the child and needs to be supported during the pregnancy and for a long time afterwards. My son had a very bad accident just a few weeks ago and has to be kept on a heart–lung machine with twenty-four hour nursing care, and you can imagine how much that costs. Now, rabbi, I don't give them any money, so why on earth should I give some to you?' JM

29 JULY

My empathic friend

My empathic friend sees the unique mystery that is me. Never fully understanding it nor too deeply exploring it, he allows it to be. He sees this mystery and knows it to be the evolving me. He sees and knows that it's mine and mine alone. He sees the possibilities for growth and allows it to happen. Sometimes the results please him, sometimes not. He sees the mystery that is me and lets it be, for me, for others and for himself. He sees me as a whole person. Not always complete and together, nor loose and lost. He sees the whole me and accepts this wholeness. This indeed makes him my friend. He sees the strengths and the weaknesses, the potential and limitations, the clear views and the blockages, the caring and the selfishness, the harmony and the discord, the saint and the sinner. He sees it all and accepts. He sees the struggle and the ease of my move towards change and the greater me, and allows it to happen at my pace. He sometimes sees just how slow it is and how many backward steps I have to retrace in an effort to get it right in my own terms. He sees me as a person who knows the value of true friendship but also as a person who sometimes lets him down. He is safe in the knowledge that I would never knowingly hurt him. So, when I do, the process of healing is co-creative. He knows that I'll try to dwell more on the recovery than on the hurt itself. He sees that in wounding I'm wounded too. He sees the sensitivity that is in me and is careful to encourage and preserve it. But he also sees the times when I'm just a little too introspective and self-centred and he makes allowances. He sees the person who needs loving, who wants to give, who needs to be needed, the searcher after truth, the child and the adult, the poet and the writer, the Marxist who reads the Bible, the guy who says he wants a lot of new experiences but is often just too lazy to move. My friend sees the paradox that is me and my efforts to work through it constructively. He sees the aggression and then frustration and my efforts to cope with such a powerful energy. He sees me growing through trying. He sees my HIV disease and does not make it the centre of his or my world. His seeing helps me to see myself so much more honestly. The strength of his growing acceptance of the total me permits me to be growingly vulnerable towards him, so allowing myself to see myself through his eyes. His 'seeing' and my acceptance of it allows the mystery that is me to remain intact and free to evolve. (*Richie McMullen*) LB

30 JULY

Food for thought

Unlike Lionel, my own culinary expertise is limited to two dishes. My father taught me how to dip sliced bread in egg and fry it. The resultant 'fritters' can be eaten with either salt or sugar, thus killing two courses with one fry up. The other is more ambitious. Smother a chicken in marmalade, pop it into a Römertopf and put it in the oven. (I can't remember for how long.) In this respect I am closer to the tradition of the ancient Rabbis, rather than the new man, as the following story indicates.

A woman took her son to a baker in Caesarea. She said to him: 'Teach my son the profession.' He said to her: 'Let him stay with me for five years and I will teach him five hundred recipes with wheat.' He stayed for five years and learnt five hundred recipes with wheat. Then the baker said to her: 'Let him stay another five years and I'll teach him a thousand recipes with wheat.' But how many recipes can there be with wheat?' Rabbi Chanina and Rabbi Yonatan were sitting together and calculating and stopped at sixty.

Moreover Rabbi Elazar in the name of Rabbi Yossi said: There was a woman in Caesarea who took her son to a cook and said to him: 'Teach my son the profession.' He said to her: 'Let him stay with me four years and I will teach him a hundred recipes with eggs.' He stayed with him for four years and learnt a hundred recipes with eggs. He said to her: 'Let him stay with me four more years and I will teach him another hundred recipes with eggs.' Rabbi Judah the Prince heard this and said: 'We have no idea what good living is!' (*Ecclesiastes Rabbah 1:8*) JM

31 JULY

The force within me

I would often pray to God. I thanked Him for my good fortune in having weathered the past months, and that now, fortified in body and soul, I had charge of sixteen young lives for whom I felt responsible. I felt these days that, in my own small way, I was part of creation: and I sensed within myself something of that vast power that was responsible for me. I felt that God frequently works out His plans through human beings, and that if only we listen to human words and voice, we can often hear Him speak. And whenever I succeeded in bringing curiosity, interest, a smile or sometimes tears into the eyes of these wretched children and felt proud of myself for it, I also thought that in my very self-praise I was praising that Infinite power which had granted me the opportunity of playing a positive role in this inferno. I felt that I had strength only because He was present in my blood and in my senses, and that so long as I realized this force within me, the Germans would be unable to touch me.

Eugene Heimler was a great therapist, who studied life, death and resurrection in the 'university' of the concentration camps. LB

AUGUST

1 AUGUST

The pub

I sometimes found warmth in a pub when I was frozen out of a place of worship. God (thank God!) is not caged by the institutions that claim Him.

Dear Mother, dear Mother, the Church is cold,
But the Ale-house is healthy & pleasant & warm;
Besides I can tell where I am used well,
Such usage in heaven will never do well.

But if at the Church they would give us some Ale,
And a pleasant fire our souls to regale,
We'd sing and we'd pray all the live-long day,
Nor ever once wish from the Church to stray.

Then the Parson might preach & drink & sing,
And we'd be as happy as birds in the spring;
And modest dame Lurch, who is always at Church,
Would not have bandy children nor fasting nor birch.

And God, like a father rejoicing to see
His children as pleasant and happy as he,
Would have no more quarrel with the Devil or the Barrel,
But kiss him & give him both drink and apparel.
(*William Blake* 1757–1827) LB

2 AUGUST

My child, we were children

I had given a lecture at a German university and was invited to a party with the students afterwards. She sat in a corner with her guitar and sang Yiddish songs. It had become almost fashionable in a Germany without Jews to rediscover this ancient language, part German, part Hebrew, and the culture that went along with it. But she sang them straight and with a kind of simplicity that cut to the heart. And then among the Yiddish some pure German, the words of Heinrich Heine (1797–1856), Germany's greatest lyric poet, though, as a Jew and a highly political animal, one of her absentee sons. It is nostalgic and witty and sad at the same time, with a beautiful newly composed melody. This translation is by Elizabeth Barrett Browning. (By the way, 'pelf' is a word for money or wealth! – I'd never heard of it either.)

My child, we were two children,
Small, merry by childhood's law;
We used to creep to the henhouse,
And hide ourselves in the straw.

We crowed like cocks, and whenever
The passers near us drew –
'Cock-a-doodle!' they thought
'Twas a real cock that crew.

The boxes about our courtyard
We carpeted to our mind,
And lived there both together –
Kept house in a noble kind.

The neighbour's old cat often
Came to pay us a visit;
(We have made the very same speeches
Each with a compliment in it.)

After her health we asked,
Our care and regard to evince –
(We have made the very same speeches
To many an old cat since).

We also sat and wisely
Discoursed, as old folks do,
Complaining how all went better
In those good old times we knew;

How love, and truth, and believing
Had left the world to itself,
And how so dear was the coffee,
And how so rare was the pelf.

The children's games are over,
The rest is over with youth –
The world, the good games, the good times,
The belief, and the love, and the truth. JM

Role reversal

When it became impossible to continue in my German school, my parents sent me to a Jewish boarding school in Sweden. It was run by a couple who were inspiring teachers and they too taught as much by the way they lived as through their lessons.

Something must have rubbed off on me in connection with teaching and learning. My first psychotherapy patient was a six-year-old little girl who would not talk. Her parents were sure that she was perfectly capable of speaking, but she had never done so at school. When she came to see me she went straight across to the sandbox and began to busy herself paying no attention to me and not saying a word. I said: 'I will get on with my writing, and when you are ready, you just tell me.' We went on like this for three sessions. She looked around a few times to see what I was doing, but remained mute. In the fourth session she turned round and said with considerable vehemence, 'Aren't you ever going to talk to me?' I said, 'With pleasure. I was just waiting until you were ready.' She wanted to play school, she was going to be the teacher and I the pupil. She was a very strict teacher, and I was a rather unsatisfactory pupil, and she had no hesitation in letting me know about it.

I learned a great deal from my child teacher about taking my cue from the patient, about allowing space and time and not putting on pressure or making her fit my wishes and expectations.

I also learned a great deal from those of my adult patients who told me when they thought I was getting it wrong and from students who challenged me. I recently met one of them again. He is a professor now, and this time it was I who did the challenging. We had both learned something about respecting and accepting criticism and challenge from those we taught and treated. (*Irene Bloomfield*, psychotherapist)

The test of any relationship is – if we 'take' from those we 'give' to. If we don't we may help our clients but we will harm ourselves, because one-way traffic enourages our egos and fantasies of power. LB

The lays of Israel

I don't know where I acquired it but from time to time I dip into a little volume of poems titled *The Lays of Israel*, by Max Boshwitz, 'Published for the author' in New York in 1925. It is quite in keeping with the volume that it is dedicated: 'Inscribed to the ever cherished memory of the dearest friend I ever had – my mother'. Apparently Mr Boshwitz lived in Memphis, Tennessee, and though of an Orthodox background, and with some command of Yiddish, he belonged to a Reform community. But for a certain amount of self-irony, and a lot of humour, he might qualify as a kind of Jewish McGonagall (see 'Poetic Gems' 12 August) – though he may not be unique in this respect.

The poems cover biblical themes, the Jewish festivals and hints on etiquette but he was also prepared to celebrate or commemorate important local events. 'The Old Shool' marks the time when the old temple on Main and Exchange Streets, Memphis, a bank before it served the congregation, was torn down to make way for a more modern structure:

> Farewell! thou old landmark! the home where Mammon swayed,
> Farewell! ye crumbling walls, wherein my Israel prayed!
> Farewell to Gothic pillars! 'twas time to hew you down;
> The pride of olden commerce, when Memphis was a town.

He dedicated a poem to the Silver Jubilee of Rabbi Max Samfield.

> With mickle joy, amidst a thousand cheers,
>   We hail thy jubilee thou good pastor!
> Thou'st been our guide these twenty-five years;
>   And lulled our moans in every disaster . . .
>
> Thou's taught thy flock along the vanished years,
>   A faith that sparkles like the pure crystal;
> That stills the sob in heart bedewed with tears;
>   When life is heavy ladened with thistle. JM

Content

5 AUGUST

So much attention is given to the 'greats' such as Shakespeare, that we deprive ourselves of the pleasure of minor masters – not least of whom is Shakespeare's contemporary, Thomas Dekker. The joyousness of his 'Shoemaker's Holiday' is wonderful for winter reading and this lyric from it, just right to ease one's mind before sleep. It can be sung too, but I, alas, can only moan it.

Art thou poor, yet hast thou golden slumbers?
O sweet content!
Art thou rich, yet is thy mind perplexéd?
O punishment!
Dost thou laugh to see how fools are vexéd
To add to golden numbers, golden numbers?
O sweet content! O sweet, O sweet content!
Work apace, apace, apace, apace;
Honest labour bears a lovely face;
Then hey nonny nonny, hey nonny, nonny!

Canst drink the waters of the crispéd spring?
O sweet content!
Swimm'st thou in wealth, yet sink'st in thine own tears?
O punishment!
Then he that patiently want's burden bears
No burden bears, but is a king, a king!
O sweet content! O sweet, O sweet content!
Work apace, apace, apace, apace;
Honest labour bears a lovely face;
Then hey nonny nonny, hey nonny nonny! LB

Over Jordan

6 AUGUST

The sad little tune that accompanies this folk song echoes the pain and resignation out of which it was written and the hope for a better life beyond the grave:

I'm just a poor wayfaring stranger,
A-trav'ling through this world of woe;

But there's no sickness, no toil nor danger
In that bright world to which I go.
I'm going there to see my father,
I'm going there no more to roam,
I'm just a-going over Jordan,
I'm just a-going over home.

The promise of a better life on the other side of the Jordan gets a more cheerful treatment in this other favourite spiritual:

Swing low, sweet chariot,
Coming for to carry me home,
Swing low, sweet chariot,
Coming for to carry me home.

I looked over Jordan and what did I see,
Coming for to carry me home,
A band of angels coming after me,
Coming for to carry me home.
Chorus.

If you get there, before I do,
Coming for to carry me home,
Tell all my friends, I'm coming too,
Coming for to carry me home.
Chorus. JM

7 AUGUST

Trifling things

Yet they are the way we get to heaven – if we deal justly with them. This is the simple message of De Caussade, the 18th century Jesuit, in his 'Self-Abandonment to Divine Providence'. No special abilities are required.

> This God of goodness has made easy of access all the necessary and common things of the natural order, such as earth, air and water. Nothing is more necessary than breathing, sleep and eating; nothing also is easier. Love and fidelity are no less necessary in the supernatural order, it cannot therefore be that the difficulty of acquiring them is as great as one thinks. Consider your life; of what

is it made up? Of a number of very unimportant actions. Well, it is just with these very things, so trifling, that God is pleased to content himself . . .

Here is the whole of sanctity. Here is the grain of mustard seed of which the fruits, because we do not recognize it on account of its tiny size, are lost. Here is the penny of the Gospel parable, the treasure which we cannot find, because we imagine it to be too far off to be discovered. LB

8 AUGUST

The house of the rising sun

When I first started learning the guitar I could only figure out about three chords. Luckily they included Em, B7 and A and I could learn to sing this song. The trouble with it is that it is so easy to sing, and to ham up, that the reality of the bitter life that lies behind it becomes almost lost. But it reflects the fate of too many women, and too many children. Versions of the song differ, but the tragedy is the same.

There is a house in New Orleans
they call the Rising Sun
and it's been the ruin of many a poor girl
and me, Oh Lord, I'm one.

My mother she's a tailor
she sews those bright new jeans.
My husband he's a gamblin' man
gambles down in New Orleans.

Go tell my baby sister,
not to do what I have done,
to shun that house in New Orleans
they call the Rising Sun.

One foot on the platform,
the other one on the train
I'm going back to New Orleans
To wear my ball and chain. JM

The distorting mirror

'Don't taunt your neighbour with your own blemishes'. (*Talmud, Baba Metzia*)

'Sinners are mirrors: when we see faults in them, we must realize that they only reflect the evil in us.' (*Baal Shem Tov*)

After the Nazi rise to power in Germany it took very little time for many of my fellow pupils at school to become enthusiastic followers of the Nazi creed. This included two girls whom I had regarded as good friends. We had acquired the nickname 'three-leafed clover', because we spent so much time together. We belonged to the same sports club and shared many interests and activities.

Within a few weeks of Hitler's victory I was told that Jews were no longer welcome and that my name had been removed from the members' list. A few days later I saw my former friends approaching, and as I was about to greet them, they crossed to the other side of the road. We never spoke to each other again.

It would have been good to think that this experience made me beware of prejudice and contempt for whole groups of people, but when I contemplated my own record I recalled an incident which now fills me with shame.

During World War Two I belonged to a Jewish platoon within the British army and was working in a military hospital in Palestine. We had a few Arab civilians working for us, doing the jobs members of the Forces did not care to do. Masud was our 'boy'. He was a silent, uncommunicative and skinny lad. Perhaps it was because of this that he was suspected of taking some leftovers without permission. The corporal in charge of provisions talked very contemptuously of Masud being just another of 'those wogs who could not be trusted not to steal your pants off you when you took your eyes off them for a minute.' I laughed and shortly afterwards told the story to one of my fellow workers, using the same denigrating expression of 'wog' about Masud as the corporal had used. We all did without thought, mindlessly, but dangerously and without remembering what prejudice, name-calling and stereotyping had done to us.

I now like to remind myself of the sayings mentioned above plus another more recent one by Sigmund Freud: 'We hate the criminal and deal severely with him, because we view in his deeds,

as in a distorted mirror, our own criminal tendencies.'
(*Irene Bloomfield, psychotherapist*) LB

10 AUGUST

Motherless child

This Negro spiritual reflects the experience of many black slaves – taken from their parents and sold everywhere. But the melancholy tune and the feeling of hopelessness fit anyone who has experienced the bitterness of exile. Strangely, singing a song like this can help ease the pain, if only for a little while.

Sometimes I feel like a motherless child,
Sometimes I feel like a motherless child,
Sometimes I feel like a motherless child,
A long way from home,
A long way from home,

Sometimes I feel like I'm almost gone,
Sometimes I feel like I'm almost gone,
Sometimes I feel like I'm almost gone,
A long way from home,
A long way from home. JM

11 AUGUST

Sullen saints

May God preserve us from sullen saints.
(*St Teresa of Avila* 1515–1582) LB

12 AUGUST

Poetic gems

Courage, singlemindedness of purpose and generosity of spirit are rare qualities to find in a single individual. When they are dedicated to some lofty ideal we have the making of a potential saint or a magnificent eccentric. William McGonagall, a handloom weaver from Dundee, perceived himself, and acted out the role, of a 'poet and tragedian', reciting his self-composed poems to any audience prepared to listen. Here is his immortal 'The Tay Bridge Disaster' which should be read aloud, while standing, with one arm raised – a Dundee accent is optional.

Beautiful Railway Bridge of the Silv'ry Tay!
Alas! I am very sorry to say
That ninety lives have been taken away
On the last Sabbath day of 1879,
Which will be remember'd for a very long time.

'Twas about seven o'clock at night,
And the wind it blew with all its might,
And the rain came pouring down,
And the dark clouds seem'd to frown,
And the Demon of the air seem'd to say –
'I'll blow down the Bridge of Tay.'

When the train left Edinburgh
The passengers' hearts were light and felt no sorrow,
But Boreas blew a terrific gale,
Which made their hearts for to quail,
And many of the passengers with fear did say –
'I hope God will send us safe across the Bridge of Tay.'

But when the train came near to Wormit Bay,
Boreas he did loud and angry bray,
And shook the central girders of the Bridge of Tay
On the last Sabbath day of 1879,
Which will be remember'd for a very long time.

So the train sped on with all its might,
And bonnie Dundee soon hove in sight,
And the passengers' hearts felt light,
Thinking they would enjoy themselves on the New Year,
With their friends at home they lov'd most dear.
And with them all a happy New Year.

So the train mov'd slowly along the Bridge of Tay,
Until it was about midway,
Then the central girders with a crash gave way,
And down went the train and passengers into the Tay!
The Storm Fiend did loudly bray,

Because ninety lives had been taken away,
On the last Sabbath day of 1879,
Which will be remember'd for a very long time.

As soon as the catastrophe came to be known
The alarm from mouth to mouth was blown,
And the cry rang out all o'er the town,
Good Heavens! the Tay Bridge is blown down,
And a passenger train from Edinburgh,
Which fill'd all the people's hearts with sorrow,
And made them for to turn pale,
Because none of the passengers were sav'd to tell the tale
How the disaster happen'd on the last Sabbath day of 1879,
Which will be remember'd for a very long time.

It must have been an awful sight,
To witness in the dusky moonlight,
While the Storm Fiend did laugh, and angry did bray,
Along the Railway Bridge of the Silv'ry Tay.
Oh! ill-fated Bridge of the Silv'ry Tay,
I must now conclude my lay
By telling the world fearlessly without the least dismay,
That your central girders would not have given way,
At least many sensible men do say,
Had they been supported on each side with buttresses,
At least many sensible men confesses,
For the stronger we our houses do build,
The less chance we have of being killed. JM

13 AUGUST

The fool

On the 13th August, 1759, Christopher Smart was shut up in Bedlam and wrote:

> For I bless the thirteenth of August in which I was willing to be called a fool for the sake of Christ. LB

14 AUGUST

Seeking whom?

God or our own spiritual satisfaction? An important question today when, after sex, money and streaking in public, mysticism is the last satisfaction – the ultimate hedonism.

This piece is taken from *Mount Carmel*, the journal of the Discalced (no-shoes) Carmelites, and the author is Fr John Bernard Keegan who brings the mysticism of St Teresa of Avila into the daily life of me and many others. Very practical, very hard hitting!

> It is true that God never does fail his friends, and to be convinced of this is a great help to perseverance in prayer, because there will be times when we will be tempted to think that he has deserted us. When all goes well there is no danger of this, since his presence is almost palpable. Our minds are filled with thoughts of him and our hearts warmed by his love, so that to pray is a pleasure and all other attractions fade. The danger then is that we may be seeking our own satisfaction rather than God, so he is obliged to withdraw his consolations in order to preserve and deepen our love for himself. Then we are cast into a darkness which seems equally palpable, and we no longer find any satisfaction in prayer or the service of God. The spiritual life seems empty and pointless, while the attractions of the world spring to life again and offer us an escape from it all. If in fact we have been seeking our own consolation in prayer, the temptation will be difficult to resist, and we could fall back into a state of mediocrity or worse. But, if it is really God whom we are seeking, we shall struggle on in spite of everything and, unknown to ourselves, the virtues will grow strong in the darkness, like plants thrusting their roots down into the earth . . . LB

15 AUGUST

Barb'ra Allen

Samuel Pepys wrote in his diary that he had enjoyed this ballad. And it is a staple of folk clubs, though it has never been quite the same for me since hearing it sung by the extraordinary John Jacob Niles. It is a hymn for anyone who has ever had the misfortune to fall in love at the wrong time with the wrong person.

In Scarlet Town where I was born,
There was a fair maid dwelling,
Made many a youth cry lack-a-day,
Her name was Barb'ra Allen.

'Twas in the merry month of May
When green buds they were swelling,
Sweet William came from the west country
And he courted Barb'ra Allen.

He sent his servant unto her
To the place where she was dwelling
Said my master's sick, bids me call for you
If your name be Barb'ra Allen.

Well, slowly, slowly, she got up
And slowly she went nigh him;
But all she said as she passed his bed
Young man, I think you're dying.

Then lightly tripped she down the stairs
She heard those church bells tolling;
And each bell seemed to say as it tolled
Hard-hearted Barb'ra Allen.

O, mother, mother go make my bed
And make it long and narrow;
Sweet William died for me today
I'll die for him tomorrow.

They buried Barb'ra in the old church yard.
They buried Sweet William beside her;
Out of his grave grew a red, red rose
And out of hers a briar.

They grew and grew in the old church wall
Till they could grow no higher;
And at the top twined in a lovers' knot
The red rose and the briar. JM

Guru

The wisest man I know lives in a semi in South Dublin. He is a recluse, a self-effacing OAP who slept in the streets of Bombay seeking wisdom.

Are you looking for a guru?

It is one of the ironies of the mystical quest that the rich Western countries are now a happy hunting ground for mass media pop gurus from the Mystic East, while India is struggling with problems of industrialization, poverty or drought. There is nothing mystical about the hordes of touts the moment you land at Bombay, the beggars like swarms of flies, and the primitive sanitation outside the cities.

You might feel that there is every reason why the up-and-coming Indian guru should migrate to the comfortable affluence and adulation of Europe and California. Indeed, one of my favourite *New Yorker* cartoons is that of the zealous American devotee who has just scaled the Himalayan heights in search of his guru, only to be told: 'I open in Town Hall November sixth, and I'm on Johnny Carson's show on the eighth. You could have saved yourself a trip.'

Many years ago, I made a trip to India and spent time living in an old temple on the banks of the river Ganges, in the foothills of the Himalayas. I had studied Hindu scriptures and religious teaching, and wanted to *live* my philosophy, to measure theory by the light of experience. I wrote in my diary: 'I want to travel several thousands of miles to reach the centre of the point *on which I am standing when I leave.*'

As guest of a local ashram, I lived on the food provided, and in return gave such service as I could. I reduced life to bare essentials, so that the inner life could override material obstacles. I took my drinking water unboiled, straight from the river in a galvanized bucket. The jungle was my lavatory. My clothing was a pair of trunks and two pieces of cotton cloth. My only books a couple of scriptures and a treatise on Indian music. I gave up my wooden divan when the mattress became infested with hundreds of bugs, and slept instead on a mat on the floor. There were a number of scorpions, which I had to try to remove without injuring them, as part of the observance of non-violence.

There were times when I was severely tested. Once I had toothache and an excruciatingly painful gum abscess. I could not sleep, and the pain continued night and day for weeks. The abscess did not burst naturally until the precise moment that the monsoon came, so that suddenly it seemed to be raining inside and outside my mouth. Another time I lay helpless for several days with a high fever, without food, in absolute squalor. I got better after I resigned myself to dying.

Yet there were also times when the sheer beauty of the Ganges and the mountains was like a dream scene that might be rolled up and taken away by some celestial stagehand. I immersed myself in the vibrations of Indian music, a metaphysical language of great subtlety and spiritual depth. I met saints and sinners, for the ashram was a world in miniature on the main pilgrim route to the holy places high in the mountain snows. I also met many hopeful Western travellers, searching for a guru.

What I found was that life itself can be the guru.

The Hindu scriptures say that the ouer guru only exists to awaken the inner guru inside everybody, that the true reality lies beyond the pairs of opposites – pleasure and pain, desire and fear. Hindu *sadhana* or spiritual discipline does not differ substantially from the Christian tradition of penance and austerity, and reveals the same spiritual landmarks.

Nowadays, with the current fashion for gurus, swamis and Maharishis, people sometimes ask me how I got on in India – did I find the right guru – was it enjoyable – did I find what I was searching for? – and so on.

It is very difficult to explain! I usually just say politely – Oh yes, it was most enjoyable, and I did find what I was looking for.
(*Leslie Shepard*) LB

17 AUGUST

A birthday present

I met the writer of this poem, Batsheva Dagan, when she came to England from Israel to work with young people. She has become a leading authority of teaching children about the Holocaust, a subject that cannot be ducked in the Jewish world, and yet must be approached with the greatest sensitivity. It cannot be ducked in the Jewish world because the effects are still there – on those who experienced and survived it and on those who have come after them. A colleague in Holland has to work with the nightmares of the grandchildren of those who survived. But the Holocaust is no longer the only genocide and 'survivors' and their children will also need to learn from people like Batsheva – and from this poem that she wrote for her friend Zosia.

It was a special present
A birthday present
In a concentration camp
In a place contemptuous
Of the right of man to live
A place where time was measured
By the roll call
For line upon line of prisoners.

It is difficult to describe such a present
But it's possible to explain its great value,
Although it was only a drawing, a bit of bread and a poem.
All this was given as a gift
For an 18th birthday.
From Zosia to me, who were there together
And dreamed of a life without fear.

What can be given as a gift
for a friend's birthday?
There wasn't even a shop
In that terrible, isolated place.
There was no money to use
Food was divided into portions.

But Zosia knew how to write poetry
And to make others happy
With the treasure she carried in her heart
In peace and in war
So she worded a poem for a birthday
A special present.

The drawing showed a laden table
Roast chicken, borscht and cabbage,
Fruit juices and all kinds of wines
A mouth-watering sight.
In addition an apple and honey.
What a sight for sore eyes.

But it was only in the imagination
That the good taste was in the mouth, on the tongue,
In reality it was just a thin slice of bread
Black bread with a sliver of sausage
But it had the taste of a delicacy
Tastier than anything on that table.

The slice of bread was eaten and is gone
Not a crumb remained.
The paper disappeared like dust in a breeze
But deep inside it was all engraved.

The poem was hidden in the heart
Waiting for the day to emerge
To tell the story of a friend
To whom thanks are due.
The poem was filled with blessings and encouragement
For a new life in a free world.

And the poem was kept
As a wonderful gift, a precious gift
A sign of love
A symbol of hope
As a sign of remembrance,
Because Zosia was missing on the final march. JM

18 AUGUST

Good prayer (See, 11 January)

Prayer the Churches banquet, Angels age,
  Gods breath in man returning to his birth,
  The soul in paraphrase, heart in pilgrimage,
The Christian plummet sounding heav'n and earth;
Engine against th' Almightie, sinners towre,
  Reversed thunder, Christ-side-piercing spear,
  The six-daies world transposing in an houre,
A kinde of tune, which all things heare and fear;
Softnesse, and peace, and joy, and love, and blisse,
  Exalted Manna, gladnesse of the best,
  Heaven in ordinarie, man well drest,
The milkie way, the bird of Paradise,

Church-bels beyond the starres heard, the souls bloud,
The land of spices; something understood.
(*George Herbert*) LB

19 AUGUST

Again Jerusalem, and again

If places have a certain spirit, Jerusalem has it in abundance. The Rabbis taught that ten measures of beauty came into the world and nine of them went to Jerusalem (*Kiddushin 49b*). But what kind of beauty? We project upon it our collective expectations – from eternal holiness to political real estate. My own feelings oscillate from intoxication to claustrophobia to despair and back again. One very famous Jewish writer lost a touch of his charisma when he made the mistake of saying that he loved Jerusalem – when he wasn't there. But I can understand his feelings.

When I had a sabbatical I was happy to discover the anonymity of Tel Aviv. In Jerusalem it is hard to remain detached, you have to identify with some group or other, and certainly no religious position is neutral. So I stayed away for four months and then visited for a couple of days. On bus number 425, returning to Tel Aviv, I wrote this poem.

Nevertheless
it is still possible to fall in love with
Jerusalem
all over again.
Despite everything.
Despite the fear in the streets of the old.
Despite the anger in the streets of the new.

For any hidden courtyard
any vista
any crowded corner
can snatch away your breath
by its sheer . . .
density.

It is not the holiness,
for that was always a political commodity,
nor its age alone.
It is something else:

a sad mocking at our pretensions
and a wonder at our dreams.
To have invested so much
in a couple of hills and valleys,
to have suffered so much to possess them
and done such harm to hold them
in the name of so many gods,
so much hope and greed.

So boast not of unity,
promise no eternity,
where Jerusalem is concerned,
for she will outlive our rhetoric
and lose even the memory of our passing –
another relic
for antiquarians to ponder
and archaeologists tenderly to reconstruct.

No,
better to tread softly,
woo her with care
and give the love we feel
to all her many children. JM

20 AUGUST

The call in the night

Sleep would not come, but there was no restless irritation. The night was peaceful, still and timeless in that strange House of Reconciliation in post-war Germany. I lay and listened to the silence. God was in the silence and something was being asked of me. But what? Must I accept without knowing where it would lead? Throughout that deep night I listened to the voice that was not yet a voice and as light was dawning I gave my promise. I would do whatever was being asked of me.

Later, much later, a stranger from a different faith told me that he had spent that very night in a desperate prayer for help in that same mysterious house. Perhaps, somehow, it had been his voice that I had heard crying in the darkness. I do not know, but for a short while our souls touched each other, and neither of us could tell which was the giver and which the receiver. (*Daphne Richardson*)

Formerly, Assistant Secretary of West London Synagogue – now a writer and my friend. LB

21 AUGUST

Travellers' tales

Before there was Baron Munchausen there was, in about the third century, the celebrated Rabbi, Rabbah bar bar Chanah. His travellers' tales include the following:

> Once we were travelling on a ship and saw a fish whose back was covered with sand out of which grew grass. We thought it was dry land, an island, so we went up and baked and cooked on its back. But when its back got heated it turned and if we had not had the ship nearby we would have drowned! (*Baba Batra 73b*)

He had close encounters with other large animals, including a frog the size of a fortress that was swallowed by a snake that was in turn swallowed by a raven that perched in a tree of quite extraordinary size.

> Once we were travelling on board a ship and saw a fish into whose nostrils a parasite had entered! The water threw up the fish on to the shore where it destroyed sixty towns, provided food for a further sixty towns and sixty towns salted the remains. From one of its eyeballs they took three hundred kegs of oil. When we returned twelve months later we saw them cutting beams from the skeleton and rebuilding the towns that had been destroyed. (*ibid*)

On another occasion he saw a bird standing up to its ankles in water while its head reached the sky. He thought the water was not deep but a heavenly voice informed him that a carpenter's axe was dropped into the water seven years before and had not yet reached the bottom!

In the desert he was taken to a hole in the ground from which smoke emerged. He dipped a piece of wool in it and it was singed. He was told to listen and heard voices – the sons of Korach who had rebelled against Moses in the wilderness and been swallowed up by the earth. Apparently they travelled around the underworld every thirty days and could be heard saying: 'Moses and his teaching are truth and we are liars.'

Some of his colleagues added similar tales, especially about the

'Leviathan', the sea monster that will be slain to provide a banquet for the righteous in the messianic time. Which leads to a joke about the consequences of being super-pious.

In the messianic time as well as 'Leviathan' the main course at the banquet will be the 'Great Ox'. Which raises the following question: given the great care Jews take in the slaughtering of animals for food, who will slaughter the Great Ox. The answer: 'Mosheh Rabbenu!', 'Moses our teacher'. But then some pious Jews expressed doubts whether even Moses would be able to do it with sufficient skill to satisfy their stringent requirements. In that case, 'The Holy One, blessed be He', God himself, would slaughter the Great Ox to ensure that it was absolutely *kosher*, ritually fit for eating. But then if that is the case, why was Leviathan also on the menu? Because even if God Himself were to slaughter the Great Ox, there are some Jews from Frankfurt who would not trust that it was *kosher* enough – so for them there's fish! JM

22 AUGUST

Woodbine Willie (The Rev Studdert-Kennedy)

Woodbine Willie didn't only cheer up soldiers in the First World War. The suffering he witnessed in the trenches drove him deeper. I came across this poem in the writings of an Anglican nun and it spoke to me.

The Kiss of God
It was not death to me,
Nor aught the least like falling into sleep.
It was nothing to joy upon
Nor yet to weep.
It was an infinitely perfect peace
Wherein the world entranced
Stood quite still
Outside of time and space:
And like the changeless, everchanging face
Looked kindly on me
As I lay
And waited on His will.
It was not night
Nor day –
But bright and rainbow colours
Of an everlasting dawn

Down from the golden glory light
That shone in his great eyes.
The mysteries of the earth
Lay open like a book,
And I could read
But slowly, as a small child reads
With an often upward look
that pleads
For help – still doubtful of the truth
Until he sees it mirrored
In the answering eyes of Love.
So I looked up to God
And while I held my breath,
I saw Him slowly nod,
And knew – as I had never known aught else,
With certainty sublime and passionate,
Shot through and through
With sheer unutterable bliss.
I knew
There was no death but this,
GOD'S KISS
And then the waking to an everlasting love. LB

23 AUGUST

Responsibility

Rabbi Joshua said: I was once defeated by a little girl. I was walking by the way. I saw a path through a field made by other travellers and I walked along it. A little girl said to me: 'Isn't this a field (and not to be trampled on)?' 'No,' I replied, 'it is a path that has already been made.' She answered: 'Because others damaged the field, will you do the same?' (*Eruvin 53b*) JM

24 AUGUST

The gate – the geäte

William Barnes remained a country curate. He was the humblest of men who wrote in the Dorset dialect on the fringes of fashionable English. But as the sincerity breaks the archaic grammar and forgotten words, the sense of generations passing like the countryside seasons, stirs up compassion and the recognition of God.

The Geäte A-Vallèn To

In the sunsheen ov our summers
  Wi' the häytime now a-come,
How busy wer we out a-vield
  Wi' vew a-left at hwome,
When waggons rumbled out of yard
  Red wheeled, wi' body blue,
As back behind 'em loudly slamm'd
  The geäte a-vallèn to.

Drough day sheen for how many years
  The geäte ha' now a-swung,
Behind the veet o' vull-grown men
  An' vootsteps ov the young.
Drough years o' days it swung to us
  Behind each little shoe,
As we tripped lightly on avore
  The geäte a-vallèn to.

In evenèn time o' starry night
  How mother zot at hwome,
And kept her blazing vier bright
  Till father should ha' come,
And how she quickened up and smiled,
  And stirred her vier anew,
To hear the trampèn hosses' steps
  And geäte a-vallèn to.

There's moonsheen now in nights o' Fall
  When leaves be brown vrom green,
When to the slammèn of the geäte
  Our Jenny's ears be keen,
When the wold dog do wag his taïl,
  An' Jeän could tell to who,
As he do come in drough the geäte,
  The geäte a-vallèn to.

And oft do come a saddened hour
  When there must goo away
One well-beloved to our heart's core,
  Vor long, perhaps vor aye:
An' oh! it is a touchèn thing
  The lovèn heart must rue,
To hear within his last farewell
  The geäte a-vallèn to. LB

25 AUGUST

Taking a stand

This Rabbinic comment on a somewhat obscure verse from the Book of Ezekiel is an uncomfortable reminder of what it means to take responsibility for our society.

> 'Go through the city, through Jerusalem, and put a mark upon the foreheads of the men who sigh and groan over all the abominations that are committed in it'. (*Ezekiel 9:4*)
>
> The Holy One said to the angel Gabriel: Go mark the foreheads of the righteous with an X of ink so that the angels of death do not harm them, and the foreheads of the wicked with an X of blood so that the angels of death do harm them. Hearing that, Justice spoke up and said: 'Lord of the Universe, what is the difference between them?' God answered: 'These are the wholly righteous and those the wholly wicked.' Justice replied: 'Lord of the Universe, how can You call them wholly righteous? They could have protested against the wickedness of others but did not!' Said God: 'But I know that even if they had protested no one would have listened to them.' Said Justice: 'Lord of the Universe, You knew it but did they?' (*Shabbat 55a*) JM

26 AUGUST

The cloud of unknowing

> It's not what you are, nor what you've been, that God looks on with mercy, but on what you would like to be. (*The Cloud of Unknowing*)
>
> Thank God for that!

No one knows who wrote *The Cloud*. It was written in the 15th century not for the general reader but specifically for intending recluses or hermits. It's strange how it has become a modern bestseller, to be bought by commuters at railway stations. LB

27 AUGUST

Ownership

The medieval moralists were not prepared to mince words as the following passage, by Jonah Ibn Janach (11th century Spain), indicates. The image comes straight from today's newspapers of the looting that follows any disaster, whether natural or caused by human folly. Unlike Ibn Janach's spectators, today's victims are less likely to be compensated.

> We are held responsible for everything we receive in this world, and our children are responsible too. The fact is nothing belongs to us, everything is God's and whatever we received we received only on credit and God will exact payment for it. This may be compared to someone who entered a city and found no one there. He walked into a house and there found a table set with all kinds of food and drink. So he began to eat and drink thinking, 'I deserve all of this, all of it is mine, I shall do with it what I please.' He did not even notice that the owners were watching him from the side! He will yet have to pay for everything he ate and drank, for he is in a spot from which he will not be able to escape. JM

28 AUGUST

Silence

I found God again one winter afternoon in Oxford. I was sheltering from the rain in a doorway, the door opened and I found myself in a Quaker meeting for farmers. My friend Henry Dyson is a Quaker and a teacher on many levels, an honest shrewd Yorkshireman. I trust him.

This is his experience of what lives in Quaker silence.

> It was Easter day and I was visiting Whitby. There is an old Quaker meeting house there and I went along for Meeting for Worship. Out of a deep silence came troubled ministry. One Friend said she couldn't accept the historicity of the Resurrection of Jesus and therefore couldn't call herself Christian. After some time a man got up and said 'Christian' was a term which should be applied by others and not used as a defensive shield by oneself.
>
> The final speaker changed my life, an old friend got up and movingly said that her only son had been killed in a car crash some

months before – 'My heart is broken, but it is broken *open* – this is my resurrection and hope.' All present were united in a deep Silence beyond theological debate and words. LB

29 AUGUST

It is bitter

This was told to me in the name of Rabbi Israel Salanter, a nineteenth century Lithuanian scholar who founded a movement to encourage the study of ethical literature and to emphasise these aspects of Jewish life.

> A true believer should never say: *'Es ist schlecht'* (It is bad). But there may be times when one may say: *'Es ist bitter'* (It is bitter). JM

30 AUGUST

Humour

To live alongside the One or the All requires a sense of humour to make such an unequal relationship work. Jews and Catholics have jokes and Anglicans have wit. Here is the Quaker variety.

> The most important thing about Quakers is the Silent Worship which is its unifying force. At a meeting for Worship where the Silence has been broken many times by Ministry which was political, contentious and irrelevant, a Friend brought unity by standing up and saying, 'I never argue religion with a Roman Catholic, politics with a communist and music with a gramophone.'
>
> Everyone laughed and we were united in our joy. (*Henry Dyson*)

LB

31 AUGUST

The loves of Judah Halevi

When Jews lived in Muslim Spain in the Middle Ages there was a great flowering of creativity. Judah Halevi (before 1075–1141) was an outstanding poet and philosopher, and his life became the subject of folklore because of his journey to the land of Israel, then under the control of the Crusaders. The legend has him die in Jerusalem, trampled to death by a horseman as he kissed the stones of the city; it may be that he died in Alexandria awaiting the boat to take him on the last leg of his journey.

Some 800 of his poems have been preserved – religious poetry, but also laments on the death of people he knew and poems expressing his feelings about his friends. Most anthologies make a distinction between his 'religious' and his 'secular' poetry, though the latter clearly caused some embarrassment to the Victorian scholars who began to collect and translate his works into English.

In 1851 M. H. Breslau published a collection of poems from the Bodleian Library in Oxford. He introduces one of Halevi's love poems as follows:

> Some of the metaphors may, perhaps, sound rather extravagant to a modern ear, but we ought not to forget the age and the locality when and where it was composed. It appears that the author wrote it on separating from the beloved one to whom he was sincerely attached, and who had engaged his warmest affections. He portrays her beauty and charms with an oriental pencil, and in oriental colours. He is full of amorous feelings, such as would scarcely be expected from a Rabbi of the middle ages; and we are by no means ashamed to discover these pure sentiments of love and attachment in our great master, Rabbi Judah Halevi; but we, on the contrary, rejoice that this beautiful poem has been preserved in manuscript.

Another beautiful short poem is introduced somewhat coyly by the title: 'A couplet . . . to Ophrah, to whom the Rabbi appears to have been attached';

> Ophrah washes her garments in the water of my tears,
> And dries them by the sun-rays of her beauty;
> She required not the water of wells, after having the water of my
>   eyes,
> Nor the sun, after the beauty of her countenance.

But our Victorian translator, though faithful to his texts, seems unable to attach a heading to a number of love poems when the object of Judah Halevi's love is not a lass but a lad.

> *A couplet by the same author*
> The day I played with him on my knees,
> He saw his image in the apple of my eye.
> Ah, the deceiver kissed my eyes –
> It was not me he kissed, but his own image. JM

SEPTEMBER

The morning paper

Reading the morning paper, and the reports of pompous declarations, I remember the warning words of Rudyard Kipling at the turn of the century when Victoria was still on the throne and the Empire was at its greatest. It amazes me how the old 'imperialist' got away with it! The power structures of our time, whether of the left or right, ignore such words at their peril.

God our fathers, known of old,
  Lord of our far-flung battle-line,
Beneath whose awful Hand we hold
  Dominion over palm and pine –
Lord God of Hosts, be with us yet,
Lest we forget – lest we forget!

The tumult and the shouting dies;
  The Captains and the Kings depart:
Still stands Thine ancient sacrifice,
  An humble and a contrite heart.
Lord God of Hosts, be with us yet,
Lest we forget – lest we forget!

Far-called, our navies melt away;
  On dune and headland sinks the fire:
Lo, all our pomp of yesterday
  Is one with Ninevah and Tyre!
Judge of the Nations, spare us yet,
Lest we forget – lest we forget!

For heathen heart that puts her trust
  In reeking tube and iron shard,
All valiant dust that builds on dust,
  And guarding, calls not Thee to guard,
For frantic boast and foolish word –
Thy mercy on Thy People, Lord! LB

2 SEPTEMBER

My name is Ozymandias

I resented having to learn poems by heart at school. It seemed an awful effort. I was far too shy to recite them aloud later and somehow the various verses always got scrambled up. Now, of course, I regret that I did not learn more, as fragments pop into my mind at appropriate moments, though usually I can't remember what came before or after. One poem, or at least some lines, still stays with me although I had totally forgotten that 'Ozymandias' was written by Shelley. The 'two vast and trunkless legs of stone' that stand in the desert might have inspired the image of the head of the Statue of Liberty sticking out of the sand in one of the 'Planet of the Apes' films. Certainly the description of such remains mocking the posturing of emperors still hits home wherever leaders put on airs.

Ozymandias Of Egypt
I met a traveller from an antique land
Who said: Two vast and trunkless legs of stone
Stand in the desert. Near them, on the sand,
Half sunk, a shatter'd visage lies, whose frown
And wrinkled lip, and sneer of cold command,
Tell that the sculptor well those passions read
Which yet survive, stamp'd on these lifeless things,
The hand that mock'd them and the heart that fed;
And on the pedestal these words appear:
'My name is Ozymandias, king of kings:
Look on my works, ye Mighty, and despair!'
Nothing beside remains. Round and decay
Of that colossal wreck, boundless and bare,
The lone and level sands stretch far away. JM

3 SEPTEMBER

A knee

A knee goes through the world alone
An ordinary knee, nothing more.
It isn't wood, it isn't tin
Just an ordinary, nobbly knee.

It once belonged to a man
Who got shot up in a war
And now alone his knee remains
Like a holy relic.

So it wanders through the world alone
An ordinary knee, nothing more.
It isn't wood, it isn't tin
Just an ordinary knee, nothing more.
(*Christian Morgenstern* 1871–1914)

This poem reminds me of the First World War my father fought in, the Cenotaph and poppies in my lapel. Another reminder is the last moments of *All Quiet on the Western Front*, when the dying soldier reaches for a flower. O the dreadful waste of war! How the flower of Europe was butchered twice in the 20th century. LB

4 SEPTEMBER

Teachers

Had God's revelation not been given to us, we could have learned modesty from the cat, honesty from the ant, chastity from the dove and good manners from the cock. (*Eruvin 100b*) JM

5 SEPTEMBER

At sea

You pray very sincerely when you're at sea. You pray for what you really want, not what you think you ought to want. This prayer was scribbled by a sane sailor in Tudor times. I know exactly how he felt. This is the version I know.

O Westering Wind, when wilt thou blow?
  In drops the rain doth light.
O Christ that my love were in my arms,
  And I in my bed tonight. LB

Senses

Abraham Ibn Ezra (see the section under his name on 9 January), composed this little hymn to God and to the senses through which we perceive God.

> Every form you see gives testimony: there is none beside God.
> Every sound your ear hears sings God's praise.
> Every odour you smell tells of God's work
> and everything you taste reveals the mystery of God's greatness.
> Your hands are faithful witnesses to touch God's great wonders
> and your mind that thinks and reflects has its origin from God. JM

7 SEPTEMBER

Staring

A very important activity! I sit in Euston Station precinct, watching the frantic arrivals and departures, the joyous and tearful meetings. From this Human Comedy, I learn compassion. Being a townsperson, I prefer to stare at cafés, not cows!

Leisure

What is this life if, full of care,
We have no time to stand and stare.

No time to stand beneath the boughs
And stare as long as sheep or cows.

No time to see, when woods we pass,
Where squirrels hide their nuts in grass.

No time to see in broad daylight,
Streams full of stars like skies at night.

No time to turn at Beauty's glance,
And watch her feet, how they can dance.

No time to wait till her mouth can
Enrich that smile her eyes began.

A poor life this if, full of care,
We have no time to stand and stare.
(*W. H. Davies* 1871–1940) LB

8 SEPTEMBER

In praise of silence

Rabbi Abin said: When Jacob of the village of Neboria was in Tyre he interpreted the phrase in the Psalms 'Praise is silence for You, O God' (*Psalm 65:2*) as meaning: silence is the height of all praises of God. For God is like a jewel without price; however high you appraise it, still you undervalue it. (*Midrash Psalms* 19:2) JM

9 SEPTEMBER

An old person's alphabet

Y is for YOU, whom most of the time I love. I view you with exasperation because you, like me, continue to make the same mistakes over and over again and rarely learn from them. I view you with gratitude, because you are all so different and I am constantly reminded that we are all capable of almost anything. I view you with hope, because ultimately I trust you individually to deal kindly and sympathetically with those of us who are old and getting older. I know I can depend on you, because you too will be old one day.

From *Dr Wendy Greengross* – 'agony aunt' to me and to all who wrote in to the radio programme *'Have You Got Problems!'* LB

10 SEPTEMBER

A good guest

Since so much of life revolves around eating it is not surprising that the Rabbis had something to say about etiquette:

A good guest, what does he say?

'How much trouble my host has gone to for me! How much meat he put before me! How much wine he put before me! How many cakes he put before me! And all this trouble was only for my sake!'

But a bad guest what does he say?

'How much trouble has my host gone to for me? One slice of bread I ate? One piece of meat I ate? One cup I drank? All the trouble he took – it was only for his wife and children.

(*Berachot 58a*) JM

Kamikaze

I wish I could remember his name. He was a Japanese, the current boyfriend of a friend of my mother. The couple must have been over for tea. I suppose I was in my early teens and allowed to join with the 'grown-ups'. Some way through the afternoon he began to talk about his life and it turned out that he was a failed kamikaze pilot.

I suppose that his failure was self-evident or he would not have been around to tell the tale. All I know about such things is derived from war documentaries I saw a long time ago, how Japanese pilots would fly suicide missions – ramming their planes, loaded with explosives, into allied ships. This gentleman set off on his mission, some time towards the end of the war, was about to dive his plane, said to himself the Japanese equivalent of 'to hell with it', turned round and went home.

I have no idea what a personal sacrifice of honour and pride that must have meant – or anything about what happened to him subsequently in Japan. I recall him only as an urbane, kindly man, who was very willing to answer the inevitable questions that came from a curious young adult about this extraordinary event.

Even that tale would have been enough to anchor him in my memory but he went even further. I had some vague awareness of the martial arts – this was long before kung fu movies and the astonishing Bruce Lee. He proceeded to show the basic stance, feet apart, knees slightly bent, a posture that enabled one to move in any direction and react in any way even . . . And he proceeded to do a forward roll on our living room carpet and come up in the identical position at the other end of the room. I think I had a go as well with less grace and success.

But what a moment! And what a 'grown-up' to take a child's questions so seriously and respond so generously.

I only appreciated how unusual and special this quality was a few years ago when I visited some friends in New York. We'd met in Israel years before. Their daughter, now married, was present and said she remembered me. Because I had sat down with her and had a proper conversation – and that was very rare in her experience, for a 'grown-up' to treat a child like an adult.

I couldn't remember the episode and I'm delighted that a younger me had the common sense and openness to do it. Perhaps at the back of my mind was my Japanese failed kamikaze pilot and the attention he had been willing to show me. I know many adults who are simply overgrown children, perhaps because there are not enough children who are treated as not yet grown adults. JM

12 SEPTEMBER

Reassured

'For all will be well, and all will be well, and all will indeed be exceedingly well.' (*Visions of Anchoress, Julian of Norwich, 15th century.*)

It's nice to be reassured by heaven, for the world often doesn't seem to work out like that. Julian of Norwich was no fool. She had common sense as well as the uncommon kind – so I believe her. LB

13 SEPTEMBER

Discovering truth

When I was young, I used to think that truth was something one discovered by study and discussion, and that only clever people could teach it.

But clever people told me that truth was only relative (as if this was some absolute truth in itself) and it seemed that truth meant whatever one wanted it to mean. I might never have come to terms with truth if I had not been so unhappy that I was forced to take stock of myself and find out certain uncomfortable personal truths.

Growing up can be a painful process in which impulses and emotions are shaped into a character structure that does not change very much throughout later life. As a child, I was bullied by an elder brother and took it out on my young sister. The emotional pattern of anxiety, despair and hostility remained with me as I grew up, underlying all my language and ideas, which became a system of defence and attack in my dealings with other people. I reacted as if *they* were actually the brother, sister, or the parents for whose sympathy we competed.

It took a long time to identify this process, because in the search for the truth about oneself, the old habits of impulse are not usually questioned. Language and ideas are a superstructure that develops *after* the impulses, and because habitual impulses feel familiar, there is no guilt feeling at using words for self-justification. Only by understanding my own defences and evasions could I learn how to do without them in a grown-up world that was not the same world as my childhood. And I had to recognize habitual impulses before they were triggered by situations in the present that had the same shape as past problems.

In this process, I began to see clearly how other people too were caught in the same emotional trap of habitual reaction, like actors always playing one role. The everyday world of social relationships, business and politics was riddled with people playing nursery games with grown-up toys, always finding a good excuse for power games of defence, attack, pride, self-assertion, ambition and secret hostility, always criticizing and reacting to others but not understanding themselves.

I could recognize the social reformer projecting his own inability to reform himself, the Casanova unable to form a single worthwhile adult sexual partnership, the friend secretly hostile, the confident man over compensating inner doubts, the religious entrepreneur, merchandising metaphysical real estate for prestige and self-esteem, the revolutionary and terrorist whose love of violence stemmed from childhood hatreds and feelings of inferiority. It was not what they said or how they posed that was important, but only the emotional shape of their actions and reactions. I learnt that one understands other people in proportion to how well one understands oneself.

Sometimes one can help other people to gain insight, but often their fear of truth is too great. Personal relationships can be like a dangerous espionage game of hidden motives and secret commitments, with truths that cannot be revealed openly.

This is one kind of relative truth, but there is a larger truth, an absolute which embraces the whole cosmos with all its contradictions and the tragi-comedy of individual terms of reference. It is that truth which mystics and saints have tried to show us. To the extent that one can remove personal barriers to understanding, some part of that total truth can make its way through.

We do not personally discover the ultimate truths of life, but if we can open ourselves to them through self-awareness, *they* may be able to discover *us* and overwhelm our individual limitations.
(*Leslie Shepard*, my teacher) LB

14 SEPTEMBER

Restraint

The following is by Rabbi Israel Salanter (see 'It Is Bitter' – 29 August).

> Not everything that is thought should be said.
> Not everything that is said should be written.
> Not everything that is written should be published. JM

15 SEPTEMBER

Giving

Someone told me of a saying of the great philosopher Wittgenstein. 'Poverty was such a blessed virtue, he did not want to deprive anyone he liked of it.' It seemed to me (and it still in part does) one of those clever-clever remarks dons make. But this experience of my Quaker friend Henry Dyson made me consider it again more carefully. It is true that the warmest companionship I ever had was in London's poor East End.

> When I was nineteen I travelled in India as well as working on a scheme which was set up to teach people in villages how to sink wells to improve the water supply. I have been in many villages which were on the verge of starvation yet they would always offer a small item of food or drink to a visitor. Giving came naturally and was a part of their everyday experience as human beings. I have seldom experienced such kindness in the West – those sincere and smiling people taught me how to give in the right spirit. LB

16 SEPTEMBER

September melodies

In autumn comes the Jewish New Year when the whole world stands in judgement before God. The poem 'September Melodies' evokes the solemnity of this time and weaves it into a picture of the changing face of nature as winter approaches.

The original was written in Yiddish at the end of the last century by Morris Rosenfeld, known as the 'Poet Laureate of Labour' for his depiction of the tragic life of immigrants to America in the sweatshops.

The translator, Leo Wiener, who devoted much of his life to collecting and preserving Yiddish literature, introduces him in the first collection of Rosenfeld's poems to appear in English, in 1898, *Songs From The Ghetto*:

> Mr Rosenfeld was born in 1862 in a small town in Poland, where his ancestors had been fishermen. He has received no other education than that which is allotted to all Jewish boys of humble origin. While well read in German and English literature, he masters only his native Yiddish. He went early to England, to avoid military service, and there learned the tailor's trade. Thence he proceeded to Holland where he tried himself at diamond grinding. He very soon after came to America, where for many weary years he has eked out an existence in the sweatshops of New York. It is there he has learned to sing of misery and oppression. His health gave out, and he had to abandon the shop for the precarious occupation of a Yiddish penny-a-liner. In the meantime he has developed Judaeo-German versification to unknown proportions. Of the merits of his poetry let the reader judge himself.

Rosenfeld continued throughout his life to write and despite the success of his poems, many of which became popular songs, he never escaped from the bitter struggle to earn a living. The simple rhyming scheme of the original Yiddish is lost in translation.

The ram's-horn has blown his blast, there falls a dismal weather; the young grass withers in the field; the tree loses its leaves.

The earth soon becomes naked and bare, there is an end to its glory. The bird sings in the large forest and calls to the first prayers of mourning.

He sings so sadly, so sweetly, no doubt a song of parting, and that touches and tears your heart.

The woods rustle, the wind blows, terror seizes the dreamers: the day of judgement has come now on little trees and big trees.

O people! Trees of the forest! Do you hear the howling of the storm? Whether young or old, late or soon, you will all be mowed down!

Oh, 't is cold and windy, there is an end of summer! The flowers wither in the valley; all beauties disappear, and suddenly all is rocked into slumber of death.

The storm hurls down the dry leaves, and disperses the dead flowers. The forest rustles its last confession, and a little later even the holiest song will cease.

The birds sing their song of passage and turn their eyes towards the ocean. Beloved, where do you fly? Pray, tell me how far away? and tell me when will you return?

The woeful melodies are poured forth in bitterness, and the painful answer is: 'We all know only, we must fly away, but God knows of coming back!' JM

17 SEPTEMBER

F is for fear

'F' stands for words ministers like me never mention. My friend Dr Wendy Greengross wrote her own alphabet. This is her entry for 'F'.

> F is for FEAR of ageing in the wrong way. We all know 70-, 80- and 90-year-olds who seem to have got it right. They seem to live FULL lives, with plenty of people around and not too much in the way of pain and disability. We get smitten by FEAR about the way we may be forced to live and the way in which we may be forced to die. We are unsure whether euthanasia is an answer and whether, when we get there, we will have the means, the fortitude and the courage to see it through. F is also for FRANK AND FULL DISCUSSION, which usually means someone saying something unpleasant. We try to remember that F is for FUN, giving freedom to the child that is somewhere within us all. LB

18 SEPTEMBER

The 'how'

I needed a sermon for the approaching Jewish High Holy Days. Reluctantly I agreed to go to the opera. Rosenkavalier seemed more like a mannered musical comedy than an opera. And indeed that was how it was first intended. But as Hofmannsthal and Strauss worked on it, one secondary character grew and grew to their own astonishment and in the end the young lovers finding each other has less substance than a grande dame facing up to age and the giving up of youth.

It happens to us all. It is built into life. All we can control is the 'how' of acceptance. Squealing and screaming, or with adult dignity. That is our only choice.

I found my sermon, though my congregation found my choice of text surprising.

Marschallin (The Field Marshal's Wife) (alone)
There he goes, that pompous wretched man
and wins the pretty young thing and a small fortune too
as if it was fated.
And imagines to himself that he's the one who has given something away.
But why am I so upset? That's just the way the world is.
I can also remember a girl
who, fresh out of a convent, was forced into holy matrimony.
(*takes her hand mirror*)
Where is she now? Yes,
look for the snows of years gone by!
I say it like that
but can it really be
that I was that little Resi
and that one day I'll be an old woman . . .
the old woman, the old Marschallin!
'Look! There goes the old Princess Resi!'
How can that be?
How does He do it, the dear Lord?
While I stay always the same.
And if He must do it like this
why does He have to let me watch it
so fully aware. Why can't He conceal it from me?
It is such a mystery, so great a mystery,
and we are simply here to endure it.
And in that 'how'
the whole difference lies . . . LB

(*New translation by* JM)

19 SEPTEMBER

Brief encounter

How often does it happen? A train ride. A chance encounter with some-one. An instant rapport, a feeling that we have known each other forever. The excitement of sharing thoughts and ideas. And then the parting – aware that there is no future together. Because each returns to another life and other commitments or simply because there was no way to keep in touch, or even an unwillingness to go beyond this moment, to take the risk. And later the sadness and regrets – the might-have-beens. When eyes meet like that, when smiles are answered, when some intuition can anticipate so much of what the other will say – it is a very deep mystery about our humanity. Or else, as the biologists explain, it is simply hormones, a biological pre-conditioning of the mating instinct, one of nature's little tricks to encourage the preservation of the species. So was it simply biology or actually a soul mate who was tantalizingly close and then lost?

I was twenty-seven when I wrote this song, so the biology was beginning to wear a bit thin. I have no idea anymore where the train was going or who she was or anything about her. Bertolt Brecht has a rather unkind poem about an afternoon making love with a woman in the open air, with a little cloud hovering overhead. Now he cannot remember her face or name, but he remembers the cloud. Perhaps all such encounters are destined to end that way till the 'right one', or at least the one we're prepared to take a chance on, comes along. But in gratitude for all the delicious excitement of the encounter and all the wistful regret when it is over, here is that little song.

Met her on a passing train
Hardly time to learn her name
May never see her again
But we shared some dreams
But we shared some dreams
And nothing really seems the same, the same.

Eager hope and open eyes
Living in the next surprise
Sad because an old love dies
Speaking without words
Speaking without words
Laughing at absurd replies, replies.

Talked of cities we had known
Talked about the way we've grown
Talked of things we cannot own
When we turned away
When we turned away
Noticed how the day had flown, had flown.

Strangers meeting sometimes find
A smiling face you think is kind
One that will not leave your mind
When you have to part
When you have to part
Leave some of your heart behind, behind. JM

Preparation

20 SEPTEMBER

Every day during the month of Ellul I read Psalm 27.

One thing have I asked of the Lord,
That do I seek after;
That I may dwell in the house of the Lord
All the days of my life . . .

Lord, it is Your face that I seek:
Do not hide Your face from me . . .

Had I not believed
To look upon the goodness of the Lord
In the land of the living.
Wait for the Lord.
Be strong and let your heart take courage;
And wait for the Lord. (*Rabbi Daniel Smith*)

'Ellul' is the Hebrew month when rabbis prepare themselves for the Jewish High Holy Days with their self-examination and call for repentance, forgiveness and change. The outer religion of committees and accounts gives way to the inner religion of salvation and judgment.
LB

Hunting

21 SEPTEMBER

Hunting animals for sport is a subject that arouses quite unexpected emotions from those both for and against it. So it is nice to see the careful, reasoned approach to the question that comes out of the Jewish legal tradition. In the eighteenth century, Rabbi Ezekiel Landau was the leading interpreter of Jewish law, a man of extraordinary knowledge and authority. He was approached by a rich Jew who had an extensive estate which was swarming with wild animals. Was it permissible to hunt these animals as a pastime or would it mean breaking Jewish laws against cruelty to animals?

The answer is complex and includes quotations from the rulings of earlier authorities. But it gives the flavour of the system in operation, the careful weighing of opinions and the respectful examination of all possible objections. Nevertheless Landau's opposition to the very idea of hunting for pleasure comes across most strongly.

> Rabbi Israel Isserles in his Responsa (legal answers) (back in the sixteenth century) has already considered this problem. He shows that only in the following cases will the rules of 'Cruelty to Animals' not apply – when the act is done to bring a tangible benefit to people, or when the victim is killed outright . . .
>
> That applies to the legal aspect of the issue. But I am surprised that you felt the need to ask such a question. We find in the Torah that only fierce characters like Nimrod or Esau are known as hunters, never Abraham, Isaac and Jacob or their descendants. Rabbi Weil (quoted by *Rema Orach Chayyim 223*) has already pointed out that the usual blessing on donning new clothes should not be recited when putting on a fur coat. Such a blessing might make it appear that killing animals is not only accepted but considered desirable, which goes against the verse 'God's tender mercies are over all His works' (*Psalm 145:9*).
>
> It is true that Rabbi Moses Isserles (who commented on the major codification of Jewish law, the *Shulchan Aruch*) remarks that the reason given is weak. But it is only weak because the fact of putting on the fur coat does not necessarily imply that the owner directly caused the killing. The fur may be of animals who died a natural death. And he agrees with the decision of Rabbi Weil. But I cannot understand how a Jew could even dream of killing animals merely for the pleasure of hunting, when he has no immediate need for the bodies of the creatures.
>
> Some have tried to justify the hunting of wild animals on the basis that they are likely to injure people. They base their views on the statement of Rabbi Eliezer (*Sanhedrin 2a*): 'Whoever is quick to destroy them has done a worthy deed'. But there are two mistakes here. First, because the final decision in the discussion in the Talmud does not agree with Rabbi Eliezer. Secondly, as Resh Lakish explains, Rabbi Eliezer only refers to animals which have already shown themselves to be dangerous to people.
>
> The suggestion has also been made that this attitude to beasts only refers to those who have an owner and are therefore looked after and to some extent tame. So that where there is no owner such an animal is considered to be dangerous and liable to do harm. So it is permitted to kill them even on the Sabbath.
>
> But this is also a mistake and does not really affect the case before

us. It is only true when these wild animals are found in places inhabited by people so that they are a menace to society. It is certainly not a worthy act to hunt them in their own haunts. It is, instead, something governed by lust. There is one exception made in the case of someone who earns a living from hunting by selling the furs or skins. The animal world is under the rule of human beings to provide for their needs. So it makes no difference whether we take the life of clean animals for food, or kill unclean animals for their skins and furs. But when the act is not based on any such consideration, it is simply an act of cruelty! JM

22 SEPTEMBER

Spinoza

I rarely dip into the writings of Spinoza – but it is usually when I want to be startled out of complacency. He was one of the first of the 'moderns', but today we are supposed to live in a 'post-modern' age. Since a post-modern age seems to include large doses of very pre-modern ideas, especially when it comes to religion, maybe he can still surprise us – as in this extract from his chapter 'Of the interpretation of religion'. It comes from his *Theologico-Politico Treatise*, published in 1670.

When people declare, as all are ready to do, that the Bible is the Word of God teaching man true blessedness and the way of salvation, they evidently do not mean what they say; for the masses take no pains at all to live according to Scripture, and we see most people endeavouring to hawk about their own commentaries as the word of God, and giving their best efforts, under the guise of religion, to compelling others to think as they do: we generally see, I say, theologians anxious to learn how to wring their inventions and sayings out of the sacred text, and to fortify them with Divine authority. Such persons never display less scruple or more zeal than when they are interpreting Scripture or the mind of the Holy Spirit; if we ever see them perturbed, it is not that they fear to attribute some error to the Holy Spirit, and to stray from the right path, but that they are afraid to be convinced of error by others, and thus to overthrow and bring into contempt their own authority. But if men really believed what they verbally testify of Scripture, they would adopt quite a different plan of life: their minds would not be agitated by so many contentions, nor so many hatreds, and they would cease to be excited by such a blind and rash passion for interpreting the sacred writings, and excogitating novelties in religion. On the contrary, they would not dare to adopt, as the teaching of Scripture, anything which they could not plainly deduce therefrom: lastly, those sacrilegious persons who have dared, in several passages, to interpolate the Bible, would have shrunk from so great a crime, and would have stayed their sacrilegious hands.

Ambition and unscrupulousness have waxed so powerful, that religion is thought to consist, not so much in respecting the writings of the Holy Spirit, as in defending human commentaries, so that religion is no longer identified with charity, but with spreading discord and propagating insensate hatred disguised under the name of zeal for the Lord, and eager ardour . . .

Every result of their diseased imagination they attribute to the Holy Spirit, and strive to defend with the utmost zeal and passion; for it is an observed fact that men employ their reason to defend conclusions arrived at by reason, but conclusions arrived at by the passions are defended by the passions. JM

23 SEPTEMBER

I do not know its name

Before Heaven and Earth existed there was something undefined but already perfect.

How calm it was and formless! Self-sufficient and unchanging; all fore-reaching without effort – the Universal Mother.

I do not know its name, but for title call it Tao. (*Lao Tze*) LB

24 SEPTEMBER

Freedom of thought and speech

This motto appears on the front of Spinoza's *Theologico-Political Treatise* in the translation by R. H. M. Elwes.

A THEOLOGICO-POLITICAL TREATISE
CONTAINING CERTAIN DISCUSSIONS
WHEREIN IS SET FORTH THAT FREEDOM OF THOUGHT
AND SPEECH NOT ONLY MAY, WITHOUT PREJUDICE
TO PIETY AND THE PUBLIC PEACE, BE GRANTED;
BUT ALSO MAY NOT, WITHOUT DANGER
TO PIETY AND THE PUBLIC
PEACE, BE WITH-
HELD. JM

25 SEPTEMBER

Our parentage

Thus we have given to man a pedigree of prodigious length, but not, it may be said, of noble quality. The world, it has often been remarked, appears as if it had long been preparing for the advent of man; and this, in one sense is strictly true, for he owes his birth to a long line of progenitors. If any single link in this chain had never existed, man would not have been exactly what he now is. Unless we wilfully close our eyes, we may, with our present knowledge, approximately recognize our parentage; nor need we feel ashamed of it. The most humble organism is something much higher than the inorganic dust under our feet; and no one with an unbiased mind can study any living creature, however humble, without being struck with enthusiasm at its marvellous structure and properties. (*Charles Darwin,* The Descent of Man 1871)

We should not be so snobbish as to disown our ancestors, our distant relatives. LB

26 SEPTEMBER

Open rebuke and hidden love

In the Middle Ages there was a flowering of Jewish commentary on the Bible. In Christian France and Germany, Rashi (an acronym for Rabbi Shlomo ben Yitzchak. 1040–1105) was the undoubted master – and when the first Hebrew Bible was printed it contained his commentary. Rashi was the great carrier of previous Rabbinic traditions of interpretation, though casting them into a new, more systematic mould. In Spain the great philosopher and philologist Abraham Ibn Ezra (1093–1167) offered a more rational, critical and controversial approach, with a degree of detachment that allowed him to recognize the literary conventions and structures of the biblical text. And then came Nachmanides, Rabbi Moshe ben Nachman, (1194–1270) who argued with great respect and love with both of his illustrious predecessors, and introduced his own mystical strand of interpretation.

In his preface Nachmanides defines his relationship to these two great masters – the phrases in italics are quotations or reworkings of Biblical verses. (For terms such as Mishnah, Talmud and Midrash see the Glossary)

I will set before me as illumination
the lights of *the pure candelabrum*,
the commentaries of Rabbi Shlomo (Rashi),
a crown of glory and a diadem of beauty.
distinguished in his ways,
in Scripture, Mishnah and Talmud.
His is the right of the firstborn.
in his words I will meditate,
infatuated by love of them,
and with them we will have
debates, investigations and examinations,
in his plain explanations
and Midrashic interpretations,
and every obscure allusion
which is mentioned in his commentaries.
And with Rabbi Abraham the son of Ezra
we shall have *open rebuke and hidden love*. JM

27 SEPTEMBER

The horse

Jews claimed a holy history I knew, but reading history at Oxford, I discovered I had inherited another holy history as well – an English or Angle-ish one. The friendship of the Anglo-Saxon King Oswin and his Celtic bishop, Aidan, glowed from the pages of Bede. In a dusty library I was warmed by their goodness. It was another world from the petty gains and losses of petty kingdoms and their so-easily forgettable war-lords.

King Oswin had given an excellent horse to Bishop Aidan, on which he might either cross the streams of rivers or perform a journey in case of any other pressing necessity, although he usually went on foot. A short time after, a poor man meeting the bishop, and asking alms, he dismounted, and ordered the horse, regally caparisoned as it was, to be given to the poor man, for he was very compassionate, and a cherisher of the poor, and, as it were, a father of the wretched. This being told the king, he said to the bishop, when they were about to go in to dinner, 'How was it, lord bishop, that you gave a kingly horse, which it became you to have for yourself, to a poor man? Had we not very many horses of less value, and of other sorts, which would have sufficed for gifts to the poor, without your giving that horse to them which I chose for your special possession?' To whom the bishop answered immediately, 'What do you say, O king? Is that foal of a mare dearer to you than that son of God?' After which words they went in to dine. And the bishop, indeed, sat down in his own place. Forthwith the king, for he had come from hunting, began to warm himself, standing at the hearth with his attendants; and suddenly, whilst he was warming himself, remembering the words which the bishop had said to him, he ungirded his sword, and gave it to a servant, and, approaching with haste, threw himself before the bishop's feet, desiring that he would be reconciled with him, 'for never hereafter', said he, 'will I say anything of this, or judge what or how much of our money you may give to the sons of God.' The bishop, seeing this, was much alarmed, and immediately arising, lifted him up, assuring him that he was quite reconciled to him, if he would only sit down to his meat, and lay aside his sorrow. And whilst the king, at the bishop's bidding and request, recovered his joyousness, the bishop, on the other hand, began to grow sad, even to the shedding of tears; whom when his presbyter asked, in his own country's language, which the king and his domestics did not understand, why he wept, 'I know,' said he, 'that the king will not live long, for I never before this saw a humble king. Whence I perceive that he is soon to be snatched out of this life, for this nation is not worthy to have such a ruler.' And not long after, the dire presage of the bishop was fulfilled by the sad death of the king, concerning which I have spoken above. (*Bede's Ecclesiastical History*) LB

Thank you very very very much

I'm not sure how to cope with 'Have a nice day!' It seems to belong to a very special American style of marketing – put on a smile and make like you're happy. You know it's phoney, but at the same time at least it's nicer than the indifference, grunt or grudging nod you tend to get in Britain. I once saw an American teacher of travelling salesmen (I don't know what the term would be today – direct retail persons?) explaining how to approach a potential client. 'You have to give them *sincere appreciation,*' he said. 'Why every night when I come home to my wife I say to her, Doll, you're more beautiful today than the first time we met! That's what I mean, *sincere appreciation!*' Well, don't knock it till you've tried it.

Showing appreciation is very important, and in this area, too, the Americans have got it down to a fine art. So much so that I was puzzled then delighted to come across a 'Report on the Committee on Thanks', in a yearbook. Presumably the task of the committee, which must have laboured long and hard in its deliberations, was to find as many different ways as possible of saying thank you, preferably without repeating yourself. (It could become a new panel game.) I have omitted the names since, given the marvellously general nature of the gratitude expressed, they could well be interchangeable. The template is available for a small fee.

> To all those who have made this conference a stimulating and enriching experience, we wish to express our heartfelt appreciation.
>
> We are grateful to our President . . . for his guidance during the past year and for his timely, cogent and comprehensive message. We are indebted, as always, to our tireless and selfless Executive Vice President . . . for his constant devotion and sensitivity in so many areas of creative endeavour. To the staff of the conference itself, who work behind the scenes, we would acknowledge our gratitude.
>
> Because of the painstaking research and provocative presentation of the past week, we feel deepened and charged with a renewed sense of purpose and calling. The diverse lectures were particularly of benefit at this historic . . . conference. The wide range of topics, the perspective they have given us, have made our travels here highly worthwhile. For this and so much more, we should like to thank the program chairman . . . and his able and diligent committee. We should also like to commend the special interest group for the

pre-convention sessions . . . at this critical period. We take note of the momentous visit of . . . whose appearance among us has given renewed impetus to the prospects for the joint efforts of our . . .

To our cherished colleagues of . . . and their congregations – especially their sisterhoods and chairman of hospitality Mrs . . . – for their reception we would make special mention. Their attention to our many needs, their warmth and graciousness, have made us feel most welcome. We should also like to comment on the beauty of the service for our opening session. To these who made this possible, a heartfelt word of appreciation.

We are delighted that Mr . . . was again with us. For the coverage which the . . . newspapers extended to us, we should like to note our gratitude at this time.

In the final analysis, our most adequate expression of appreciation will be manifested by our renewed efforts gained here to stress the teaching of what we are, not of what we have; to emphasize that character, stature, and reverence for personality are the essence of life and that success should be measured in terms of what we give and permit others to achieve rather than what we are able to acquire for ourselves alone.

Respectfully submitted,

. . . Chairman

The report was adopted

I sometimes wonder how God copes with this kind of thing twenty-four hours a day. JM

29 SEPTEMBER

The pious temptation

The greatest religious temptation is to love one's own more by loving others less. Millions have died in religious wars because of this tempting short cut. LB

Do not attach yourself to any particular creed exclusively, so that you may disbelieve all the rest; otherwise you will lose much good, nay, you will fail to recognize the real truth of the matter. God, the omnipresent and omnipotent, is not limited by any one creed, for, he says, 'Wheresoever ye turn, there is the face of Allah' (Koran 2.100) Everyone praises what he believes; his god is his own

creature, and in praising it he praises himself. Consequently he blames the beliefs of others, which he would not do if he were just, but his dislike is based on ignorance.
(Ibn al-Arabi) Karen Armstrong.

30 SEPTEMBER

Transcendent – immanent

This deceptively simple hymn is for me the profoundest in the Jewish liturgy. Its date is not certain, nor is the author. It says that the transcendent, unknowable God of the first three stanzas is the personal Saviour of the last two stanzas. No evidence is cited but the simplicity makes one believe the unknown author's experience. It is the simplicity of great spiritual sophistication.

Eternal Lord who ruled alone
before creation of all forms,
when all was made at His desire
then as the king was He revealed.

And after everything shall end
alone, in wonder, will He reign,
as once He was, so is He now,
the glory that will never change.

He is the One, no other is
to be compared, to stand beside,
neither before, nor following,
His is the strength and His the might.

This is my God, my life He saves,
the rock I grasp in deep despair,
the flag I wave, the place I hide,
He shares my cup the day I call.

Within His hand I lay my soul
both when I sleep and when I wake,
and with my soul my body too,
my Lord is close I shall not fear. LB

OCTOBER

Life's journey

Solomon Ibn Gabirol belongs to that élite group of philosopher/poets who flourished in Muslim Spain in the eleventh century. He is best remembered for his religious poems that still adorn the Jewish prayer-book, especially during the penitential season that climaxes with the Day of Atonement.

Man enters the world and knows not why,
and rejoices and knows not the reason,
and lives and knows not how long.
In his childhood he walks in his own stubbornness,
and when the spirit of lust begins in its season
to stir him up to gather power and wealth,
then he journeys from his place to ride in ships and tread the deserts,
and to carry his life to dens of lions, walking among wild beasts.
And when he imagines his glory is great
and mighty the spoil in his hand
quietly steals the spoiler upon him, his eyes open and there is nothing.
At every moment he is destined to troubles that pass and return,
and at every hour evils, at every moment chances and every day terrors . . .

The man to whom these things happen,
when shall he find a time for repentance
to scour away the rust of corruption?
For the day is short and the work is great,
and the task-masters urgent, hurrying and scurrying,
and time laughs at him and the Master of the House is pressing.
So I pray to You, my God,
remember the distresses that come upon man,
and if I have done evil may You, Yourself, do me good at my end
and not repay measure for measure, to man whose sins are measureless
and whose death is a joyless departure. JM

2 OCTOBER

Sermon material

Just before the High Holy Days with sermons outlined but waiting to gell in my own mind as well as on my lined notepad,
I received from my granddaughter Clio just the right perspective.

Clio is just three years old and has a delightful personality. She has a sturdy body and an equally sturdy sense of independence.
It was Sunday morning a few days before Rosh Hashanah (the Jewish New Year) and the day before Clio and her family had to leave our home after a lovely summer to return to theirs. To help her mother with packing I offered to take Clio to a new adventure playground in nearby Regent's Park. She enthusiastically agreed but when I offered to help her with her sandals she quickly said, 'I can do it by myself.'

When we got to the playground there was a new and very high climbing frame. 'Clio, let me help you get on it,' I offered. She shook her head. 'No grandpa, I can do that by myself.' And so she did. When she then reached the top of this very high frame it suddenly became dramatically clear to her that she couldn't come down alone. After a few attempts to gain a foothold but failing and then with her legs dangling, she called down, 'Grandpa, now I need some help.'

And that was exactly the point I wanted to make with my preaching this year and thanks to Clio I was able to find the right set of images and words. (*Rabbi Hugo Gryn.*)

'Out of the mouths of babes and sucklings'. It's not the rabbi's own scripture. But it's the same though! LB

3 OCTOBER

More from the passionate jew

Rabbi Izak Goller (see previous entry on 4 February) was a highly controversial figure. He was a fiercely loyal Jew, and therefore a fiercely critical one of Jewish failures, but he could also recognize in the uniqueness of his Jewish religious identity something shared by all human beings. He prefaces his second book of poems, 'A Jew Speaks', published in 1926, with the statement:

The Author hopes that God will shew to him and to his congregation, to Israel and to the nations more mercy than may reasonably be expected.

The following prayer from this volume was composed for Yom Kippur, the Day of Atonement, a twenty-four hour fast that marks the climax of the Jewish penitential season. He mentions a couple of technical terms: *Shulchan Aruch*, a codification of Jewish law; *shabbos* – the sabbath day; *tephillin* – boxes containing biblical verses that are placed on the forehead and arm during the morning prayer.

Understanding
God
I am an average Jew of to-day.
Tonight – tomorrow – I shall mutter a tenth of the prayers that wise Jews of old have composed, and I shall understand one-tenth of my mutterings,
And half of that tenth will be a matter of indifference to my present reality,
Or even repugnant.
I would therefore
Today
Pray to You truly, sincerely, privately,
As my need induces me,
And the language I understand best can best express.

God,
It is not for bread, luxuries, individual necessities that I pray,
I am not so vain, so selfish,
Nor do I vision You as a philanthropic institution.
No. It is not that.

I take no credit for being a Jew.
My birth and upbringing were beyond my control.
If I had been born and bred in another faith, my average lethargy would probably have left me an adherent to that faith.
And yet I am proud to be a Jew, proud of the Jew's historic connection with You and Your unity, to preach which is our mission;
And I believe that the perfect understanding of the unity of God will give us also the Unity of Man.

Yet I am only an average Jew!

I believe in the utter divinity of the Pentateuch – more or less.

I obey the laws of the *Shulchan Aruch* – more or less.

I subscribe my dues to the Synagogue, to our charitable institutions, even to the Zionist Organization – since the Balfour Declaration.

And I keep the *Shabbos* and wear my *tephillin* regularly – more or less.

I would perhaps do more, preserve more – reform more – be, in short, more enthusiastic.

Only I don't know what, I don't know how, I see no certain way forwards:

I do not understand.

God,

Religionists, I know, will condemn me for speaking to You so easily, calmly, comfortably, familiarly.

They will snarl at my prayer as blasphemy;

But they will not make me understand

That to You who observe my most inmost thought,

I should not speak easily, calmly, comfortably, excitedly even, familiarly.

My father,

An old-fashioned Jew,

Will tonight beat his breast and sob to You a confession of unutterable sins – he will wail penitently: *I have sinned! I have sinned!*

I shall read those words mechanically, beat my breast perfunctorily, and think of the bright lights, the reader's fine voice, the many people, the stuffiness of the synagogue, the last *bon mot.*

What virtue is absent from me that I am so cold, without that abandon, without that ability to loose my soul from its materialism?

God,

It is not that I am foolishly proud,

That I don't know how comically insignificant in the cosmic scheme is this 'I' of mine;

Nor am I so heavily oppressed with my littleness as to forget that an infinitesimal fraction of the Life-force that is so utterly You lives even in me, making my hands to work and my brain to think.

No, it is not that. What then?

I do not understand.

God,
I who am an average Jew of to-day am also an average man of today.
The world is racked with sorrow and pain and foolishness,
Progress marches ever upon the still quick carcasses of humanity;
Nations just arisen from the shambles eye each other again, malevolently, fearfully;
Men, nations, distrust, deceive and deal harshly one with another;
Man's laws oppress man's natural instincts:
Circumstances breed more sin than the Devil could ever have planned;
Dead customs fetter living souls;
The cleverest brains sow to reap destruction.
Why?
I cannot understand.

God,
I have done wrong and I have tried to amend.
I have been weak, sneakish, spiteful – but why go on?
You know all my greatness and all my meanness,
What I have striven to do and what I have failed to do.
I have done evil – why?
I do not understand.

God,
I am not alone in my bewilderment
Men like me, whether Jew or Gentile,
– I am only an average man –
Do evil for lack of this one thing.
Nations ravage and slaughter
For lack of this one thing –
Understanding.

Therefore,
God,
I do not ask of You riches, health, not even fame;
Nothing for myself alone;
But, as an average Jew,
As an average man,
I pray to You, calmly,
With all the intensity of my being,
That this Atonement Day
That will grant the world –
UNDERSTANDING. JM

4 OCTOBER

The synagogue that was too full

At the end of the High Holy Days which are so heady and spiritually intense and with the memory of the synagogue full of men, women and children to overflowing still fresh in the mind, I think of this cautionary tale.

Of the great Rabbi Baal Shem Tov coming to a village in Galicia, perhaps just at this time of the year, two and a half centuries ago. How his carriage was met and escorted in fine style to the synagogue, and the whole community waiting inside, and as the door was opened the Rabbi seemed to struggle to get in. 'I am sorry', he said 'your synagogue is too full and there is no room for me here.'

'No, no,' protested the elders, 'the seat of honour is reserved for you . . .'

'Your synagogue is too full of your prayers . . . you come, you pray, you make many resolves – but when you leave they don't go with you into your homes and streets and places of work . . . It's too full . . .' And with that he got into his carriage and left.

And my prayer – that some of the fine and noble things we want to do and be, that they will happen and not remain merely pious hopes. (*Rabbi Hugo Gryn*)

Hugo was 'educated' in Nazi concentration camps. He survived spiritually as well as physically and is the radio and television representative of Jewish vitality, experience and good humour. I think I would have been broken by such an 'education'. LB

5 OCTOBER

Harvest festival

The autumn harvest is celebrated in the Bible by taking certain branches and fruits and living for a week in lean-to huts, 'tabernacles'. The rabbinic tradition elaborated on all these details. The 'fruit of goodly trees' (*Leviticus 23:40*) is identified as an *etrog*, a citrus fruit, the 'branches of palm trees, boughs of leafy trees and willows of the brook' become respectively the *lulav* (palm branch), *hadasim* (myrtle) and *aravot* (willows). They are bound together and waved in six directions during the morning service. But why these and why tie them together?

The tradition offers its own explanation and suggests a model for solidarity and tolerance.

> Just as the *etrog* has taste and a pleasant fragrance, so there are in Israel people who are both learned and strictly observant; like the *lulav* whose fruit has taste but no fragrance, so there are in Israel people who are learned but are not fully practising; as the myrtle has a pleasant odour but is tasteless, so there are people of good deeds who possess no scholarship; as the willow is neither edible nor of agreeable fragrance, so there are those who are neither learned nor possessed of good deeds. The Holy One says: So as to make it impossible for Israel to be destroyed, let all of them be bound together as plants are bound into a cluster, so that the righteous among them will atone for the others. (*Pesikta Rabbati 51:2*) JM

6 OCTOBER

The right question

When I was a child, I found religion very boring. Intense poverty and the usual childhood rivalries and power games were painful realities that dominated my life. During adolescence I was acutely unhappy, suffering from painful shyness, sex hang-ups and suicidal depression. I left school at 15 and got a dull underpaid job.

From time to time, well-meaning friends encouraged me to visit their churches, but I found the hymns banal, the services boring and irrelevant to my problems. And so many of the faithful seemed shallow, hypocritical or merely ambitious to shine in the organization. Another kind of family rivalry and power game . . .

After a number of years, I managed to get some psychoanalysis. I won't say it dramatically solved all my personal problems, but after a year of introspection they lost some of their emotional charge and no longer obsessed me.

I became aware that *everybody* seemed to have troubles too. I began to look at life with clearer vision and ask all kinds of questions: Who were all these people, including myself? What we were doing here? What was our real destiny? Did we have to keep playing childish emotional games in an adult world.

I thought a lot about it during a long period of serious illness. It was a kind of meditation.

I looked at myself and my reactions as if I was a stranger.

I discovered that it was possible to separate impulses from self-justifications, emotions from ideas, truth from evasion. What tricks we play on ourselves! Yet behind all the trivial everyday entanglements of ego, self-indulgence and ambition, I could dimly sense a mysterious majestic region of meaning and purpose in the universe and in individual lives.

One day it all came together. I suppose you could call it a religious experience, although that sounds a bit pretentious. *I simply became aware that God exists.* What God? Which religion? I didn't know. I only realized that once you grew out of the petty pains of self-interest, of hopes and fears, something vaster rushed into consciousness, transforming the understanding.

From the sublime to the ridiculous. Religious insight might be very moving, but I still had to eat drink, go to the lavatory and earn a living. There was something comic as well as cosmic in the contrast of infinite truth and the millions of little human beings like myself – loving, hating, humble, ambitious, all so firmly tied to a limited identity and ego, flipping through life like a host of Charlie Chaplins!

Could these two worlds be reconciled – the cosmic and the comic?

Once more the answer came. The sublime and the ridiculous were two poles of one great reality, and the secret lay in being yourself without being wholly identified with the part, like an actor giving the performance of a lifetime but still unattached, willing to let it go, as we all must when we leave this world theatre. One's everyday responsibilities and ideals were still a priority, but underneath them was a deeper purpose.

From then on, in between earning a living and fulfilling my social obligations, as I saw them, I began to study scriptures, Western and Eastern. They became inspiring reading. I found that faith and knowledge need not be something to take on trust, but only echoes of what one already knew to be true deep within oneself. Somehow I had stumbled on a master key to religion from the inside.

Religion was really a matter of asking the right questions in the right way. (*Leslie Shepard*) LB

This is your truth

It was our privilege to know Eugene Heimler. Born in Hungary in 1922, as a young man he was taken to Auschwitz. He belongs to that rare group of survivors who managed to transmute their bitter experience in the death camps into positive lessons that could be given to others. Before the war he had been a published poet; now he turned again to writing and his book *Night of the Mist* recalls the camp experience and *A Link in the Chain* the stages of his recovery.

After the war he settled in England, became a psychiatric social worker and pioneer of his own form of short-term therapy. The quest for meaning in our lives was central to his work and he dedicated himself to addressing social issues like the problems that arise with unemployment. A deeply religious man, he was always available to support the young rabbis newly emerging from the Leo Baeck College as they sought to understand what was the task of a rabbi in this new post-war European world. His sudden death from a heart attack was a tragic loss.

But he had faced death before as this poem of his attests. It was translated by Tony Rudolf from the verse drama *The Storm*.

This is your truth: doubt and faith together.
Uncertainty is your only certitude.
Death and life together are the truth
like two sides of a coin named destiny.
There is no start, no end, only continuance
and no solutions within the bond of flesh.
Yet pain and death will teach you secret words
and the dreadful truth hidden within your soul.
Be not afraid of fear. But trust.
Faith is no mirage: Die now.
And come to life again.
Seek, search, suffer.
And then rejoice. This is your fate
as long as the earth revolves in space. JM

8 OCTOBER

Journey of the night

I kissed his warm cheek and, with my love brimming over, wished him God's blessing on this journey of journeys. Then, softly I crept away and rested, waiting for all that needed to be done the following morning. The night sister wept.

They had moved him to the mortuary chapel and the body was cold and looked like marble. My love had gone, leaving only an empty shell. The tears raged through me and nothing could stop them. Blinded, I groped my way back to the bleakness of our house bereft of his presence. Somehow I got the door open and forced myself inside. And most wonderful of mysteries, he was there waiting for me. His spirit had flown straight home. His love as clear and strong as ever. There was a veil, but there would be no dividing. Not now; not ever! (*Daphne Richardson*, my friend and former secretary) LB

9 OCTOBER

Scholars

There is a magnificent certainty about the statement below by the Rabbis. By 'scholar' they mean someone who studies Jewish tradition and teaches it to his generation. Actually tradition knows of three kinds of leadership, all deriving their authority from God: the crown of kingship (political leadership), the crown of priesthood (the maintenance of ritual and religious tradition, the regular service of God) and the crown of the Torah (of learning, of the critical perspective of the prophet and the possibility of renewal). A proper society flourishes when all three kinds of leadership interact with each other.

A scholar takes precedence over a king of Israel, for if a scholar dies no one can replace him, while if a king dies, all Israel is eligible for kingship. (*Horayot 13a*) JM

Violence!

10 OCTOBER

Civilization is thin. Underneath violence lurks, both inside us and in the outer world. When it breaks out, something greater than repressing is required. An incident recounted by the Quaker Henry Dyson.

> A friend of mine was walking her dog on Cannock Chase in Staffordshire when she was suddenly attacked by a young man. He shoved a stick down her throat and left her for dead. She was discovered some time later and her life was saved although her voice is now only a whisper. The young man was caught. He had been refused entry to join the army on the day he had attacked and was angry with the world. He was imprisoned and after some months my friend was given permission to visit him, although she was a complete stranger to him. She met him and they talked and tried to make sense of what had happened. She said she forgave him and that, as a Christian, she prayed for his well-being. Three weeks later the young man hanged himself in his cell. LB

Who knows?

11 OCTOBER

An elderly Jew set out one morning for synagogue. He was stopped by a policeman who asked him where he was going. 'I don't know,' replied the old man. So the policeman arrested him for vagrancy and took him off to the station. He spent the night in a cell and appeared the following morning before the judge. 'What is this man accused of?' he asked the policeman. 'Well, when I stopped him in the street and asked him where he was going he said that he did not know, so I arrested him for vagrancy.' The judge turned to the old man and asked him what he had to say for himself. 'I'm a religious man,' he explained, 'and I am very aware that my life is in the hands of God. So when the policeman asked me where I was going, all I could honestly answer was that I did not know. And I was proved right, because I thought I was going to synagogue but I ended up in jail!' JM

12 OCTOBER

Spoiling my day

But I've seen many people coping tranquilly with their own impending death. They've not been superhuman, but ordinary people who have found comfort in being able to bring their lives to a close, and live out the last of their days and months being able to talk to those they love about how life would be without them. It may sound extraordinary and perhaps those people are unusual in having faith in themselves and the people around them, or a strong, religious faith. But faith itself is an unknown quality. It's a bit like jumping into the water and not being certain whether you can swim or not. When they do, most people stay afloat. The real problem is that we sometimes don't get the chance to jump, but get pushed. On the whole, I believe that faith is a risk worth taking. Otherwise you might get left with deathbed instructions, like the old man who, on dying, wanted his wife to promise him that she would drive to the cemetery in the same car as his sister whom she detested. Reluctantly, she agreed. 'All right,' she said. 'I'll do it, but it will completely spoil my day.'

Dying nearly always spoils the day; the important thing is that death doesn't destroy the living, and that they are not left with too many regrets and too many things that were left unsaid.

(*Dr Wendy Greengross*, doctor, therapist, lecturer and trustee of the Cheshire Homes) LB

13 OCTOBER

A good read

This particular, rather bitter, little joke could have taken place in any number of societies – and though it is told about antisemitism, it could apply to any kind of racism today.

A Jewish gentleman was shocked to see his Jewish friend sitting in the cafe reading an antisemitic newspaper. When he asked him why, he got the following reply.

'When I read a Jewish newspaper what do I find? That Jews are being persecuted in some part of the world. That there is assimilation everywhere and the Jewish people is disappearing. That Jews can't get jobs because of antisemitism. That the Jewish family is breaking down and that divorces are on the increase. That Orthodox Jews hate Reform Jews, that anti-Zionist Jews are fighting Zionist Jews. It just makes me depressed.

'But when I read the antisemitic paper what do I find? That the richest people in the world are the Jews. That Jews control the banks, the media and the government. That Jews all stick together and have never been so united. And that there is a very successful Jewish conspiracy to take over the world. I tell you, it cheers me up!' JM

14 OCTOBER

Stanzas

The stanzas of Angelus Silesius (Johann Scheffer) are worth learning by heart. They seem jingles, but they are the textbook of spirituality.

Two eyes our souls possess
While one is turned on time
The other seeth things
Eternal and Sublime. LB

15 OCTOBER

Dearest Annie

Grace Aguilar (1816–1847) wrote a number of novels but also some religious works for Jewish women. She came from a Marrano family, Jews who had been forced to convert to Christianity at the time of the Inquisition but had kept up their Judaism in secret. Her book *The Jewish Faith* was composed as a series of letters addressed to a friend Annie, a younger woman who was losing her religious convictions. The full title already indicates something of its flavour:

THE
JEWISH FAITH;
ITS SPIRITUAL CONSOLATION, MORAL GUIDANCE,
AND IMMORTAL HOPE
WITH
A BRIEF NOTICE OF THE REASONS FOR MANY OF
ITS ORDINANCES AND PROHIBITIONS.

A SERIES OF LETTERS
ANSWERING THE INQUIRIES OF YOUTH.

Grace was ill most of her life and died suddenly on a visit to Germany at the age of 31. So there is a certain poignancy about the following passage from one of the last letters in the book, on the importance of the belief in immortality.

> Dearest Annie, cultivate, encourage, listen to, this internal voice, that it may attain such ascendancy as to render it equally impossible to disbelieve in immortality as to disbelieve in God. I believe there are very few, if any, who, were the question put, would deny a belief in a future existence: they cannot; for we find they often believe in spite of themselves. But, would we be better, happier, wiser, this belief ought not to be merely tacitly held as an article of creed, which concerns us little here below, but should be so ever present, so intimately twined with our being, that it would explain at once every seeming contradiction in the ways of God, as displayed in the affairs of men. It would throw a halo over the history of the PAST; teach us to bear calmly with the difficulties and seeming injustice of the PRESENT, and look to the FUTURE with such strong faith, that hope would seem certainty, and bereavement itself lose its deepest anguish. It would not render us careless or indifferent to the aspect of this life, as some sensualists assert. It would urge us beyond every other incentive to remove misery and vice from our fellows, that the animal might be subdued and the intellectual and spiritual obtain their intended superiority. But it is a subject but too often lost in the pressure of the world. We do not instil it sufficiently into the minds and hearts of our children, and so in manhood, though it may be believed, it fails to become their guide. We think it a subject connected only with suffering and death, that this world is, or ought to be enough for our enjoyment, and more than enough to occupy our thoughts. But all this is false and mistaken reasoning. This world is a chaos of darkness and misery, and injustice and wrath, without the belief in another; while with that belief its very clouds are illuminated by the light of Heaven gleaming through, and every seeming contradiction, tending to the furtherance of that divine rule of love and justice, which we *know* we shall understand above . . .
>
> Dearest Annie, I could write on this most important and most solemn subject, to us Hebrews especially, more and more, in the inexpressible longing to bring its peace, its joy, its comfort home to you, whose early trials and eager heart need it so strongly, but hand and brain both fail. I can only reiterate; seek, strive, pray for this precious blessing, a firm and ever acting belief in this Immortality,

which God's holy word proclaims, and His grace will grant to the full.

I remain,

Your affectionate and true friend,

Inez Villena JM

16 OCTOBER

A birth

Our English literature has a holy origin, its innocence worth pondering in the sophisticated world of modern publishing with its celebrity prizes and competing copyrights.

In the monastery of the abbess Hild was a certain brother especially marked by Divine grace, since he was wont to make songs suited to religion and piety, so that whatever he had learnt from the Divine writings through interpreters, this he in a little while produced in poetical expressions composed with the greatest harmony and accuracy, in his own tongue, that is, in that of the Angles. By his songs the minds of many were excited to contemn the world, and desire the celestial life. And, indeed, others also after him in the nation of the Angles attempted to compose religious poems, but none could equal him.

For he himself did not learn the art of poetry from men, or by being instructed by man; but, being divinely assisted, received gratuitously the gift of singing, on which account he never could compose any frivolous or idle poem, but those only which pertain to religion suited his religious tongue. For having lived in the secular habit unto the time of advanced age, he had never learned anything of singing. Whence, sometimes at an entertainment, when it was determined for the sake of mirth that all should sing in order, he, when he saw the harp approaching him, used to rise in the midst of the supper, and, having gone out, walk back to his home.

Which when he was doing on a time, and, having left the house of entertainment, had gone out to the stables of the beasts of burden, the care of which was entrusted to him on that night, and there, at the proper hour, had resigned his limbs to sleep, a certain one stood by him in a dream, who saluting him, and calling him by his name, said, 'Caedmon, sing me something.' Then he answering said, 'I know not how to sing; and for that reason I went out from the entertainment and retired hither, because I could not sing.' Again he who was talking with him said, 'Yet you have something to sing to me.' 'What,' said he, 'must I sing?' The other said, 'Sing the beginning of created things.' Having received this reply, he immediately began to sing verses in praise of God the Creator, which he had never heard, whereof this is the purport: 'Now we must praise the Author of the celestial kingdom, the power of the Creator and His counsel, the deeds of the Father of glory. How He, being eternal God, was the author of all wonderful things; who first created heaven for the sons of men, as the roof of their dwelling and afterwards created the earth, being the omnipotent guardian of mankind.' This is the sense, but not the exact order of the words which he sang in his sleep, for songs, however excellently composed, cannot be translated from one tongue into another, word for word, without some loss of their beauty and spirit. Moreover, on his rising up from sleep, he retained in memory all that he had sung in his dream, and presently added to it more words of song worthy of God, after the same fashion.

And coming in the morning to the steward who was set over him, he told him what a gift he had received; and having been brought to the abbess, he was ordered, in the presence of many learned men, to declare his dream and to repeat the song, that it might be tested, by the judgment of all, what or whence it was that he related. And all concluded that a celestial gift had been granted him by the Lord. And they interpreted to him a certain passage of sacred history or doctrine, and ordered him to transpose it, if he could, into poetical rhythm. And he, having undertaken it, departed, and returning in the morning, brought back what he was ordered to do, composed in most excellent verse. Whereupon presently the abbess, embracing heartily the grace of God in the man, instructed him to leave the secular habit, and to take the monastic vow; and having, together with all her people, received him into the monastery, associated him with the company of the brethren, and ordered him to be instructed in the whole course of sacred history. And he converted into most sweet song whatever he could learn from hearing, by thinking it over by himself, and, as though a clean animal, by *ruminating;* and by making it resound more sweetly, made his teachers in turn his hearers. (*Bede's Ecclesiastical History*) LB

Dialogue

Interfaith dialogue has become a growth industry, though only a few years ago it was seen as a kind of worthy but irrelevant activity for a few slightly odd individuals on the liberal end of their religious tradition – so near the end that they risked falling off altogether. Thankfully things have changed and the real challenges and opportunities that arise when people of good faith meet their counterparts from other faiths are very clear. So much so that a theologian like Hans Küng can try to help us find a new global ethic under the motto:

> No peace among the nations
> without peace among the religions.
> No peace among the religions
> without dialogue between the religions.

There's a story told about a religious man who learnt this truth from overhearing a conversation between two peasants. One says: 'Ivan, do you love me?' 'Of course I love you,' replies his friend. 'Then do you know what causes me pain?' 'How could I know such a thing?' 'Then you do not truly love me!'

One of the first steps in dialogue is learning what causes the other pain, including what we ourselves do. It is a novel definition of 'love', but worth trying out. JM

An open mind and heart

For all embracing ecumenism and tolerance, you have to go to a Moslem.

> My heart is capable of every form.
> A cloister for the monk, a fane for idols,
> A pasture for gazelles, the votary's Kabah,
> The tables of the Torah, the Koran.
> His camels, still the one true faith is mine.

(From *Ibn al-Arabi*, 12th century. Told to me by my ecumenical friend, Karen Armstrong.) LB

The poet in the kitchen

19 OCTOBER

Some friends in Budapest invited me out to lunch. 'Not a tourist restaurant', they said, 'but one for local people'. The menu was full of familiar and not so familiar dishes. I only gave a casual glance at the section labelled 'Wild Boar', since this was obviously not going to conform with the Jewish dietary laws. And there I saw it, under the label: Roast Wild Boar 'Bakony' Style:

> The tender braised wild boar joins the golden yellow dumplings in a gravy made with mushroom and sour cream.

What delicacy, what poetry! How long had the chef mulled over the precise wording of this little hymn to the perfect marriage of tastes and textures? How little we appreciate the artistry of the food we consume. What would our poet in the kitchen have made of a hamburger in a bun? How would our sensitivity change if we had to compose such a menu for every meal that we so casually eat? JM

No 'plaster saint'

20 OCTOBER

> I first met the woman I am going to call Mother Bianca in 1965, when I was a twenty-year-old nun who had just made her vows of poverty, chastity and obedience. Mother Bianca was Mistress of the Scholasticate, the next stage of rigorous training for the religious life. She was dying of cancer. When I knelt at her feet for the first time, she had been given three weeks to live. In fact, with extraordinary will-power, refusing all painkillers lest they cloud her judgement, she hung on for nearly a whole year. When I looked up at her that first day, I found myself smiling with genuine pleasure at one of the most serene faces I had ever seen in my life. I would say now that it was the face of somebody who had little ego and no hidden agenda to promote or defend herself. All I knew then was that her face was utterly kind.
>
> There was not much kindness in convent life as I knew it. It was thought that young women needed toughening up, so that they did not depend on human warmth and friendship. I had been quite shattered by the experience of the novitiate, which in those days

resembled spiritual trench warfare and it was Mother Bianca who began the process of putting me back together again. I cannot remember how she did this, because it was (and this is an important point) so unobtrusive. Without making any great song and dance about it, she managed to convince me that I was not the worthless, spineless person I feared. When we all knelt round her bed at the end to say goodbye, she kept me behind the others to tell me that I was a good girl and that I was to remember that she had said so. After she died, it was clear that she had made all sorts of other people – including people outside the convent who had only a very tenuous connection with her – feel better about themselves. What they recalled most was the extraordinary kindness and attentiveness of her face, which was, I suppose, numinous – a reflection of the compassion of God.

Yet the wonderful thing about Mother Bianca was that she was no plaster saint and it was impossible to put her on a pedestal. She was often ratty and impatient (and not just because she was in constant pain). She had a good but not a remarkable mind and the little homilies she had to give us were actually rather boring. She was also quite cranky. She could become incoherent with rage, for example, if one of us broke a ninepenny jug from Woolworths. The result was that we became so anxious that year that cups, glasses and plates slipped through our hands as though they were coated with butter. On one pouring wet day, she became incensed by the state of the garden and had us all, in our dripping long black cloaks, weeding all afternoon in the downpour, while she rattled on the window to urge us on.

When people ask me if I regret my years in the convent, I always think of Mother Bianca and I say no. One of the reasons why I left was that I realized that I could never be as good a nun as she, even though she was no pattern religious. Above all, she taught me the value of kindness. It did not take me long, after leaving the religious life, to learn that kindness was in short supply in the outside world too, even (indeed, especially) among religious people. We can spend so much time defensively boosting our own congregation (often at the expense of others), glorying in being *right* and virtuously obeying laws about food and sex that we forget that charity and loving-kindness are the greatest of the commandments and that, as Wordsworth said, it is the 'little unremembered acts of kindness and of love' that make us worthy of our humanity. (*Karen Armstrong*)

Religion seeks truth on the higher slopes, but is not very good at honesty on the lower ones, which is why Karen Armstrong is so important for me. You need both to write *A History of God*. LB

21 OCTOBER

Stencl

He was a fixture at any Jewish gathering – the poet Stencl. You would find him standing in a corner somewhere selling his Yiddish poetry magazine *'Losh'n und Leb'n'*, 'Language and Life'. He edited it, wrote most of the copy and sold it, a one man labour of love. Long after his death a life-size cut-out of a photograph of him used to stand in the hallway of the temporary rooms of the Museum of Jewish Life on the top floor of my college. Many's the time I would be startled into thinking he was standing there.

I once went to visit him with a novelist friend from Israel and his young son. We had heard that Stencl had a regular meeting in the old building of the Bernard Baron Settlement in the East End. At the switchboard they directed us to the third floor. But we came out of the lift into an empty hallway. The lift door shut, it was pitch black with no windows even to guide us, and somewhere ahead of us the stairs. We listened and heard the faint sound of voices from the floor below. We groped our way to the staircase and carefully descended, the voices getting louder and clearly singing something. On the floor below, equally dark, a thin strip of light was visible beneath a door at the end of the corridor. We opened it carefully to find a small group of elderly people, Stencl standing in front of them beside the piano. They were singing lustily in Yiddish an old Bundist socialist song: 'We are the youth, we are the spring!'

Stencl greeted my friend whose writings he knew and admired. And then felt around in his pockets for a sweet for the little boy – but all he could find were his heart pills.

The journey in the dark, the voices streaming out from beneath the door, the sheer energy of these eighty-year-olds seemed like a strange dream at the time. But what power and what generosity of heart from another age. They were quite right in their song – it is all a matter of the spirit. 'We *are* the youth, we *are* the spring!' JM

22 OCTOBER

Yearning

. . . this gray spirit, yearning in desire
To follow knowledge like a sinking star
Beyond the utmost bound of human thought.
(*Alfred, Lord Tennyson: Ulysses*)

I have chosen this because it expressed the need we have to go on and continue to explore, never giving up. (*Karen Armstrong*) LB

23 OCTOBER

Is he a clown or is he really wise?

It is said that a good piece of literature helps us discover things within ourselves that we might never have recognized otherwise. The same applies to people who get beneath our skin in some way.

It was a youth conference and I was only just out of my teens. There was a young man present who seemed out of sync with everyone else. Something he said cut through me like a knife: 'Life is a game of snakes and ladders. You climb the ladders and kill the snakes!'

But he inspired a song, since those were my composing days. And of course it is a kind of projection on to him of the concerns that his strangeness evoked in me.

Is he a clown or is he really wise
And all his lifetime merely a disguise
Behind the face he changes every day
He's not sure why he wants to stay.

Chorus:
And if sometimes he's angry
And sometimes feels afraid
He cannot always reach beyond
The way that he is made.

Sometimes it's clear and sometimes hard to find
What to believe and what to leave behind
What's true today tomorrow is a lie
The truth for which so many die.

Chorus:
A moment's pause to make a little sense
Between the hours of endless consequence
With not much more to keep the thing alive
Than just the habit to survive.

Chorus:
A dream can be a lonely place to hide
But even dreams can safely be denied
When all is done and when he has awoke
Perhaps he will enjoy the joke.

Chorus:
And if sometimes he's angry
And sometimes feels afraid
He cannot always reach beyond
The way that he is made.

I don't know what happened to him but the song remains to evoke him and to haunt me – and also to offer a bit of necessary comfort: we cannot always reach beyond the way that we are made. JM

24 OCTOBER

Phoebe Lawton

One of the most illustrious but at the same Time one of the most difficult Christian duties is 'To love our Enemies' and to pray for the Welfare and Amendment of them 'who do spitefully use and persecute us.' As therefore Love and Charity towards all such is so repeatedly and strongly enjoined by our blessed Lord, we are under indispensable obligation to comply with it, and if we duly observe this precept, we shall soon find the beneficial effects of it.

Which is very true – even for non-Christians. Phoebe embroidered this as a sampler in 1800 which I found in a junk shop one hundred and sixty years later. I read it most days. LB

25 OCTOBER

Passing strangers

The gallery was closed. I was heading back to my car, vaguely aware of a tall, grey-haired, bespectacled gentleman approaching me, dressed in a light raincoat and carrying a large artist's folder. He stopped and addressed me: 'Well, wouldn't you know! Abbey Road!'

I quickly ran through my computerized memory of friends and acquaintances trying to identify him. He looked familiar but did I really know him? The accent was slightly American. Nothing registered. He went on: 'And that shop is still there!'

That seemed to be all he wanted to say. Just a visitor coming back to an old haunt and happy to say a word to another human being. I said: 'Good luck!' He said: 'God bless you!' and walked on.

Strange how something so inconsequential, so human, can cheer you up for a whole day. JM

26 OCTOBER

Martha Lawton (1800)

Filled with praise of him who gives the light
And draws the sable curtain of the night
Let placid slumbers sooth each weary mind
At morn to wake more heavenly more refined
So shall the labours of the day begin,
More pure more guarded from the snares of sin.

Martha embroidered these verses in Ackworth School in 1800 – a Quaker establishment, I'm told. They are surrounded by alphabets which modestly display her skill. I read them before going to bed, because I should like to wake 'more refined'. I do not know the author of the verses. LB

27 OCTOBER

That's show business

A lot of my parents' friends were in, or on the fringe of, show business. Many of them were ex-patients of my father's whom he had treated with hypnosis for anything from stagefright to stopping smoking. He became an Honorary Water Rat, when that was restricted to only a dozen non-show business people, and acted as the GP for the Victoria Palace Theatre. So from an early age my sister and I would go with him backstage on a Wednesday night during the interval of the current Crazy Gang show to visit Bud Flanagan and the rest of the Gang. We only ever saw the same part of the show from backstage – the last number of the Tiller Girls before the interval. Then back to the dressing room and these strange, completely round little men, dressed only in their underwear, sitting in front of their make-up mirror with a TV on in the background.

In a way it must have been a bit disillusioning, certainly a cure for believing the apparent glamour from the other side of the footlights. But there was also the pride of being an 'insider', however temporarily, in someone else's world. They were always very kind to us kids and asked how we were – though they had nothing to offer since the only drinks available were alcoholic. After a brief chat, my dad would look at the latest sprains they had acquired from their strenuous performance, give them another prescription for sleeping pills and we'd leave.

Bud's real name was Robert Winthrop, a Jew from the East End. In the army he had run into antisemitism, particularly from his sergeant. When he went into the music halls he took the sergeant's name, Flanagan, so that if they laughed at him he would be getting his own back.

I was proud, as only a thirteen-year-old can be, that Bud Flanagan, and some other comedians of that vintage, came to my barmitzvah. When Lionel and I were preparing our first prayerbook together, I decided to return the compliment, and put a quote from Bud's autobiography in the study anthology. He wrote that show business had been good to him but the biggest bonus had been to make people laugh and forget their troubles for a few hours. Next to it I put this astonishing piece by the Chasidic master Nachman of Bratslav:

> There are men who suffer terrible distress and are unable to tell what they feel in their hearts, and they go their way and suffer and suffer. But if they meet one with a laughing face, he can revive them with his joy. And to revive someone is no slight thing.

So here's to all the comics and comedians, performers and artistes, who revive us with their joy. JM

28 OCTOBER

Tombstones

> To subsist in lasting Monuments, to live in their productions, to exist in their names, and praedicament of *Chymera's*, was large satisfaction unto old expectations and made one part of their *Elyziums*. But all this is nothing in the Metaphysicks of true belief. To live indeed is to be again our selves, which being not only an hope but an evidence of noble believers; 'Tis all one to lie in St *Innocent's* Church-yard, as in the Sands of *Aegypt:* Ready to be any thing, in the extasie of being ever, and as content with six foot as the Moles of *Adrianus*.
>
> *Lucan*
> *– Tabesne cadavera solvat*
> *An rogus haud refert –*

My thoughts exactly as I walk away from a funeral to unrobe in the vestry. But I don't express them in the grandest English prose. These lines conclude the Urn Burial of Sir Thomas Browne (1605–1682) – the most addictive mine of misinformation ever. LB

29 OCTOBER

But you forgot to remember

If I had not heard this from the lady herself I would have said it was just a story. She was walking in the street when a man called to her by name. He started talking, and clearly knew her, but she could not place him. She went through her friends from various social and work circles – nothing! A few minutes later her dilemma registered with him as well. 'You don't remember me, do you?' he asked. 'I'm terribly sorry,' she said. 'I'm your ex-husband!'

In her defence she pointed out that some years had passed, his hair was different and he had replaced his glasses with contact lenses.

Of course that is only an extreme example of a familiar kind of lapse that all of us might have. But for clergy and politicians it can be fatal. Not to remember someone is pretty devastating to the person you forgot and it doesn't do your reputation for caring much good either. Nevertheless there are strategies. One showbiz solution is to call everyone 'Darling,' irrespective of gender. A slightly less compromising alternative is 'dear'. Even better is to cultivate a reputation for forgetfulness, so bad that everyone immediately introduces themselves fully convinced you will never recall them.

I think it was Abraham Lincoln who devised a couple of useful tricks. A sound opening was always to ask: 'And how's the old condition?' That was guaranteed to get you enough information to guess their identity or avoid it entirely. His other approach was to ask the individual's name. When the offended person offered his surname, he would apologize: 'No, I know that, of course, but what was your first name'! The same applied if the first name was offered.

But I take my hat off to the clergyman in America, I forget the denomination, who avoided the problem by avoiding meeting people. When forced to make a 'house call', he would sit in his car outside the house till he was sure no one was in, or had seen them leave. Then he'd drop one of his printed cards through the letterbox. 'The Revd So and So called while you were out and leaves behind his blessing.' JM

30 OCTOBER

Breath of peace

I had walked on ahead of the rest of the party – the only Jew amongst a group of Christian pilgrims – as we reached a promenade that overlooked the magic that is Jerusalem. I gazed at the wonderful view of the Old City and then moved on again, for one brief moment virtually alone in that popular tourist area. But I was not quite alone. A few paces away stood a tall hawk-faced Arab. He made no move towards me but watched me in silence, wrapped in stillness. He was an old man – white-bearded, stern and dignified. We gazed at each other, caught up in a meeting. Solemnly, I gave him his own ancient greeting: 'Salaam'. The old face transformed into a blazing smile and swift as lightening his hand shot out and caught up mine and kissed it. There was a burst of movement. The rest of my party had caught up with me. I moved on. But the moment has stayed with me. The beauty and the wonder of it, Jew and Arab drawn together heart to heart by the word 'peace' – the traditional greeting of his people and mine. If only it could always be so. (*Daphne Richardson,* my friend and former secretary, a Jewess who became secretary to the friars of a Carmelite sanctuary.) LB

Seven ages – at least

Shakespeare gave us the 'seven ages of man', but over a thousand years earlier the Rabbis had discovered the same pattern to our lives. They found in the opening words of the Book of Ecclesiastes ('vanity of vanities, all is vanity') an allusion to seven stages in our life:

> Rabbi Shimon ben Elazar said, the seven 'vanities' correspond to the seven 'worlds' which a man sees in his life. One year old, he is like a king, everyone hugs and kisses him. At two and three he is like a pig who puts his hand into every dirty place. At ten he skips about like a young goat. At twenty he neighs like a horse. He marries a wife and he is burdened like a donkey. He has children and his face becomes aggressive like a dog as he goes out to earn bread and food. He grows old, and he becomes bent double like a monkey.
> (*Ecclesiastes Rabbah 1:1*)

In the Middle Ages an unknown Hebrew writer turned the idea into a poem to contemplate on the most solemn day of the Jewish calendar, the Day of Atonement. It is pretty sobering but it may be worth reading once a year.

> Son of the ground, let him remember his origins,
> For at the end of his life he will return to his childhood.
>
> At the age of five they say: good luck to him,
> His virtues rise up to the sun.
> He rests between the breasts of his mother and never wishes to leave them.
> The shoulders of his father become his chariot.
>
> What instruction do you give to the child at ten?
> He is still a bit young, but soon he will grow and remember.
> Speak to him gently so that he learns
> You are his parents and family whom he enjoys.
>
> How sweet are the days of the twenty-year-old,
> Agile as a young deer skipping over the mountains.
> He laughs at the instruction of his teachers
> A young gazelle is for now his only trap and snare.

At thirty he falls into the arms of a woman.
Suddenly he sees that he is caught in a net.
From all sides he is assailed by darts,
The caprice of his children and his wife.

Bowed and servile he reaches forty,
Content with his lot, whether bad or good.
He runs on his journey, leaving friends behind,
Dedicating all his time to his work.

At fifty he thinks of the vanity of his life,
Alarmed that the days of mourning are approaching.
All the wealth of the world is despised in his eyes
For he is scared that his end draws near.

Don't ask what happens at sixty!
His actions are no longer clear and precise.
For the powers that remain are weakening
And cannot sustain him in his struggle.

If he manages to make it to seventy
His words are neither audible or comprehensible.
He is only a burden to his neighbours
Those who look after his health and well-being.

At eighty he's a bother to his children.
Neither his eyes nor heart function well.
He's despised by those who know him and mocked by his
neighbours.
Bile is in his cup and bitterness in his bread.

After this he is thought of as already dead.
Happy the person who is no more than a passing stranger
In his heart neither feelings nor thoughts.
The reward for his soul will be in the life beyond. JM

NOVEMBER

Faith and identity

I had embraced Jewish tradition in a serious way when I was thirteen. It was with the fervour of somebody volunteering to join a crusade. This was not a bad thing because a lot of positive energy went into learning about my faith and developing an identity which could not easily be shattered – so I thought. The more tiresome aspect could be better explained by my poor mother who had not actually intended to immerse herself into all details of Jewish dietary laws but found she had to when suddenly a second fridge appeared in the kitchen with three full pages of instructions how to keep a kosher home. I still admire her for her patience with which she endured those surprises which kept overwhelming her over the years whenever the ingredients of my faith identity changed.

In those days I belonged to a small synagogue in Lower Bavaria which served as a safe haven for a couple of families who had narrowly escaped the Holocaust but somehow never managed or wanted to leave Germany. It came as a slight surprise to the congregation's president when I told him at the age of 16 that I felt becoming a rabbi might make a difference for the German Jewish community. I remember the moment during a Yom Kippur (Day of Atonement) service when the old man took my arm and we sat in a pew at the back of the little building which had survived the 1938 'Reichskristallnacht' and always been a little too big for the remaining couple of Jews in that area.

'My son,' I heard him with a serious tone trying to discourage my conviction that the rabbinate was for me, 'I do not like to disillusion you but I dare say that not anybody who prays in front of this ark does it for religious reasons. They use the Jewish tradition to mourn their families whom they survived and by using those old forms they try to come to terms with their guilt for being still alive. There is no faith here but only loneliness and grief.'

A few months later he and his wife died. When they found them in their flat there were still their packed suitcases in the corridor which they had always ready in case they had to leave the country in haste. It was a sign of a fragile coexistence with their non-Jewish environment. And it was a Jewish identity defined less by traditional teaching and more by the overwhelming facts of 20th century history . . .

In time I learnt from my own experience that the development of a religious identity is an ongoing process, a never-ending personal trip to find God between the boundaries of modern organized religion. And I seem to find Him in the most unusual places nowadays – at any rate it's not in my mother's kitchen anymore. (*Walter Homolka*) LB

2 NOVEMBER

Sodom

Everyone knows what the sin of Sodom was. Or do we? It is not mentioned explicitly in the Bible and the idea that it was homosexual activity is actually a Christian tradition. The Rabbis thought it was something much worse – a total abuse of the laws of hospitality. The Sodomites were prosperous, and did not want to share what they had with wayfarers. So they devised some nasty ways of getting rid of them. The following stories about their wickedness also introduce Abraham's servant Eliezer who managed to take them on and beat them at their own game.

They used to look with envy on wealthy men, put them near a leaning wall and push it over on them! . . . They used to entrust balsamum into the keeping of a wealthy man which he would place in his storeroom. In the evening they would come and smell it out like dogs and rob them . . . (The Rabbis record that this explanation was taught by Rabbi Jose in Sepphoris, and the following night there was an outbreak of crimes there using this method!).

There were four judges in Sodom, Shakrai, Shakurai, Zayyafi and Mazle Dina . . . If someone wounded his neighbour they would say to the victim: 'Give him a fee for bleeding you.' Whoever crossed on the ferry had to pay four *zuzim*, but someone who crossed through the water had to pay eight *zuzim*. Once a certain fuller came there. They said to him: 'Give us four *zuzzim* for the ferry.' 'But' he said 'I crossed through the water.' 'Then you have to give us eight *zuzim*!' He refused so they assaulted him. He went to the judge who ordered: 'Give them a fee for bleeding you and the eight *zuzim* for crossing through the water.' Eliezer, Abraham's servant, happened to be visiting Sodom and was attacked. When he went before the judge he was ordered to pay his attackers a fee for bleeding him. So Eliezer took a stone and hit the judge! 'What was that for!' demanded the judge. Said Eliezer: 'The fee you now owe me (for bleeding you) pay to the man who attacked me!'

They also had beds on which travellers slept. If the guest was too long they shortened him by cutting off his feet. If too short, they stretched him! When Eliezer, Abraham's servant, came along he escaped by saying that he had made a vow since the day of his mother's death never to sleep on a bed.

If a poor man came to Sodom every resident gave him a *denar* with his name on it. But they would never sell him any food. When he starved to death they all came and collected their coins.

They had another agreement amongst themselves that whoever invited a stranger to a meal would be stripped of his garments. When Eliezer came there, a banquet was in progress, but they gave him nothing to eat. So he went and sat down next to someone at the end of the table. They asked him: 'Who invited you here?' So he turned to the man next to him and said: 'You invited me'. The man was scared that he would be stripped of his garments, so he grabbed them and fled. And Eliezer repeated this with each of the Sodomites till they had all left and he ate the whole meal.

A certain girl gave some bread to a poor man. When the Sodomites heard this they smeared her with honey and put her on the top of the wall, and bees came and devoured her. That is why the Bible says: 'And God said, the cry of Sodom and Gomorrah, because it is great.' It was the cry of this girl, which led to the destruction of the cities. (Based on *Sanhedrin 109b*) JM

3 NOVEMBER

The dying city

Remember also your Creator in the days of your youth, before the evil days come, and the years draw nigh, when you will say, 'I have no pleasure in them'; before the sun and the light and the moon and the stars are darkened and the clouds return after the rain; in the day when the keepers of the house tremble, and the strong men are bent, and the grinders cease because they are few, and those that look through the windows are dimmed, and the doors on the street are shut; when the sound of the grinding is low, and one rises up at the voice of a bird, and all the daughters of song are brought low; they are afraid also of what is nigh, and terrors are in the way; the almond tree blossoms, the grasshopper drags itself along and desire fails; because man goes to his eternal home, and the mourners go about the streets; before the silver cord is snapped, or the golden bowl is broken, or the pitcher is broken at the fountain or the wheel broken at the cistern, and the dust returns to the earth as it was, and the spirit returns to God who gave it. Vanity of vanities, says the Preacher; all is vanity (*Ecclesiastes 12:1–8*)

That's the way the world ends. Reconcile yourself to it! LB

4 NOVEMBER

Antiques

I once saw an antique shop with interesting things in the window and dropped in. I asked if the owner had any Jewish ritual objects, not expecting much response. To my surprise he was both positive and regretful at the same time. Yes, from time to time he got Jewish ritual objects but he had very little at the moment.

For example, sometimes he had small seven-branched candlesticks. Ah, I pointed out, those, of course, aren't actually Jewish. He looked a bit bewildered so I explained. In the Temple in Jerusalem there used to be a large seven-branched candlestick, the *Menorah*. But since the destruction of the Temple, Jews were forbidden to reproduce the things that were in the Temple. You could make a picture of the *Menorah* but not a three-dimensional model. The candelabra you find in Jewish homes has eight branches for use during the Festival of Chanukah which lasts for eight days – and it has an extra ninth branch as well, usually in front, where the candle was kept that is used to light the others. Any seven-branched candlestick was either Christian or simply an ornament.

He did not look convinced. Still, he pointed out, he had this large glass beaker with a Star of David engraved on it, obviously used for Jewish ritual purposes. I had a look. 'Nice', I agreed, 'but not Jewish – probably it belonged to a Masonic lodge.'

He disappeared into the back of the shop and returned with a plastic bag. 'I have a *shofar*, a ram's horn,' he said, perhaps a little hesitantly by now. Yes, Jews do blow a ram's horn during the Jewish New Year. But this one was carved so that the large open end looked like the mouth of a crocodile. If it had ever been a *shofar*, which seemed very unlikely, someone had long since made it quite unacceptable.

He dipped into the bag again. 'How about this?' 'This' was a wooden pair of tongs, shaped like a blunt pair of scissors, with a kind of scruffy eagle carved on it. 'What is it?' I asked. 'Well I've seen carvings like this on other Jewish ritual objects' he explained, 'so it's probably something ritual as well.' It might have been a kind of candle snuffer, I suppose, but since there is no Jewish candle-snuffing ritual, I had to turn that one down as well.

Finally he found a mantle, used to cover the 'scroll of the law' that is kept in the ark in a synagogue. That at least was Jewish and we all cheered up a bit. But it certainly wasn't worth the price he had paid or the price he wanted.

I felt rather sorry for him, though I suspect that he will still label the same objects as 'Jewish' in the hope of finding a less knowledgeable (and argumentative) customer. He reminded me of those people in the Middle Ages who made a tidy sum out of selling bits of the 'original cross' and other relics. They played on the genuine piety of others and the desire to come closer to some religious object. It is a narrow line between wanting to beautify one's religious life by owning such things and turning them into objects of superstition or worship.

But wherever people care a lot about something, there's usually someone around to make a buck as well. So the next time you are offered a genuine, hand-crafted, oil-anointed, doubly-blessed, sanctified and purified ritual whatsit – ask for a second opinion. JM

5 NOVEMBER

Sex

We live in a world which foists upon us, whether we like it or not, a great deal of explicit sexuality. Most of the time, most of us endeavour to cope intellectually as sensibly as possible, with a barrage of titillation and excitement, but if we are honest with ourselves, we realize that we are aroused by some things, and repulsed by others; violence, deformity and sexuality have a wide range of effects on different people, and it is necessary for each of us to be in touch with our own feelings, and be able to accept them, even if these conflict with responses that we would like to have. If we are unable to understand and accept our own feelings, we may be extremely disturbed and angry when we find them in other people . . .

Sex and marriage often go together, but they are unfortunately not an indissoluble partnership. Sex and sexual feelings are a healthy and normal part of human personality, and some people need to give expression to this side of their nature, irrespective of their marital status, if they are to be able to live fulfilling and rewarding lives. This

does not mean that indiscriminate sexual experience or promiscuity is to be encouraged, for it is usually safer for sexuality to be part of a caring relationship, even if the relationship itself is comparatively ephemeral. The full and complete expression of sexual love occasions extreme vulnerability, and if there is no caring, those involved can be exploited or hurt.
(*Dr Wendy Greengross*, doctor, therapist, lecturer and Trustee of the Cheshire Homes.) LB

6 NOVEMBER

Cause of death

There are few things more obvious, or more thought-provoking, than this little medieval story. When someone lost his brother he was asked: 'What was the cause of his death?' He answered: 'Life.' JM

7 NOVEMBER

At the crossroads

When I was eighteen, I was on my way to buy some potatoes in Dial Road, Tranmere. It was early one winter evening and the crossroads (which was as busy as ever) had to be negotiated in two stages with a pause at the central reservation.

As I waited for a gap in the traffic, my meditation on the evening menu was interrupted by a blinding flash. It was *not* a Pauline revelation – I had been hit in the rear by a speeding car.

Stunned by the hit and run, I pulled myself together and walked nonchalantly into the vegetable shop where I was greeted by the waiting customers with a mixture of gaping stares and consoling gestures.

They were surprised at my composure. *I* was surprised by their great concern. They told me that I had been thrown into the air, turned half-somersault, and had bounced off the bonnet of the car. I had simply not registered the details of the collision.

You see, because I had not seen the approaching vehicle, my muscles were so relaxed that I had escaped without any lasting damage. I was a very lucky man that night!

Sometimes, we waste so much time worrying about the bad things that *might* happen to us that we tense-up spiritually and

forfeit our flexibility and resilience. Perhaps if we relaxed a little and stopped imagining the worst, we might then develop the resilience to face real disaster should it take us unawares.
(*Norman Davies* whom I first met in a Carmelite Priory.)

He was at the harmonium and I was surprised out of my moody meditations by the sweep of Mahler. We were both 'at the crossroads', I found out later, which was a bond. Another bond is that we both converse with God. LB

8 NOVEMBER

Nuremberg

The name of the city of Nuremberg conjures up the history of Nazi Germany. The Nuremberg laws defined the racial 'purity' of the Nazis and prevented any relationship with Jews; the Nuremberg rallies were part of Hitler's strategy of winning the hearts and minds of the German people through displays of power and massive appeals for loyalty; the Nuremberg trials marked the end of the Nazi story as the leaders were found guilty of crimes against humanity.

So it is appropriate that the city should host an international conference on education towards peace. I gave my paper, attended some of the other lectures, met a lot of nice people and joined them for an inter-faith service in one of the oldest little churches in the nearby town of Fürth. (Jews were already banned from living in Nuremberg in the Middle Ages, but were allowed to create a settlement in Fürth. Till the Nazi period some five synagogues functioned there, only to be destroyed during 'Crystal Night' in 1938.)

The service had no particular pattern, simply a series of readings and songs from the Christian, Jewish, Islamic and Buddhist traditions. The mood was serious, with the conference members outnumbered by local people. A simple and moving occasion, celebrating a new mood of mutual respect and recognition between the different religious groups that make up our pluralistic Western European society.

Into my copy of the printed order of service, someone had slipped a little piece of paper – and others turned up afterwards in other copies. It said, in German and somewhat scrambled English: Dear Friends of Peace, it is written: 'Neither is there salvation in any other: for there is none other name under heaven given among men, whereby we must be saved, Jesus Christ! (Acts 4:12)' There followed a little poem in

German exhorting us to seek Jesus, and added a postal address for more information. In brackets at the end was the phrase (Keine Sekte) which I presume means that this organization is not a 'sect'.

I never know whether to laugh or to cry when I come across such notices. I cannot doubt the sincerity of the people who composed it – and went to all the trouble of slotting it into about 600 orders of service. On the other hand, to misunderstand the lesson of such an interfaith service so completely, with its recognition of the equality of all paths to God, is a desperately sad reminder of how much work there is to do in this area. I say 'misunderstand', but they clearly did understand the dangers posed by interfaith dialogue to any monolithic understanding of the path to God. Still to address us as 'Friends of Peace' and end with 'Christ is a Peachemaker' (sic), does seem too much of a contradiction.

The Christians I showed it to were either amused or distressed. That it took place in Nuremberg made the whole thing just that bit more macabre. I don't think they won many converts that evening, but I hope that at least they enjoyed the service. JM

9 NOVEMBER

Thou shalt love thy neighbour as thyself (Leviticus 19:18)

Rabbi Dr Albert Friedlander is the gentlest colleague. 'But what happened to your bitterness and anger?' I asked him, for he had spent his childhood in Nazi Berlin. He said this:

> I learned to fear the world in a small room in Berlin, hiding from those who wanted to hurt and kill me because I was a Jew. It was the 'Night of Crystal', the national pogrom of November 1938, when the Nazis dropped all pretence and earnestly began to destroy the Jewish people. For years, it had been difficult for me to walk through the streets – a small Jewish child could always be attacked. But I grew up in those November nights. I examined the fear I felt, the great insecurity and self-doubt which sometimes made me think: 'Perhaps I am a terrible person; perhaps they are right!' In the darkness, I came to the decision that they were wrong. I loved my family and God. I was compassionate. I had talents. From that moment on I was determined to love myself, so that I could love others. LB

On seeing destruction

The Rabbis taught that one should say a blessing over bad things as well as over good. It is not so easy to see the hand of God in both of these parts of our experience, and harder when seeing others who have been victims of inhumanity. The following is a strange blessing which looks for hope in a time of disaster. It is to be recited on seeing synagogues which remain after a destruction.

> Blessed are You, our Living God, Sovereign of the universe, who '(destroys the possessions of the proud and) preserves the portion of the defenceless.' JM

Remembering

> *For a woman*: God full of compassion whose presence rests over us, grant perfect rest beneath the shelter of Your wings, with the holy and pure, who shine like the stars in the heavens, to . . . who has gone to her everlasting home. Master of mercy, cover her in the shelter of Your wings forever, and bind her soul into the gathering of life. It is God who is her heritage. May she be at peace in her place of rest.

> *For a man*: God full of compassion whose presence rests over us, grant perfect rest beneath the shelter of Your wings, with the holy and pure, who shine like the stars in the heavens, to . . . who has gone to his everlasting home. Master of mercy, cover him in the shelter of Your wings forever, and bind his soul into the gathering of life. It is God who is his heritage. May he be at peace in his place of rest.

You can also light a candle. LB

12 NOVEMBER

Matador

A youth magazine I once helped edit used to send someone round to synagogues on a Saturday morning to listen to the sermons and then write up a kind of 'theatre crit.' They were usually pretty devastating. Part of me sympathizes with the rabbis concerned – it is no easy thing to preach week after week. Part of me sympathizes with the congregants, usually either bored or battered.

One crit. remains forever in my mind – I knew the rabbi and it was true. It goes as follows:

> The rabbi stands like a matador before the great issues of our day.
> And as they rush towards him, he steps aside and lets them pass!

JM

13 NOVEMBER

Joy

> From the Silence of Time, Time's Silver borrow,
> In the heart of Today is the word of Tomorrow
> The Builders of Joy are the children of Sorrow.
> *(William Sharp 1856–1902)*

> 'Those who sow in tears shall reap in joy' *(Psalm 126:5)*

Also confirmed in everybody's experience. LB

14 NOVEMBER

The hunter and the bird

This story comes from a medieval Jewish collection of fables – but the theme is universal.

A hunter once caught a bird, but when he was about to kill it the bird said to him: 'If you set me free, I'll teach you three wise rules to live by: never regret what is past; never believe the unbelievable; never reach for the unattainable.'

The hunter released the bird and it flew up to the top of a tree. The bird thanked him but then added that it had a pearl in its stomach worth a million *zuz*.

Regretting that he had let the bird go the hunter tried to climb the tree, but towards the top the branch snapped and he fell to his death. So the bird had the final word: 'You didn't listen to what I said! You set me free, so why regret what is past. I am so small, how could I possibly have such a valuable pearl within me – never believe the unbelievable! And I warned you never to reach for the unattainable – yet you tried to climb the tree!' JM

15 NOVEMBER

One more step

One More Step
One more step along the world I go,
One more step along the world I go,
From the old things to the new
Keep me travelling along with you.
Chorus

And it's from the old I travel to the new,
Keep me travelling along with you.

Round the corners of the world I turn,
More and more about the world I learn
All the new things that I see
You'll be looking at along with me.
Chorus

As I travel through the bad and good
Keep me travelling the way I should.
Where I see no way to go
You'll be telling me the way, I know.
Chorus

Give me courage when the world is rough,
Keep me loving though the world is tough,
Leap and sing in all I do
Keep me travelling along with you.
Chorus

You are older than the world can be
You are younger than the life in me
Ever old and ever new,
Keep me travelling along with you.
Chorus

I sing this on the way to work, as I travel through the bad and good of my own thoughts and the world outside me. It also helps a lot of anxious people like me. It turns our morning commuter journey into a pilgrimage. For which I thank my friend Sydney Carter who has allowed me to include it. LB

16 NOVEMBER

Gentlemen

A friend of mine in Germany, a doctor, has a rather graphic illustration in her loo showing the spray effect. The following message is in the loo of another friend in London. It's a nice reminder that spirituality begins with showing concern for others – and is nearer to everyday realities than we usually think.

Gentlemen. If your aims are unfocused, you will miss your target.
Please think of those who follow you . . .
Clean the rim of the seat and replace both lids.
Thank you. JM

17 NOVEMBER

Plod

'No wonder of it: sheer plod makes plough down sillion shine.'

I studied these lines of a Gerard Manley Hopkins poem in an English Literature class at school.

My teacher explained that the poet was referring to the beauty of a field etched by the hard labour of a farmer.

When we devour a meal that took hours to prepare . . .
When we take our folded socks from the drawer . . .
When our dishes have miraculously returned sparkling to the cupboards . . .

Do we see the 'plod' of a partner's care, or do we take the 'sillion shine' for granted? (*Norman Davies*) LB

18 NOVEMBER

Committee

There's a running joke in the Jewish community about how much Jews enjoy sitting on committees. One variation in my circles suggests that more people are willing to join a committee to discuss what should take place in the services in the synagogue than actually attend the services themselves. I suppose that in a secular society a committee is more familiar territory and therefore feels safer than a religious service where a God you don't quite believe in is being praised in a language you don't understand – and you don't get a chance to argue the point. So sometimes we put in a prayer or a study passage at the start of the committee to evoke the 'right' mood. That works for some, but just makes others feel uneasy; some boundary has been crossed.

But committees are 'religious' in their own way. Where else do worldly experience, and lots of different egos, come together to try to find some way of sharing in a common task – where everyone will have to give up something for a result to be obtained. It is a great human challenge and a marvellous training ground for any wish we have for improving society – politics, ambition, ideology, stubbornness, bloody-mindedness, good intentions, ingenuity and common sense all have their place and all are contained within a formal structure that holds the worst emotions in check and allows the best solutions to emerge – on a good day!

So here's to one of the greatest 'orders of service' yet offered to suffering humanity, with its awareness of absent friends, its commitment to the honest recording of what people actually said, its sense of the continuity of life beyond the committee itself, its promise of encounters yet to come and its courteous parting:

Apologies
Minutes
Matters arising
Agenda items
Any other business
Date of next Meeting
Vote of thanks to the Chair. JM

The truss

The horrors of religious persecution in England did not match the horrors of the Holocaust in quantity – about five hundred Protestants were martyred under Mary and five hundred Catholics under Elizabeth. But in quality they were equal.

Sometimes one detail is more than enough to taste the evil of the whole, just as one girl, Anne Frank, stands in for six million fellow Jews.

I read the original printing of *Foxe's Book of Martyrs* in Worcester Cathedral. One detail stood out for me – Ridley's truss. Burnings used to take place close by my room in Balliol. Some say a charred door still remains. A plaque in the road outside marks the place.

This passage also taught me the true meaning of 'professor'.

In those days, a truss was a sort of supportive skirt.

> Then Master Ridley, standing as yet in his truss, said to his brother, 'It were best for me to go in my truss still.' 'No,' quoth his brother, 'it will put you to more pain: and the truss will do a poor man good.' Whereunto Dr Ridley said, 'Be it, in the name of God,' and so unlaced himself. Then being in his shirt, he stood upon the foresaid stone, and held up his hand and said, 'O heavenly Father, I give unto thee most hearty thanks, for that thou hast called me to be a professor of thee, even unto death; I beseech thee, Lord God, take mercy on this realm of England, and deliver the same from all her enemies.' . . .
>
> Then they brought a faggot kindled with fire, and laid the same down at Dr Ridley's feet. Thereupon Master Latimer said, 'Be of good comfort, Master Ridley, and play the man, we shall this day light such a candle, by God's grace, in England, as I trust shall never be put out.' And so the fire being given unto them, when Dr Ridley saw the fire flaming up towards him, he cried with a wonderful loud voice, *In manus tuas, Domine, commendo spiritum meum: Domine recipe spiritum meum.* And after, repeated this latter part often in English, 'Lord, Lord, receive my spirit.' LB

20 NOVEMBER

Sermons

> 'To everything there is a season and a time for every purpose under heaven; a time to be born and a time to die . . . (*Ecclesiastes 3:12*)

An Orthodox rabbi with a sense of humour once explained that between each of the extremes described in this famous passage there was a middle position. So that between 'a time to be born and a time to die' was 'life' itself. But what about the verse that says 'there is a time to keep silence and a time to speak' – what is the middle position? He answered: 'a sermon' – presumably because the preacher speaks but may not actually say anything.

Of course this is very unfair – as anyone who has tried to compose a sermon will know. In fact there are any number of uncomfortable anecdotes among professional preachers about the difficulty of the task. 'If you haven't struck oil after ten minutes, stop boring.' Or the lovely story told me by the Rev. Clive Thexton who on retiring from the ministry became the bursar at Leo Baeck College and supplied a generation of rabbis with Christian jokes. In this one the wife returns home from church Sunday morning and her husband asks her: 'What was the sermon about?' To which she replies: 'He didn't say.' JM

21 NOVEMBER

The ABC of charity

> Everybody is full of humanity and good nature when he can relieve misfortune by putting his hand in his neighbour's pocket. Who can bear to see a fellow creature suffering pain and poverty when he can order other fellow creatures to relieve them? Is it in human nature that A should see B in tears and misery and not order C to assist him? (*The Rev. Sydney Smith* 1771–1845)

The most witty and good-hearted of Anglicans – an English unofficial 'saint'. How comforting to meet him in heaven, which he defined as 'eating pâtés de foie gras to the sound of trumpets'. LB

22 NOVEMBER

No flowers, by request

We have quoted the Rev. Simeon Singer's advice on preaching elsewhere (see 11 July). Here are a couple more samples: they apply to anyone who thinks he has a message to put over.

> Take the advice of an old preacher, and don't address your flock as if they were a herd of giraffes. Be not over lavish in the use of figures, and images, and tropes. They are dangerous things to deal with in quantities, and they often fall out with one another, making sad havoc of such sense as you may have put into your sermon. Don't mistake a florid style for eloquence and grace. Besides, it does not suit the English taste, and is usually an outrage upon the English language. That preacher was a fortunate man who, before he had got to his second sermon, received from a candid friend a line cut out of a newspaper column of death advertisements, 'No flowers, by request,' and took the hint.
>
> Do not get into the habit of scolding people in the pulpit, whether they be present or absent. The absent don't know, and the present, after a while, don't care. Reserve rebuke for rare occasions, and it will be more effective. JM

23 NOVEMBER

A walk

If you lift up your eyes to the hills, you might not need other scriptures.

> I'll walk, but not in old heroic traces,
> And not in paths of high morality,
> And not among the half-distinguished faces,
> The clouded forms of long-past history.
>
> I'll walk where my own nature would be leading:
> It vexes me to choose another guide:
> Where the grey flocks in ferny glens are feeding;
> Where the wild wind blows on the mountain-side.
>
> What have those lonely mountains worth revealing?
> More glory and more grief than I can tell:
> The earth that wakes *one* human heart to feeling
> Can centre both the worlds of Heaven and Hell.
>
> (*Emily Bronte*) LB

Little white lie

24 NOVEMBER

When I told this story on the BBC World Service I got a lot of shocked responses – but here goes anyway.

In the Book of Genesis, three 'angels' visit Abraham to inform him that his wife Sarah, ninety years old and barren, will have a child! Sarah overhears them and starts to laugh.

> They said to him, 'Where is Sarah your wife?' And he said, 'Look, she is in the tent.' So he (*sic*) said, 'I will surely return to you in the spring and your wife Sarah will have a son.' Sarah was listening at the entrance to the tent behind him. Now Abraham and Sarah were old, well on in life, and it had ceased to be with Sarah after the manner of women. So Sarah laughed to herself, saying, 'After I am past having pleasure, and my husband is old?' The Eternal said to Abraham, 'Why does Sarah laugh, saying, 'Shall I really give birth, since I am old?' (*Genesis 18:9–13*)

The Rabbis spotted something in the text. Whereas Sarah had said that 'her husband was old', God reported her as saying, 'since I am old'. So they explained that God had told a little white lie so as to preserve *shalom bayyit*, 'peace in the house'. (If God had reported Sarah as calling Abraham past it, real trouble might have broken out between them.)

It's in the biblical text, and the Rabbis are only making explicit what is actually there in black and white. But people got awfully fussed at the idea that God could tell a lie, even a little white one. Which is just a reminder that the Bible is much braver, and more interesting, than we sometimes give it credit for. And how sad that the first thing that seems to go when people become religious is their sense of humour. JM

Consent

25 NOVEMBER

> There is a reality outside the world, that is to say, outside space and time, outside man's mental universe, outside any sphere whatsoever that is accessible to human faculties.
>
> Corresponding to this reality, at the centre of the human heart, is the longing for an absolute good, a longing which is always there and is never appeased by any object in this world . . .

Just as the reality of this world is the sole foundation of facts, so that other reality is the sole foundation of good.

That reality is the unique source of all the good that can exist in this world: that is to say, all beauty, all truth, all justice, all legitimacy, all order, and all human behaviour that is mindful of obligations.

Those minds whose attention and love are turned towards that reality are the sole intermediary through which good can descend from there and come among men.

Although it is beyond the reach of any human faculties, man has the power of turning his attention and love towards it . . .

It is a power which is only real in this world in so far as it is exercised. The sole condition for exercising it is consent.
(*Simone Weil 1909–1943*)

Do you consent? Do you dare? LB

26 NOVEMBER

You can't take it with you

A Rabbi called Samuel had a go at his colleague Rab Judah for being too serious: 'Keen scholar! Don't delay your eating or your drinking, for this world which we are destined to leave is like a wedding.'

It seems to have been a favourite idea of the Rabbis – here is Rab advising Rab Hamnuna: 'My son, if you have the means, enjoy yourself. For there is no pleasure when you're in the grave, and death does not delay. And if you say to yourself: "I will leave a sum to my children", in the grave who is going to thank you for it! People are like the grass of the field, some blossom and some fade.'
(*Eruvin 54a*) JM

27 NOVEMBER

Gender

We need to understand each other's worlds, and not least each other's gender; how it feels to be another sex, female, male or in between. Most of us have most of them within us.

As a rabbi, I have relied on Jewish women in all my work. They have been my faithful helpers, and most of my congregation. But it is only lately I have tried to understand them.

> We follow the precepts of our mothers and are moulded by the arguments of our daughters. We sometimes feel like rudderless boats being tossed hither and thither, pulled one way by the needs of our family, pulled in another by the dictates of society, while at the same time being told that we must be our own person and make choices about our own way of life. And making choices and putting yourself first is really very difficult for someone who has been brought up to believe that a woman's role is to put someone else, husband, child or parent, before her own wishes or needs.
>
> Nowadays, we Jewish mothers are not only not trams, we're not even buses with a route to follow. Cars we're not either, because cars have more freedom than most Jewish mothers. Perhaps we are only taxis, being propelled quite haphazardly from destination to destination by something inside us insisting that we got to a particular place, only to arrive and be sent once again to yet another destination. (*Dr Wendy Greengross*) LB

28 NOVEMBER

Forward planning

'Old Chinese proverbs' seem to be available for most circumstances. I'm sure most of them are genuine, but you sometimes have the feeling that they get invented to match the circumstances. I found a version of the following, described as an anonymous poem from 500 BC, on a 'season's greetings' card sent out by a university.

> If you plan for one year ahead, then you should sow a seed.
> If you plan for ten years ahead, then you should plant a tree.
> If you plan for one hundred years ahead, then you should educate the people. JM

The worker

29 NOVEMBER

Swami Vivekananda was invited to the World Parliament of Religions held in Chicago in 1893. Reluctantly invited because Hinduism was not held to be a 'higher' religion. He never went back east but remained in the west as a missionary in reverse.

He described four paths to God: Jnana through the intellect; Bhakti, through love; Hatha, through the body; and Karma, through duty. Most religious arguments are just disputes between devotees of these different paths, though all are valid and lead to the same reality.

I think Rabbinic Judaism is an example of Karma Yoga. Vivekananda takes Buddhism as his example. The important thing is to do the work for its own sake, without reward.

> All the prophets of the world, except Buddha, had external motives to move them to unselfish action. The prophets of the world, with this single exception, may be divided into two sets – one set holding that they are incarnations of God come down on earth, and the other holding that they are only messengers from God, and both draw their impetus for work from outside, expect reward from outside, however highly spiritual may be the language they use. But Buddha is the only prophet who said . . . 'Believe not because some old manuscripts are produced, believe not because it is your national belief, because you have been made to believe it from your childhood; but reason it all out, and after you have analysed it, then, if you find that it will do good to one and all, believe it, live up to it, and help others to live up to it.' He works best who works without any motive, neither for money, nor for fame, nor for anything else; and when a man can do that, he will be a Buddha, and out of him will come the power to work in such a manner as will transform the world. This man represents the very highest ideal of Karma-Yoga.
>
> LB

Norton 1, Emperor of the United States

30 NOVEMBER

I learnt the following story from an article by Dr Louis Hermann, at the time Principal of the High School, Cape Town. He contributed it to an otherwise somewhat solemn collection of essays presented in 1942 to the Chief Rabbi, the Very Rev. Dr J. H. Hertz on the occasion of his seventieth Birthday.

It seems that one Joshua Abraham Norton, a Jew from South Africa who had emigrated to America, after a series of business disasters became convinced that he was the Emperor of the United States. This in itself is probably not uncommon, but what is less common is that the good people of San Francisco seemingly went along with this peculiar idea and took him very much to their hearts. On 17 September, 1859 he put the following proclamation in the news column of the San Francisco Bulletin:

> At the peremptory request and desire of a large majority of the citizens of these United States, I, Joshua Norton, formerly of Algoa Bay, Cape of Good Hope, and now for the last 9 years and 10 months past of San Francisco, California, declare and proclaim myself Emperor of these United States; and in virtue of the authority thereby in me vested, do hereby order and direct the representatives of the different states of the Union to assemble in Musical Hall of this City on the first day of February next, then and there to make such alterations in the existing laws of the Union as may ameliorate the evils under which the country is labouring and thereby cause confidence to exist both at home and abroad in our stability and integrity. NORTON THE FIRST, EMPEROR OF THE UNITED STATES.

Over the next twenty years he continued to produce a whole series of proclamations dealing with all issues affecting the home affairs and foreign policy of the United States. He wore a special uniform (a blue military coat with bright brass buttons and gold epaulettes, a sword of state and a tall white hat with a plume) and made public appearances where everyone treated him with due deference. He was an affable man, people enjoyed his company and those who had done business with him when he was wealthy supported him. When he died in 1880 ten thousand attended his funeral, people from all classes of society. And when the cemetery was removed fifty years later, a monument was erected to his memory.

Robert Louis Stevenson visited San Francisco in 1879 and met the Emperor. His record is not only a tribute to this man, who seems to have lived out the fantasy of so many, but also to the people of San Francisco who treated their Emperor so well:

Of all our visitors, I believe I preferred Emperor Norton; the very mention of whose name reminds me I am doing scanty justice to the folks of San Francisco. In what other city would a harmless madman who supposed himself emperor of the two Americas have been so fostered and encouraged? Where else would even the people of the streets have respected the poor soul's illusion? Where else would he have been suffered to attend and address the exhibition days of schools and colleges? Where else in God's green earth, have taken his pick of restaurants, ransacked the bill of fare, and departed scatheless? They tell me he was even an exacting patron, threatening to withdraw his custom when dissatisfied; and I can believe it, for his face wore an expression distinctly gastronomical. Pinkerton had received from his monarch a cabinet appointment; I have seen the brevet, wondering mainly at the good nature of the printer who had executed the forms, and I think my friend was at the head either of foreign affairs or education: it mattered, indeed, nothing, the presentation being in all offices identical. It was at a comparatively early date that I saw Jim in the exercise of his public functions. His Majesty entered the office – a portly, rather flabby man, with the face of a gentleman, rendered unspeakably pathetic and absurd by the great sabre at his side and the peacock's feather in his hat.

'I have called to remind you, Mr Pinkerton, that you are somewhat in arrear of taxes,' he said, with old-fashioned, stately courtesy.

'Well, Your Majesty, what is the amount?' asked Jim; and when the figure was named (it was generally two or three dollars), paid upon the nail and offered a bonus in the shape of Thirteen Star.

'I am always delighted to patronize native industries,' said Norton the First. 'San Francisco is public-spirited in what concerns its emperor; and indeed, sir, of all my domains, it is my favourite city.' JM

DECEMBER

The lesson

In Monkwearmouth I saw a picture of the Venerable Bede teaching his novices. (I know he's now been canonized but he was such a modest man I prefer his old title. 'Venerable' suits him. So many saints are being proclaimed now in the West, and so many assume that title in the East; the category of saints is becoming overcrowded. Modest 'Venerables' however remain rare.)

But back to the picture. It reminded me of a Yiddish children's song I learnt at Hebrew School, though some of my teachers weren't that gentle and threw things. But then I wasn't gentle with them either. That song was important. I learnt early on the tears, the Hebrew letters of Jewish history.

A small fire burns in the stove
And the room is hot.
And the Rabbi teaches little children
The Hebrew letters.

'Listen children, remember dearest,
What you learn here.
Repeat once more, and still once more, the sounds of
"kametz, alef, o".

When you children grow older
You'll understand for yourself
How many tears lie in these letters
And how much pain.'
(*Mark Warshawsky,* 1848–1907) LB

A guest

One time when Hillel left his students, they asked him where he was going. He replied, 'To do a kindness to a guest in my house.' They asked him, 'Do you have a guest every day?' 'Yes,' he replied, 'is not the soul a guest in the body. Today it is here, tomorrow it is gone.'
(*Leviticus Rabbah, Behar 34:3*)

In another version of this, Hillel says that he is about to do a pious deed.

What? Take a bath! His students are somewhat nonplussed till he explains that it is like someone employed to polish the statues of kings in their theatres and circuses. He gets paid for polishing them and even honoured. So how much more should we polish and wash our body which is created in the image of God (*Genesis 9:6*). (*ibid*). JM

3 DECEMBER

Sin

Black is the raven, black is the rook
Black is old Hitler the world's biggest crook.
But blacker the swine, he's worse than a louse
Who pinches the glasses from this public house.

Pub sign from the last war (World War II) – now, of course, politically incorrect. There was a shortage of everything domestic at the time so the biggest offenders were women who hid them in their handbags, to the outrage of serious drinkers. I do not know the author. LB

4 DECEMBER

Of the making of books

A poor man came to a rabbi with the manuscript of a commentary he had written on the Book of Job. In Orthodox circles it is the practice to have letters of recommendation from recognized religious authorities at the front of such a commentary and the writer asked for one. After considering the book for some time, the rabbi agreed and the commentary on Job was published.

A year later the man returned, this time with a commentary on the Book of Ruth and a similar request. The rabbi refused. 'But you haven't even looked at my commentary!' complained the man. The rabbi explained, 'I know what it will be like because I read your last one. When you come to me then you were in a terrible financial situation and I knew that you needed my recommendation to get the book published. But now you are doing quite well so it is not so important. Besides, I figured that Job had suffered so much he could put up with your commentary as well – but Ruth! why does she need to suffer?' JM

Before a picture of Jesus in prison

In prison in 1942, the Dutch Carmelite Titus Brandsma, awaiting transportation to concentration camp and death, for printing forbidden news about the deportation of the Jews, wrote these verses. He was sixty and alone, but God was with him in his cell. He had never been so content!

I hope he is canonized with Franz Jägerstätter who refused conscription because he also felt there were limits beyond which a believer could not go without losing his soul. For me both are Catholic saints of the war years.

O Jesus, as I gaze at you,
I feel again my love for you,
and that your own heart's love for me,
makes me your very special friend.

I know the suffering that love brings
and that such suffering does me good
because it makes me more like you,
and brings me to your kingdom.

I am fortunate in my fate
since I forget the suffering
knowing that this lonely state
unites me, God, to You.

Yes, you can leave me lonely here
surrounded by the chill and cold
with no comforters standing by,
because then I'll be alone with you.

Jesus, because you've come so close
I was never so near to you.
Stay with me, stay, O Jesus sweet,
your nearness makes up for all I'll meet. LB

6 DECEMBER

If I knew him . . .

Yedaiah Penini was a poet and philosopher who lived in Provence at the end of the 14th and beginning of the 15th century. The Hebrew of this aphorism by him is even pithier:

> *yedateev v'hayyeeteev*, 'If I knew Him I would be Him!' JM

7 DECEMBER

The celestial city

I used to sit for hours in The Hague in front of Vermeer's view of Delft. It was as detailed and commonplace as a tourist photograph and yet it was the celestial city of Bunyan, Vaughan and every mystic. I could never work out how he put this world and the next together without a tell-tale join.

The Dutch poet Albert Verwey (1865–1937) felt the same.

A town on the other side
with towers, gates and roofs
with great barges and quays,
cloud, shadow and sunlight.

We see from the opposite bank
even the marks in her walls
her cool colour glazes
what's distant, what's nearby.

Just as she outshines
her image in the water
so will God's city later
outshine this town of mine. LB

8 DECEMBER

The art of the parable

A 'Maggid' was a wandering preacher who would teach in the synagogues of Eastern Europe. Jacob ben Wolf Kranz (1741–1804) (see also 'Something for Nothing' 26 July) was highly skilled at commenting on the weekly reading from the Bible and illustrating it with his marvellous parables. He was once asked how he managed to find exactly the right parable to fit the situation he was describing. His reply:

> There are two ways to shoot an arrow at a target. One method is to find a wall, draw a target on it, step back and shoot. The other is to find a wall, shoot the arrow at it, and then draw the target around it. JM

9 DECEMBER

The tambourine

I have tripped over the Salvation Army at odd times in my life – when I was trying to trace a missing person, when I lost all my money in a strange town and had nowhere to sleep, and on a harbour front, when three bonneted lasses did a poker-faced dance with tambourines, so delicately decorous and yet suggestive my jaw dropped. Or was it my own lewd mind? The other matelots in the crowd looked rather roundeyed too.

Anyway I like them and respect them. And so did Vachel Lindsay (1879–1931), the poet of the American Middle West. I'd like to jig to those tambourines in heaven. I hope Vachel Lindsay does too. He was so disillusioned he committed suicide and deserved a decent break.

General William Booth Enters Into Heaven
(To be sung to the tune of 'The Blood of the Lamb' with indicated instruments.)

(Brass drum beaten loudly)
Booth led boldly with his big brass drum –
(Are you washed in the blood of the Lamb?)
The Saints smiled gravely and they said: 'He's come.'
(Are you washed in the blood of the Lamb?)
Walking lepers followed, rank on rank,
Lurching bravos from the ditches dank,
Drabs from the alleyways and drug fiends pale –
Minds still passion-ridden, soul-powers frail: –
Vermin-eaten saints with moldy breath,
Unwashed legions with the ways of Death –
(Are you washed in the blood of the Lamb?)

(Banjos)
Every slum had sent its half-a-score
The round world over. (Booth had groaned for more.)
Every banner that the wide world flies
Bloomed with glory and transcendent dyes.
Big-voiced lasses made their banjos bang,
Tranced, fanatical they shrieked and sang:–
'Are you washed in the blood of the Lamb?'
Hallelujah! It was queer to see
Bull-necked convicts with that land make free.
Loons with trumpets blowed a blare, blare, blare
On, on upward thro' the golden air!
(Are you washed in the blood of the Lamb?)

(Bass drum slower and softer.)
Booth died blind and still by faith he trod,
Eyes still dazzled by the ways of God.
Booth led boldly, and he looked the chief
Eagle countenance in sharp relief,
Beard a-flying, air of high command
Unabated in that holy land.

(Sweet flute music)
Jesus came from out the court-house door,
Stretched his hands above the passing poor.
Booth saw not, but led his queer ones there
Round and round the mighty court-house square.
Then, in an instant all that blear review
Marched on spotless, clad in raiment new.
The lame were straightened, withered limbs uncurled
And blind eyes opened on a new, sweet world.

(Bass drum louder.)
Drabs and vixens in a flash made whole!
Gone was the weasel-head, the snout, the jowl!
Sages and sibyls now, and athletes clean,
Rulers of empires, and of forests green!

(Grand chorus of all instruments. Tambourines to the foreground.)
The hosts were sandalled, and their wings were fire!
(Are you washed in the blood of the Lamb?)
But their noise played havoc with the angel-choir.
(Are you washed in the blood of the Lamb?)

Oh, shout Salvation! It was good to see
Kings and Princes by the Lamb set free.
The banjos rattled and the tambourines
Jing-jing-jingled in the hands of Queens.

(Reverently sung, no instruments.)
And when Booth halted by the curb for prayer
He saw his Master thro' the flag-filled air.
Christ came gently with a robe and crown
For Booth the soldier, while the throng knelt down.
He saw King Jesus. They were face to face,
And he knelt a-weeping in that holy place.
Are you washed in the blood of the Lamb? LB

10 DECEMBER

More lays of Israel

Max Boshwitz lived in Memphis, Tennessee and published a little collection of his own poems under the title *The Lays of Israel* (see 4 August).

Some of his introductions give a fascinating insight into his generous sympathies – such as the one for the poem 'The Dying Shame', 'Written for the Jewish Spectator':

> In 1873, when the yellow fever was hurling thousands of souls into eternity, a beautiful woman who went by the name of Frances Livingston, who had led a life of shame, was dying of this fatal disease in one of the houses of ill-fame in Memphis.
>
> She was of Jewish birth, and on her deathbed sent for Rabbi Samfield and Mr A. E. Frankland, asking these men to bury her in the Hebrew cemetery and to divide her worldly goods among the Jewish orphans.
>
> Barely had these gentlemen promised to carry out her request, than her eyes closed in death and she was buried on consecrated ground, amid the many who fell victims in the epidemic.

Another poem is dedicated 'To The Brave Lad Of The Monroe', one Ferdinand J. Kuehn, the wireless operator of the steamer who saved the life of a woman passenger by giving her his lifebelt when it sank after a collision with the Nantucket.

. . . And though this noble lad we've lost
He lives in thought sublime;
Though he has paid with life the cost,
He's carved a lasting shrine.

No act in ancient chivalry,
Can boast a greater deed,
Than she who quoths: 'he died for me!
Without an earthly meed.'

For he took off his saving belt,
A life on ship to save,
His heart to her appeal did melt,
Then sank beneath the wave!

'Tis not the life that lives its span
That shows the hero great;
But life that dies to save the man,
That goes to meet his fate.

'No trumpet's blare' his heart did sway,
Life's chances were but few
To give this precious belt away –
Meant death to him, he knew.

Yet placed he belt around her hip,
Then lowered her in sea;
While he went down the fatal ship,
To his eternity!

In thought he then his wireless wrote,
To kindred with a sigh;
'The Neptune fogs the Monroe smote,
I sink with her – goodbye!'

In his rather modest preface Mr Boshwitz compares this venture, presumably the publishing of his poems, to a ship at sea. I hope that the inclusion of these extracts will fulfil the wish of his closing words.

I steer my bark upon the open sea,
To chance the waves that may upon me break;
No gentle zephyrs may e'er come to me!
No argosies may follow in my wake.

The ships that pass may wave me no salute,
  Deride my craft that tosses on the deep;
My puling cry seems like some tuneless lute,
  Too small the sail upon the waves to leap.

My fragile boat may never mooring reach!
  The lashing gales a sailor's voyage blast;
Yet have I hope in souls that stroll the beach,
  Will find on strand a fragment of my mast. JM

11 DECEMBER

The tomb

In Westminster Cathedral lie the earthly remains of Henry Cardinal Manning, once Anglican Archdeacon of Chichester, a proud, ambitious Prince of the Church who fought for the poor. On his tomb rests the curious object of that ambition.

> The funeral was the occasion of a popular demonstration such as has rarely been witnessed in the streets of London. The route of the procession was lined by vast crowds of working people, whose imaginations, in some instinctive manner, had been touched. Many who had hardly seen him declared that in Cardinal Manning they had lost their best friend. Was it the magnetic vigour of the dead man's spirit that moved them? Or was it his valiant disregard of common custom and those conventional reserves and poor punctilios which are wont to hem about the great? Or was it something untameable in his glances and in his gestures? Or was it, perhaps, the mysterious glamour lingering about him of the antique organization of Rome? For whatever cause, the mind of the people had been impressed; and yet, after all, the impression was more acute than lasting. The Cardinal's memory is a dim thing today. And he who descends into the crypt of that Cathedral which Manning never lived to see, will observe, in the quiet niche with the sepulchral monument, that the dust lies thick on the strange, the incongruous, the almost impossible object which, with its elaborations of dependent tassels, hangs down from the dim vault like some forlorn and forgotten trophy – the Hat. (*Lytton Strachey* 1880–1932) LB

Squeamish

Having studied medicine I had to get over my squeamishness about the reality of bodily functions. I can understand people's reluctance to know about such things, though we seem to end up with a lot of lavatory humour as a result. The problem is not new, as this challenging Rabbinic story shows.

> Rabbi Huna asked his son Rabbah why he did not go to the classes of Rabbi Hisda who was said to be a very clever teacher. His son answered, 'When I go to him, he speaks of mundane things, for example about certain natural functions of the digestive organs and what one should do with regard to them.' His father replied, 'He concerns himself with the life of God's creatures and you call that a mundane matter! That's all the more reason for studying with him!' (*Shabbat 82a*) JM

Kensington Gardens

Kensington Gardens were haunted for me by the kind ghost of a civil servant turned satirist. Humbert Wolfe (1885–1940) taught me to regard both the pompous statues and the poor old men with kindness. I lived opposite those gardens and shall always be in his debt. He was a gentleman.

The Old Yachtsman
I said to the old
man, pushing a yacht
with a long pole into
the Round Pond, 'What

can be the use of
that?' 'Far more,'
the old fellow said,
'than you'd think for.

Life isn't so pretty
for old poor men
that you'd blame 'em for playing
like children again.'

Queen Victoria
Queen Victoria's
statue is
the work of her
daughter Beatrice.

The shape's all wrong,
and the crown don't fit,
but – bless her old heart!
she was proud of it. LB

14 DECEMBER

Why did Cain kill Abel?

The Bible records the first murder but there is a strange gap in the text: 'Cain said to Abel his brother . . . and it came to pass when they were in the field, Cain rose up against Abel his brother and killed him.' (Genesis 4:8) The rabbis tried to fill the gap – what did Cain and Abel talk about that led to the murder? Their answers define the same issues over which people and peoples still murder each other today.

They said, 'Come let us divide up the world'. One took the immovable property, the land, the other took the movable property. One said: 'The earth on which you are standing is mine!' The other said: 'The clothes you are wearing come from wool from my sheep!' So this one went on: 'Take those clothes off!' The other said: 'Take to the air!' In the following fight, Cain killed Abel.

Rabbi Joshua of Sichnin said in the name of Rabbi Levi: Both shared the immovable and movable property. So what did they quarrel over? Both of them said: 'It will be on my territory that the Temple for God will be built!'

But the rabbis also used the story to ask the age-old question – why does not God intervene to prevent such violent acts?

Rabbi Simeon ben Yochai examined the verse where God tells Cain, 'the voice of your brother's blood cries out to Me from the ground'. He commented: This thing is hard to say and even harder to explain. It is like two wrestlers who fought each other before the king. If the king had so wished it he could have separated them – but he did not

> do so. The one overcame the other and killed him, then cried out, 'who will plead my case before the king!' That is what God really said to Cain: 'the voice of your brother's blood cries out (not 'to me' but) against Me from the ground'. JM

15 DECEMBER

The party

I was an adolescent at a posh party where I was socially out of my depth. Awkwardly I retreated away from the chattering centre to the surrounding bookcases. To avoid embarrassment I buried my nose in a book, any book. I found myself reading the first page of *The Pilgrim's Progress.* I had read it long ago at school, but this time it spoke to me. The world was a wilderness, I felt as if I wore rags and I cried out the same question. It was the beginning of my pilgrim's progress too.

> As I walked through the wilderness of this world, I lighted on a certain place where was a den, and I laid me down in that place to sleep, and as I slept I dreamed a dream. I dreamed and behold I saw a man clothed with rags (*Isaiah 64:6*) standing in a certain place, with his face from his own house, a book in his hand, and a great burden upon his back (*Psalm 38:4*). I looked, and saw him open the book, and read therein; and as he read he wept and trembled, and not being able longer to contain, he broke out with a lamentable cry, saying, 'What shall I do?' (*Acts 16:30–31*) LB

16 DECEMBER

Social worker

Living in a 'welfare state', we take for granted some of the services available to support people in trouble – or at least we know what should be available. But so many of these provisions are only a century old, and the product of amazing pioneers, often women, who set out to help the poor and destitute of their times. One such woman was Lilian Wald (1867–1940).

In some ways her story is typical. She was the daughter of German–Jewish immigrants to the United States and led a comfortable upper middle-class life. She became a nurse and then dedicated her life to helping the immigrants on the Lower East Side of New York. As well as creating the famous Nurses (Henry Street) Settlement, she tried to tackle the roots of social deprivation, campaigning against child labour, supporting trade unions and generally being at the forefront of all attempts at social reform.

This extract from her case notes shows the effect of her day to day dedication – and the description of the problems she had to confront is no different from those in any one of the trouble spots in the world today:

> Visit and care of typhoid patient, 182 Ludlow Street. Visit to 7 Hester Street where in rooms of Nathan S. found two children with measles. After much argument succeeded in bathing these two patients and the sick baby. The first time in their experience. They insisted no water and soap could be applied to anyone with measles for seven days.
>
> Gave tickets for Hebrew Sanitarium excursion to Mrs Davis and three children, Mrs Schneider and five children for Tuesday's excursion but five of the seven children are nearly naked, I am convinced, have no apparel in their possession. So we will make their decent appearance possible for the picnic.
>
> Many of these people have kept from begging and it is not uncommon to meet families to whom not a dollar has come in in seven months – the pawn shop tickets telling the progress of their fall, beginning some months back with the pawning of a gold watch, ending with the woman's waist.
>
> The multitude of unemployed grows and many who had been able to live for the first few months are now at the end of their resources. However we are glad in one respect, that having no money to engage the midwife they allow us to furnish doctors . . . who do intelligent good work.
>
> In a rear tenement, top floor, on Allen Street, a doctor found a woman, a Mrs Weichert, crazy and ill with pneumonia and typhoid; cared for by her 14-year-old daughter. She had been crazy for some time and the husband and child had kept it secret, fearing she would be forcibly taken to an asylum were it known. Though she died in a few days, I shall always be glad that one doctor told us in time so that she was made human and decent, bedding given and the child assisted to making her dwelling fit for habitation before her end.

JM

A sane voice

17 DECEMBER

In the kitsch of Christmas (robins on twigs, cardinals carousing, reindeer) let us remember Christopher Smart (1722–1771) who saw too many visions and was put in a madhouse. This is one of them. The last lines seem to me, a non-Christian, the best summary of Christianity I know.

Nature's decorations glisten
  Far above their usual trim;
Birds on box and laurels listen,
  As so near the cherubs hymn . . .

Spinks and ouzles sing sublimely,
  'We too have a Saviour born',
Whiter blossoms burst untimely
  On the blest Mosaic thorn.

God all-bounteous, all-creative,
  Whom no ills from good dissuade,
Is incarnate, and a native
  Of the very world he made. LB

Anneliese

18 DECEMBER

She was an astonishing woman. Born in Germany in 1911, Anneliese Debray was deeply committed to the Catholic women's youth movement and continued to work with them underground when the Nazis banned the organization. After the war she became the director of the Hedwig Dransfeld Haus, a Catholic centre in Bendorf near Koblenz, and devoted her enormous energies to making it a place for reconciliation – between Germans and Poles, Germans and French, and later Germans and Jews. That is how Lionel and I came to meet her and to work with her over the years on any number of projects. Incidentally, in her spare time she and her sister raised nine orphans – she once told me, with a certain amount of pride mixed with irony, when one of her daughters had an illegitimate child, that she had just become a 'grandfather'.

My favourite memories are of sitting in her apartment at midnight at the end of a conference day as Anneliese opened a bottle of wine and emptied the contents of a tin of goulash into a saucepan. Meanwhile her impossibly aggressive dogs, Bintchen and later Blackie, would take sightings on your shoes. It was in those quiet moments, too, that she unburdened herself of some of her worries about keeping the House going and her struggles for recognition as a lay woman in a highly structured and hierarchic church.

She retired as Director having mistakenly spent too much time looking for a successor – but no one could do what she did or live up to her own expectations so she was always disappointed. When finally she let go, she found new outlets for her energies – especially in visiting Israel and seeking ways of creating understanding between Israelis and Arabs. Typically she died suddenly, on the 18th of February 1985, on a railway platform in Hamburg about to board a train for yet another business meeting. A marvellous way to go. Anneliese was a 'doer' not a 'talker'. She once wrote:

> Peace is something to be worked at daily, hourly. Through 'wishing-to-be' rather than 'wishing-to-have'; through small steps; through the courage to take initiatives, and without intermission. We need to encourage each other. JM

19 DECEMBER

Simple things

My friend and teacher Leslie Shepard sends his friends small pamphlets with his thoughts at Christmas. Unlike the usual cards with their robins, carousing cardinals and vapid words, they are pertinent to my existence. I received this at the same time as a food processor.

> We live in a sophisticated age, in which technological innovation has given us superb apparatus to take the tedium out of everyday life and enhance our leisure.
>
> Nowadays, quite ordinary homes have an elaborate cooker, perhaps a microwave oven, a washing machine, maybe a dishwasher. Even an unemployed household may have a radio or television. More affluent homes will have colour television, a video-recorder, home computer, sometimes two motor cars, and other miracles of technical convenience.
>
> Yet these wonderful products of the consumer society have not brought greater human happiness – indeed, quite the reverse.

Somehow, in spite of an amazing scientific and technical leap forward, there has been no comparable breakthrough in human behaviour and happiness. At no time in history has there been greater boredom, selfishness, cultural decadence, drug addiction and crime. Years ago, when washing clothes was a heavy task, people sang while they worked. Whoever sings while watching a washing machine?

Surrounded by technological complexity and the endless demands of consumerism, we have lost contact with simple things of life which do not have a price tag and extended credit. The world of the senses and spirit is free, and the simplest pleasures are the most enduring.

There is the warmth of sunlight after the rigours of winter, the perennial miracle of growth and renewal, the astonishing greenness of the grass. Who needs an expensive painting on the walls when you can look at the ever-changing panorama of the clouds outside the window, or the spectacle of a colourful sunset?

In a world of plenty, in which others starve, we stuff jaded palates with exotic foods, but what can compare with the taste of a slice of home cooked bread and a cup of tea? And what is the mystery of heat that transforms bread into the delight of hot buttered toast? A baked potato, preferably home grown, can be a meal for an epicure.

Our sense of smell tends to be overwhelmed by artificial perfumes, but we can still enjoy the clean fresh air of the country on a spring morning or the aroma of home cooking that is a better guide than an automatic oven. Poets have written ecstatically about the fragrance of a rose.

There is the friendly warmth of a fire in winter, and it is sad to think of so many homeless people without a place at a fireside. There is the joy of meeting old friends, and the loving contact of a friendly embrace. We should give thanks for the simple things.

I live alone and may see relatives or old friends only once a year. People say, 'Aren't you lonely?' but I tell them that I have thousands of friends in my room. I have a large collection of books, and when I want company I can always take down a good book and find pleasure in the meeting of minds and emotions. For those who spend their money on smoking or drinking instead of buying books, there are still large public libraries in most cities.

There is great satisfaction in being self-sufficient and living within one's means, avoiding unnecessary demands on the welfare state. I pay all bills promptly and if I can't afford something I do without it. Because I do not rely upon other people, I often find time and energy to do something for others less fortunate. There is a unique pleasure in helping other people. And it is good to reduce one's own needs to a minimum, to be prudent but not miserly.

Of course, life is not so easy for those trying to rear a family and meet the ever escalating costs of living and the insatiable demands of the kids. The peer group pressure and the vast industry of pop culture have more influence than parents these days, but one should still try to encourage the kids to create their own culture. Whatever they make and do themselves has more value than expensive toys rapidly discarded. And the idea of selfless service to other people may be unfashionable to kids reared on the gospel of self-indulgence, but it is ultimately more satisfying.

Too many possessions perpetuate the endless cycle of desire and fear – desire for more, and the fear of losing what one has. Better to think of possessions as something rented for a lifetime, to be used wisely but without dependence. We can't take them with us, and as one grows older it is important to discover what will last.

The way we live affects the way we die, and it is sad to see people unprepared for death, unwilling to leave and totally bewildered at what it has all meant. Yet the simple truths of life are still valid.

Beyond the world of sensory life is the deeper fulfilment of those elementary ethical laws which are the basis of great religions.

Simple pleasures reduce one's dependence on material possessions and bring great satisfaction. Lasting happiness comes from a life devoted to duty, responsibility, kindness and concern for others.

The proof is also simple. Just try it! LB

20 DECEMBER

Not by might

In the darkest moments of winter we hope for the light, and many religious traditions are built around waiting to celebrate this moment of change. In the Jewish calendar we celebrate Chanukah, the Festival of Lights, for eight days. It commemorates the struggle of the Maccabees against Antiochus Epiphanes and the rededication of the Temple in Jerusalem. Instead of focusing on the military victory, the Rabbis chose to remember a miracle, how the last flask of sanctified oil kept the candelabrum in the Temple burning for eight days till more could be prepared. The story of the rebellion is told in the Book of Maccabees and it deserves a moment's consideration – if it had failed, there would be no Judaism – or Christianity or Islam for that matter.

An eight-branched candelabrum is lit in Jewish homes during the festival, with an additional candle being added every day till all eight are burning. Light triumphs, and, appropriately, the motto of the Festival comes from the prophet Zechariah: 'Not by might, nor by power, but by My spirit, says the Lord of hosts.' (*Zechariah 4:6*) JM

21 DECEMBER

Jumping off

In a moment of bravado I decided to go parachuting and signed up at my local club. A colleague at work said there was nothing to it. 'The problem is not what happens during the first 3000 feet, but what happens during the last six inches'.

The following weekend was spent along with other students, training in the expectation that it would culminate with our first jump. In between bouts of leaping off platforms to learn how to land we had exercises to teach us what to do if things went wrong.

Then came the first jump. Along with two other trainees I got into a tiny plane, which having bumped across a grass strip, got itself up into the heavens. We reached the right altitude and made our preparations. It was at this moment that my instructor asked me, 'How do you feel?' I answered with typical British understatement, 'Just a bit anxious.' 'You mean shit-scared' was his reply. I nodded in agreement. 'Good' he said, 'now you can jump.'

Back on the ground I asked him what he had meant. 'Well,' he said, 'the first time you jump, it's quite natural to feel frightened. It is the appropriate reaction to leaping out of a flying plane. Your answer showed that you were aware of your situation and what you were about to do. If you had said that you were *not* scared, I would not have let you jump, because that would show that either you did not understand what you were about to do, or that you were so over-confident that there would be a risk that you would make a mistake and cause a serious accident both to yourself and to others.'

I learnt from that to pay much more attention to what I feel and to ask myself if what I feel is an appropriate response to the situation in which I find myself. The fact that I may feel nervous need not mean that I should not go ahead. The fact that I may feel good, or in control, need not mean that I am right, or safe.

I said to my instructor, 'Well, at least the second jump will be easier.' But he said, 'No, not at all.'

I asked, 'Why?'

He said, 'Because the first time, in spite of the training, you do not know what it is really going to be like, but the second time you do.' (*Rabbi Guy Hall*) LB

22 DECEMBER

The healing of peace

This little poem was written by Jessie Sampter, an American poet from an assimilated home who rediscovered her Jewish roots. Born in 1883 she moved to Palestine in 1919 eventually settling on a kibbutz. She did social work among the Yemenite Jews, one of whom she adopted, and wrote poems, sketching life on the kibbutz. She died in 1938. Here she turns to a biblical style yet somehow reverses so much of biblical prophecy.

I shall now come, saith the Lord,
I shall now come, O my people.
I shall come as a word of comfort,
As a counsel of consolation.
Not any more in thunders, not as a roaring of terror,
Not any more in destruction, in hunger and plague.
Not with a blast of trumpets as a fanfare of triumph,
Not with the noise and shoutings of strutting over a foe.
But I will come quietly, as a woman to her sick child,
As the words of a friend, little by little.
And I will heal your wounds with the healing of peace,
And lead you up to my mountain to prophesy, saith the Lord JM

23 DECEMBER

Therapy

The story of the Good Samaritan is told in Luke chapter 10. In the unauthorized version, there is a variant ending, because the good Samaritan is a psychotherapist. He goes over to the man who had been mugged, and gazes down compassionately. 'How dreadful,' he says, 'how terrible. The poor chap who attacked you needs so much counselling!'

Therapy, like religion, needs a little humour. I am indebted to both. LB

The band

I like discovering musicians in unexpected places – and package holidays offer good opportunities. I wrote this on a Christmas break in Albufeira.

It was Christmas Eve in Toby's
on the southern Algarve coast
and the wind was chill on the quayside
and we'd drunk our final toast.
But though the place was empty
it wasn't time to quit
for a bunch of old musicians
were finishing their set.

I don't recall their names now
or what they called the band
some silly-sounding title
only they could understand.
They must have got together
to have a little fun
or show they still could cut it
and stand there in the sun.

And sure their jokes were lousy
and they hit some notes too soon
and the mikes were playing havoc
and they sometimes lost the tune
but they didn't let it faze them
and they gave it all they had
and the energy was flowing
and you came out feeling glad.

And once or twice they gripped you
when the guy on tenor blew
or they played an old French love song
and talked the lyric through.
So those who walked out early
or weren't too much impressed
they had a pleasant evening
but maybe missed the best.

So it wasn't merely charity
or simply feeling kind
but the way they loved their music
that kept them on your mind.
The streets were almost empty
on the way to my hotel,
from the church came voices singing
a final, sweet Noel.   JM

The congregation

Eddi, priest of St Wilfrid
  In the chapel at Manhood End,
Ordered a midnight service
  For such as cared to attend.

But the Saxons were keeping Christmas,
  And the night was stormy as well.
Nobody came to service
  Though Eddi rang the bell.

'Wicked weather for walking,'
  Said Eddi of Manhood End.
'But I must go on with the service
  For such as care to attend.'

The altar candles were lighted, –
  An old marsh donkey came,
Bold as a guest invited,
  And stared at the guttering flame.

The storm beat on at the windows,
  The water splashed on the floor,
And a wet yoke-weary bullock
  Pushed in through the open door.

'How do I know what is greatest,
  How do I know what is least?
That is My Father's business.'
  Said Eddi, Wilfred's priest.

'But, three are gathered together –
Listen to me and attend.
I bring good news, my brethren!'
Said Eddi, of Manhood End.

And he told the Ox of a manger
And a stall in Bethlehem,
And he spoke to the Ass of a Rider
That rode to Jerusalem.

They steamed and dripped in the chancel,
They listened and never stirred,
While, just as though they were Bishops,
Eddi preached them The Word.

Till the gale blew off on the marshes
And the windows showed the day,
And the Ox and the Ass together
Wheeled and clattered away.

And when the Saxons mocked him,
Said Eddi of Manhood End,
'I dare not shut His chapel
On such as care to attend.'
(*Rudyard Kipling* 1865–1936) LB

26 DECEMBER

Deflation

Very necessary in religion where it's easy to hypnotize yourself or make God in your own image!

I have a fondness for Dean Inge, once Dean of St Pauls in London. With his very Anglican wit, he cut through pomposity and pretension with kindness and style.

I heard this story about him. He was accustomed on Sunday mornings to drop in unannounced to the services of his churches. After one ended, he asked the preacher courteously how he prepared his sermons. 'The first part,' said the preacher piously, 'I work out carefully myself, and the second part I leave to the inspiration of the Holy Ghost.'

'My dear chap,' said the Dean courteously, 'please don't think me blasphemous, but I far prefer your part.' LB

27 DECEMBER

Happy New Years

When I lived in Bombay I rented an apartment from a Catholic lady and her Parsee husband. Part of the agreement was that I should continue to employ their Hindu servants.

When the Jewish New Year was celebrated I invited some friends for dinner and we blessed the New Year with apple and honey; the servants were not aware that this was my way of celebrating my New Year.

Each time a different New Year came around, they tried to please me by decorating the household in the various styles familiar to them which had been taught them by their employers past and present. I remember in particular the Parsee New Year and the attractive symbols with which they decorated the lintels.

My reaction was cool as they decorated the apartment for ensuing New Year celebrations, the Moslem one and the widely celebrated Hindu one.

After all these festivals had passed and their strange master had not reacted with any particular generosity, along came Christmas when two English friends, both named Cohen, decided to stay with me on their way to Hong Kong. We arrived home from a party on Christmas Eve to find a Christmas tree and a Christmas crèche in the centre of the lounge, taken out of the landlady's storage cupboard.

In appreciation of their desire to please, we Jewish friends distributed Christmas baksheesh to the Hindu servants at breakfast on Christmas day. (*Robin Gilbert*) LB

28 DECEMBER

A prayer before going to sleep

Alice Lucas (1852–1935) is best known for her translations of medieval Hebrew poems. But she was a poet in her own right and created devotional poetry for private use and to complement the regular services. In the introduction to her book '*The Jewish Year*', published in 1898, while modest about her own compositions, she is also quite realistic about the limitations of hymns:

> Many readers of hymns criticize them as monotonous. Perhaps a similar complaint will be made against this book, especially when it is

admitted that hymns written for one day appear equally suitable for another . . . But the monotony of hymns in general is due to a deeper cause also. There is infinite variety in God's goodness, but man has but a finite faculty for giving expression to it. If there be monotony in the thoughts that animate this and every other collection of hymns, the life of man would nevertheless be the nobler and the better, if it reflected, however faintly, that monotony, that wholehearted faith, that supreme sense of God's love. This is the constant theme of hymns such as are here presented by one who is fully conscious of defects for which she alone is responsible, but who ventures to hope, that a theme so congenial to the highest and noblest ideal of Judaism may yet make these poems acceptable to those for whom they were written.

Here is her prayer before going to sleep.

Bless'd are Thou, O Lord of all,
Who mak'st the bands of sleep to fall
Upon mine eyes, and slumber press
Mine eyelids down with heaviness.

God of my fathers, may it be
Thy will, this night to suffer me
To lay me down in peace and rise
In peace, when morning gilds the skies.

From thoughts of ill my slumber keep
And, lest the sleep of death I sleep,
O lighten Thou mine eyes, for Thou,
Lord, dost with light the eye endow.

Bless'd art Thou, O Lord most high,
Who in Thy glorious majesty
And in Thy gracious love hast given
Light upon earth and light in heaven. JM

29 DECEMBER

The little match girl

It was dreadfully cold; it snowed, and was beginning to grow dark, and it was the last night of the year, too, New Year's Eve. In this cold and darkness a poor, little girl was wandering about the streets with bare head and bare feet. She had slippers on when she left home, but what was the good of that? They were very large, old slippers of her mother's, so large that they slipped off the little girl's feet as she hurried across the street to escape two carriages, which came galloping along at an immense rate. The one slipper was not to be found, and a boy ran off with the other, saying, that it would do for a cradle when he had children of his own.

So the little girl wandered along barefooted, with a quantity of matches in an old apron, whilst she held a bundle of them in her hand. No one had bought a single match from her during the whole day, nor given her a single farthing. Hungry, and pinched with cold, the poor little girl crept along, the large flakes of snow covering her yellow hair, which curled so beautifully round her face, but her appearance was certainly the last thing she thought of.

In a corner between two houses, one projecting beyond the other, she sought shelter, and huddling herself up she drew her poor little feet, which were red and blue with cold, under her as well as she could, but she was colder than ever and dared not go home, for, as she had sold no matches, her father would beat her. Besides, it was cold at home, for they lived immediately under the roof and the wind blew in, though straw and rags had been stuffed in the large cracks. Her little hands were quite benumbed with cold. Oh, how much good one match would do, if she dared but take it out of the bundle, draw it across the wall, and warm her fingers in the flame! She drew one out, – 'Ritsh!' how it sputtered and burned! It burned with a warm, bright flame like a candle, and she bent her hand round it; it was a wonderful light! It appeared to the little girl as if she were sitting before a large iron-stove, in which the fire burned brightly and gave forth such comforting warmth. She stretched out her feet to warm them, too, – but the flame went out, the stove disappeared, and there she sat with a little bit of the burnt-out match in her hand.

Another was lighted; it burned, and where the light fell upon the wall, that became transparent, so that she could see into the room. There the table was covered with a dazzlingly white cloth and fine china, and a roasted goose was smoking most invitingly upon it. But, what was still more delightful, the goose sprang down from the table, and with a knife and fork sticking in his back, waddled towards the little girl. Then the match went out, and she saw nothing but the thick, cold wall.

She lighted another; and now she was sitting under the most splendid Christmas tree. It was larger and more beautifully decorated than the one she had seen at Christmas through the window at the rich merchant's. Thousands of tapers were burning amongst the green branches, and painted pictures, such as she had seen in the shopwindows, looked down upon her. She stretched out both her hands, when the match was burnt out. The innumerable lights rose higher and higher, and she now saw, that they were the stars, one of which fell, leaving a long line of light in the sky.

'Someone is dying now,' the little girl said, for her old grandmother, who alone had loved her, but who was now dead, had said, that when a star falls a soul takes its flight up to Heaven.

She drew another match across the wall, and in the light it threw around stood her old grandmother, so bright, so mild, and so loving.

'Grandmother,' the little girl cried; 'oh, take me with you! I know that you will disappear as soon as the match is burnt out, the same as the warm stove, the delicious roasted goose, and the Christmas tree!' and hastily she lighted the rest of the matches that remained in the bundle, for she wished to keep her grandmother with her as long as possible, and the matches burned so brightly, that it was lighter than day. Never before had her grandmother appeared so beautiful and so tall, and taking the little girl in her arms, in radiance and joy they flew high, high up into the heavens, where she felt neither cold, hunger, nor fear, for they were with God!

But in the corner between the two houses, in the cold morning air, sat the little girl with red cheeks and a smiling mouth. She was frozen to death during the last night of the Old year. The first light of the New Year shone upon the dead body of the little girl which sat there with the matches, one bundle of which was nearly consumed. She has been trying to warm herself, people said, but no one knew what visions she had had, or with what splendour she had entered with her grandmother into the joys of a New Year.

(Hans Christian Andersen 1805–1875) LB

30 DECEMBER

Deathbed

This poem by Robert Herrick used to frighten me. But the deaths I've witnessed in hospitals and hospices are no longer fraught. Thank God for morphine!

His Litanie, to the Holy Spirit

In the houre of my distress,
When temptations me oppresse,
And when I my sins confesse,
    Sweet Spirit comfort me!

When I lie within my bed,
Sick in heart, and sick in head,
And with doubts discomforted,
    Sweet Spirit comfort me!

When the house doth sigh and weep,
And the world is drown'd in sleep,
Yet mine eyes the watch do keep;
    Sweet Spirit comfort me!

When his Potion and his Pill
Has, or none, or little skill,
Meet for nothing, but to kill;
    Sweet Spirit comfort me!

When the passing-bell doth toll,
And the Furies in a shoal
Come to fright a parting soule;
    Sweet Spirit comfort me!

When the tapers now burne blew,
And the comforters are few,
And that number more than true;
    Sweet Spirit comfort me!

When the Priest his last hath pray'd
And I nod to what is said,
'Cause my speech is now decay'd;
    Sweet Spirit comfort me!

When (God knowes) I'm tost about,
Either with despaire, or doubt;
Yet before the glasse be out,
    Sweet Spirit comfort me!

When the Tempter me pursu'th
With the sins of all my youth,
And halfe damns me with untruth;
    Sweet Spirit comfort me!

When the flames and hellish cries
Fright mine eares, and fright mine eyes,
And all terrors me surprize;
Sweet Spirit comfort me!

When the Judgment is reveal'd,
And that open'd which was seal'd
When to Thee I have appeal'd;
Sweet Spirit comfort me! LB

31 DECEMBER

Arrival and departure

As we enter the world, so we depart:
We enter the world with a cry, and depart with a cry.
We enter the world weeping, and leave it weeping.
We enter the world with love, and leave it with love.
We enter the world with a sigh, and leave it with a sigh.
We enter the world devoid of knowledge and leave it devoid of knowledge.

It has been taught in the name of Rabbi Meir. When we enter the world our hands are clenched as though to say: 'The whole world is mine. I shall inherit it.' But when we leave our hands are spread open as though to say: 'I have taken nothing from the world.' (*Ecclesiastes Rabbah*) JM

GLOSSARY OF THE JEWISH TERMS AND REFERENCES

A number of the passages in this book come from ancient Jewish sources and we thought it might be helpful to explain them. One tip, the letters 'ch' are pronounced as in 'Lo*ch* Lomond'. The sayings and opinions of the Rabbis were transmitted orally, often for many generations, before being collected in writing over a period of 800 years, from about a century before the birth of Jesus till about 700 CE. (CE stands for the 'Common Era' and is the Jewish term for AD. So BCE means 'Before the Common Era').

The word *Torah* comes from a verb meaning 'to shoot arrows at a target'. It means 'pointing in a direction', so it is best understood as 'teaching', though that includes laws as well. At first the term was used to include the Five Books of Moses only, but then it came to mean the whole of the Hebrew Bible, and then all subsequent Rabbinic teachings. So it is a general term for anything that can be considered as part of the revelation of God.

The thoughts of the Rabbis were put together in two different kinds of collections. The first is a series of huge volumes known as the *Talmud*. It is a collection of Rabbinic debates on legal matters, but with all sorts of side remarks on current issues and additional ideas thrown in. It seems haphazard at first, but it is actually carefully crafted and is a unique literary form of its own. Its starting point is the '*Mishnah*', a codification made in the 2nd century CE of current Jewish law ('oral' traditions claimed to have been handed down by Moses alongside the 'written' traditions in the Bible). It is organized in six 'orders' and the Talmud contains the Rabbis' detailed analysis of these laws and a discussion on how to apply them to current situations. There are two editions of the Talmud, one completed in Palestine (the *Yerushalmi* (Jerusalem) Talmud) in about 400 CE and a more elaborate version edited in Babylon (the Talmud *Babli*) which was completed between 100 and 300 years later.

The other kind of collection is called *Midrash*, and is a more diverse group of materials, including verse by verse analysis of biblical passages and meditations on them, some of these being something like the notes of sermons. The Midrash also contains both legal and ethical material, and not a little humour, folklore and fantasy. Most of the following terms which have cropped up in the book refer to 'orders' of the Talmud or collections of Midrash.

Thus Baba Batra, Baba Metzia, Berachot, Derech Eretz Zuta, Eduyot, Eruvin, Horayot, Kiddushin, Pesachim, Sanhedrin, Shabbat, Succah and Yoma are all 'tractates' of the Talmud dealing with different subjects. There is one independent section of the Talmud which collects the sayings of the Rabbis. It is called the Sayings (or the Chapters) of the Fathers, and already has its own commentary, called Avot D'Rabbi Nathan.

Genesis Rabbah, Exodus Rabbah, Leviticus Rabbah, Deuteronomy Rabbah, Midrash Psalms and Ecclesiastes Rabbah, as their names would suggest, are 'Midrashic' collections commenting on these particular books of the Bible. But other more varied collections are Mechilta (Beshallach refers to the Biblical section on which this particular passage has commented), Pesikta D'Rav Kahana and Sifra.

Of course Rabbinic activity, of commentary and legal discussion, did not stop with the completion of the Babylonian Talmud – in fact its very nature, which stimulates argument, meant that it too required commentaries! Moreover, by the middle ages, the law had developed so far that the great Spanish Rabbi Moses Maimonides felt the need to collect it together in a more systematic way and produced a monumental codification called the *Mishneh Torah*, also quoted in this book. But that was eventually superseded in the 16th century by another legal code called the *Shulchan Aruch*. This too had a commentary added, so that one of our references is to the commentary of the *Rema* (Rabbi Moses Isserles 1530–1572) on the section of the Shulchan Arush called *Orach Chayyim*, the Path of Life.

All of which merely reminds us that there is a huge weight of Jewish tradition behind us (or on top of us, depending on how you see it) – but what a rich mine of law and lore it contains!

EPILOGUE

Lionel and I take it in turns to compose the prologue or epilogue of the books we write or edit together. After collaborating for almost thirty years on different projects we have a pretty good idea about how the other works, so when we started this book we each went off to find our 180-something passages.

But when we started putting them together we found ourselves disagreeing strongly. Lionel thought that my stuff was too 'Jewish' and would prove inaccessible to many people; I thought that he had included too many Christian references! Both of us were happy with passages by or about Muslims or Eastern religions!

Rather than come to blows, which would be inelegant and not a little undignified, we tried to figure out what was going on. We came to the conclusion that this battle reflected a similar problem that we had both faced as Jewish boys growing up in an English Christian environment. We were each the product of two different cultures that were just beginning to fit together, and each of us in his own way had found out how to live with these two backgrounds that had nurtured us. We then realized that this was a growing situation for many people today, here and around the world, whose roots lay in one particular culture or place or nation, but who now lived in another. How do you preserve the identity, culture or faith of your family and background, when you are fully immersed from childhood in a different world entirely? And is the only solution to give up one for the sake of the other, to deny an essential part of your own make-up? Because whether we like it or not, both of them continue to affect the way we think and act.

So suddenly this book became a challenge to understand how we had managed to live between these two worlds – what parts of each had shaped us and still had an influence on us.

We both re-examined what we had produced so that the different parts of ourselves would be fairly represented, and accessible to anyone who wanted to journey through the year with us.

Since Lionel and I have had such different personal journeys, we assume that we will carry on arguing about such things for as long as we continue working together. These kinds of tensions between us are really within us as well, so they cannot just be 'solved' – life is far too complicated for that. The best we can do is try to find our own 'centre' that is secure enough to enjoy the interplay between the bits that have helped form us. But at least knowing what these tensions are, and that they are real and increasingly common is quite helpful. We don't have to be their victim. It's just the price we pay for living at this end of the twentieth century.

So I hope these fragments pieced together from our fractured identities will be of use.

Jonathan Magonet

ACKNOWLEDGEMENTS

The acknowledgements pages constitute an extension of the copyright page.

The authors and publisher acknowledge with thanks permission to reproduce copyright material. Where available, copyright information is listed below:

Karen Armstrong for her contributions (31 May, 29 September, 18 October, 20 October and 22 October).
Michael Billig for his contribution (13 January).
Irene Bloomfield for her contributions (3 August and 9 August).
Sydney Carter, Stainer & Bell Ltd and Hope Publishing Co. for the song 'One More Step', © 1971 Stainer & Bell Ltd, London, England. Administered in the USA and Canada by Hope Publishing Co., Carol Stream, IL 60188, USA. All rights reserved.
Batsheva Dagan for the poem 'A Birthday Present'.
Norman R. Davies for his contributions (8 June, 7 November and 17 November).
Livinus Donohoe for his contribution (7 February).
Henry Dyson for his contributions (28 August, 30 August, 15 September and 10 October).
Albert H. Friedlander for his contributions (9 November and 1 May).
GMP Publishers Ltd for the extract from *Living with HIV in Self and Others* by Richie McMullen, Gay Men's Press 1988.
Robin Gilbert for his contribution (27 December).
Wendy Greengross for her contributions (9 September, 17 September, 12 October and 5 November).
Hugo Gryn for his contributions (2 October and 4 October).
G. D. Hall for his contribution (21 December).
C. K. Holman for her contribution (21 July).
Dr Walter Homolka for his contribution (1 November).
Revd Malcolm Johnson for his contributions (23 January, 8 April, 7 July and 15 July).
Bernard Keegan for the extract taken from *Mount Carmel*, published

by St Luke's Priory, Wincanton, Somerset.

Mary Kelly for her contributions (6 April and 12 April).

W. J. Kirkpatrick for his contributions (25 July and 27 July).

Brendan McAllister for the extract from *Death, Peace and Justice*, Corrymeela Community Paper, Corrymeela 2 May 1992.

Paul Murray and the Dedalus Press for the poem 'A Note on Human Passion' taken from *The Absent Fountain*, Dedalus Press 1991, © Paul Murray.

John Newbury for the poem 'Water'.

Roderic Owen for his contribution (13 March).

D. Richardson for her contributions (20 August, 8 October and 30 October).

Leslie Shepard for the passage 'Guru', broadcast in 'Thought for the Day', BBC Radio 4, 20 April 1977, and other contributions (13 September, 6 October and 19 December).

A. D. Smith for his contributions (3 July, 5 July and 20 September).

Clive Thexton for his contribution (20 November).

Graham Tyler for his contribution (19 July).

André Ungar for his contributions (23 February, 25 February and 7 March).

Routledge for extracts from *Waiting on God* and from *Gateway to God*, both by Simone Weil.

Alexandra Wright for the extract taken from ULPS News Vol. 16, No 7 March 1989.

Every effort has been made to trace copyright owners, and the publishers apologize to anyone whose rights have inadvertently not been acknowledged. This will be corrected in any reprint.